Changing Patterns of
Sexual Behaviour

Changing Patterns of Sexual Behaviour

*Proceedings of the Fifteenth Annual
Symposium of the Eugenics Society
London 1978*

Edited by

W. H. G. ARMYTAGE
*Division of Education,
The University, Sheffield, England*

R. CHESTER
*Department of Social Administration,
The University, Hull, England*

JOHN PEEL
*Teesside Polytechnic,
Middlesbrough, Cleveland, England*

1980

- 2 OCT 1980

Academic Press
A Subsidiary of Harcourt Brace Jovanovich, Publishers
London · New York · Toronto · Sydney · San Francisco

ACADEMIC PRESS INC. (LONDON) LTD.
24/28 Oval Road,
London NW1

United States Edition published by
ACADEMIC PRESS INC.
111 Fifth Avenue
New York, New York 10003

British Library Cataloguing in Publication Data
Eugenics Society. Annual Symposium, 15th, London, 1978
  Changing patterns of sexual behaviour.
  1. Sex – Congresses
  I. Title II. Armytage, Walter Harry Green
  III. Chester, Robert IV. Peel, John, b. 1930
  301.41'7   HQ21   79–42830

  ISBN 0-12-062650-0

Text set in 11/12 pt VIP Baskerville, printed and bound
in Great Britain at The Pitman Press, Bath

Contributors

W. H. G. ARMYTAGE, *Division of Education, University of Sheffield, Sheffield S10 2TN, England*

P. T. BROWN, *Frederick Chusid and Company Limited, 35–37 Fitzroy Street, London W1P 5AF, England*

ROBERT CHESTER, *Department of Social Administration, University of Hull, Hull HU6 7RX, England*

ANN CRAFT, *Department of Psychology, Bryn y Neuadd Hospital, Llanfairfechan, Gwynedd LL33 0HH, Wales.*

MICHAEL CRAFT, *Bryn y Neuadd Hospital, Llanfairfechan, Gwynedd LL33 0HH, Wales.*

CHRISTIE DAVIES, *Department of Sociology, University of Reading, Whiteknights, Reading RG6 2AA, England*

E. M. ETTORRE, *Addiction Research Unit, Institute of Psychiatry, 101 Denmark Hill, London SE5 8AF, England*

CHRISTINE FARRELL, *Department of Applied Social Studies, The North London Polytechnic, Holloway Road, London N7 8DB, England*

PAUL H. GEBHARD, *Institute for Sex Research Inc., Indiana University, Morrison Hall 416, Bloomington, Indiana 47401, USA.*

MICHAEL KINGHAM, *Department of Health Studies, The Polytechnic, Coach Lane, Newcastle upon Tyne NE7 7XA, England*

DAVID MORRISON, *Department of Social Science and Humanities, The City University, St. John Street, London EC1V 4PB, England*

KURT SCHAPIRA, *Department of Psychological Medicine, Queen Victoria Hospital, Newcastle upon Tyne NE1 4LP, England*

K. L. SOOTHILL, *Department of Sociology, University of Lancaster, Bailrigg, Lancaster LA1 4YL, England*

MICHAEL TRACEY, *Centre for Mass Communication Research, University of Leicester, 104 Regent Road, Leicester LE1 7LT, England*

CHRISTOPHER WALKER, *Department of Social Administration, University of Hull, Hull HU6 7RX, England*

Preface

This volume contains the proceedings of the Fifteenth Annual Symposium of the Eugenics Society. Its theme is changing patterns of sexual behaviour and it is the first of a planned trilogy, subsequent volumes in which will be devoted to reproductive behaviour and to infant care and child rearing.

We are grateful to all who took part in this symposium and we are glad to acknowledge our debt to Miss Eileen Walters who organized the event and prepared the typescripts for publication.

on behalf of the Eugenics Society

W. H. G. ARMYTAGE

R. CHESTER

JOHN PEEL

JANUARY 1980

Contents

Beyond Ecstasy:
Sex and Moral Protest

DAVID MORRISON and MICHAEL TRACEY

Department of Social Science and Humanities,
The City University, London, England
and
Centre for Mass Communication Research,
Leicester, England

When we were attempting a theoretical understanding of Whitehouse's concern with sex, a colleague offered us his own version. He based his theory on research done in the United States which had looked at the relationship between changing moral attitudes and temptation. The researchers measured attitudes to cheating among sixth graders (11-year-olds). The pupils were then given an exam which was competitive, with prizes for winners, such that they could not win without cheating. As one might have anticipated, some cheated and some did not, but when the researchers came next day to measure attitudes to cheating they found that those who had cheated in the exam had become more lenient, and those who had not had become harder in their attitude to cheating. His theory about moral campaigners and sex was, rather prosaically, "Thus, expect moral campaigners to be those who fancied it and didn't—not those who never would."

This has the appeal of the familiar. Many people, we suspect, may feel that Whitehouse's concern with sexual attitudes and sexual behaviour is somehow a product of her own sexual difficulties. What we wish to argue in this paper is that to explain Whitehouse-on-sex one must go beyond individual psychology and into the total social world which she inhabits.

Within Britain there can be very few people who have not heard of Mary Whitehouse. Her periodic sorties against the mass media have hoisted her to the position of a national figure, viewed by many as a self-appointed unofficial guardian of public morals. Whatever one's personal view of Whitehouse, it ought not to obscure the fact that she

1

speaks for thirty-two thousand formally aligned members of her organization, the National Viewers and Listeners Association (NVALA). Perhaps of more importance though, in terms of cultural analysis, is that she strikes a chord which reverberates sympathetically in the minds of many, many thousands more. She is, ironically, a creation of the very mass media which she condemns, but nevertheless has a basis in reality removed from any phenomenological conjurings of the media itself. The very fact of her existence is a product of, and witness to, very real changes within the moral structure of British society since the end of the Second World War; changes based on fundamental shifts in the location of moral authority.

A Symbolic Crusade

Whitehouse and NVALA are, in the public mind, primarily concerned with cleaning up television. To view the movement purely in this light, however, is to fall into the definitional trap sprung by the mass media. It is not a view adopted by the members and neither is it one shared by ourselves. Instead, the movement is more appropriately seen in terms of a symbolic crusade (Gusfield, 1972; Zurcher et al., 1971). The symbol and organizing point of the movement may well be the mass media, but the substance and content of the protest rests in a complex process of *cultural alteration* of which the mass media is only one, albeit important, part. However, the driving force and rationale, the meaning the movement has for its members, is far removed from the mundane everyday world occupied by the mass media.

To understand why television created this indignant sense of moral outrage, it is first necessary to understand those values and beliefs held by the members, which in their eyes television so grossly and indecently assaulted. There is no better entry point into the mental world of NVALA than an examination of their sexual attitudes, for there is crystallized a view of mankind which is at variance with not only popular conceptions but also recent legislative reforms governing social behaviour. The variance and disagreement is with a world that has increasingly come to be viewed as an empirical construct stripped of any higher meaning than that which individuals bring to it. For example, the demands by the pro-abortion women's groups that they be allowed to control their own bodies is, so far as NVALA is concerned, based on the fallacious argument that their bodies are theirs to control; likewise the arguments of the Divorce Act of 1969 with marital breakdown rather than marital offence as the basis for divorce is also antithetical to NVALA's way of thinking. Similarly the BBC of Hugh Greene, its Director General from 1960–69, appeared to lurch further and further into secular and anti-establishment attitudes, especially with its drama and comedy satire programmes (Tracey, forthcoming).

Behind the rhetoric lay a much deeper concern and it was not with this or that law, this or that TV programme. It was with the whole state of modern society and, more specifically, with what has been called the "Death of God".

Change and Revolt

Traditional religion, its symbolism, its rituals, its institutions and its social importance, has been eroded under the twin processes of industrialization and urbanization (Cox, 1965; Wilson, 1966). Historically, in the long march of secularization, those closest to the heartland of industrial production were the first to be brought under secular influence, not in any intellectual sense, but rather in terms of simply ceasing to view the world from a religious perspective. The angels fell from heaven not because of any philosophical onslaught but because of the demands of the modern industrial complex which, as Weber so brilliantly recognized, produced its own relentless logic which shattered not only traditional ways of behaving but also traditional ways of thinking. As more and more areas of life have been brought under industrial control the area of religious thought retreated to become an enclave mentality. No longer was it a living part of national culture but a fossilized expression dusted down to function on state occasions or to mark those solemn moments in life of birth, marriage and death.

What industrialization managed to do, which chain and fire never achieved, was to undermine the plausibility structures by which religious belief could retain its meaning since to exist in a "particular religious world implies existing in a particular social context within which that world can retain its plausibility" (Berger, 1973). This goes to the heart of the social problem faced by Whitehouse and NVALA, and offers the clue as to why television takes on a demonic importance for them.

Members of NVALA are intensely religious. Their religious beliefs structure their lives and offer the firmest commitment to the aims and expressions of the organization. Being disproportionately composed of women, of middle-age and beyond, living in rural areas or on the fringes of cities, and drawn overwhelmingly from the ranks of the middle classes, they form a classic sociological paradigmatic fit between social location and the retention of religious belief. Cut off from the mainstream of social movement, they exist in backwaters of belief. Their relative physical and cultural isolation has acted as a dam against erosion from the main currents of the secularization processes; however, the changes in the content of television in the sixties acted as the sluice gate to contemporary cultures which threatened to flood and overrun those social barriers which persisted. As the relentless logic of industrial society expanded, religious beliefs and practices vacated an ever-increasing number of institutions until its last resting place, the bunker of traditional religious belief, became the home and the self-enclosed world of the local church. Even the bunker, though, was not safe from the ubiquitous television screen whose values violated the sanctity of even the most Christian house with material which Whitehouse once informed us "one wouldn't have allowed in by the front door". The secure world of the home no longer afforded a protective cocoon against the values of the outside world. Thus, the very structural marginality which had acted as protection now provided the root of protest. Not only did television threaten them by directly challenging their beliefs, values and suppositions, but it acted as a double agent by alerting them to just how 'un-godly' British society had become. As Christians, protest became therefore both a necessity for survival and a duty. Their world had to be saved, but in doing so it was necessary to save the rest of the world since television as a cultural product did not exist in isolation from the culture which produced and consumed it. Thus NVALA became an attempt at religious revival, the reconquering of the world for God.

The Sexual Wilderness

Although the members would deny the charge often levied against them that they are obsessed with sex, they are nevertheless deeply concerned *about it* and *by it*. The members are well aware of, and object to, their public image of individuals who are easily shocked, yet in general and despite occasional protestations to the contrary, they are embarrassed by the sexual content of the mass media. As one member related:

"You don't always know what is coming on, but so often something that seemed to commence in an acceptable sort of way, invariably before it's finished there's something which is completely uncalled for, where it will develop into the sort of thing where sex entered into it and which is unnecessary, and you feel embarrassed if you have friends in."

Another member, when asked if he watched television much, replied:

"We haven't watched for some time now because it hasn't been working. It broke down and we decided not to have it mended because it caused such embarrassment waiting for something obscene to appear."

In fact, when we asked members what they objected to on television, sex was *always* raised as an important category, but when pressed to detail their specific objections we were often confronted by embarrassed vagueness. For instance, in one case when we asked what he found objectionable in general, we were greeted with the comment "you know", accompanied by knowing winks. One expression of ignorance clarification merely took the form of re-emphasized "you knows", more winking and "that", used as a euphemism for sex. Admittedly, this particular member was an extreme example of reluctance, or perhaps inability, to discuss his specific objections. Indeed, he could not even bring himself to mention the word sex. In general, though, it was difficult to follow through and discover exactly what it was about certain sexual content to which they objected and were embarrassed by. Methodologically, it should not be presumed that such reluctance to 'discuss' was the preserve of the women members who, perhaps finding our male company disconcerting, refused to talk. The male members exhibited similar reticence.

It would appear that what they objected to was the portrayal of material which confronted them with sex as a physical act, as Whitehouse once commented to us, "Why can't they walk past the bedroom door". Another member expressed her objection as "Well, one gets thoroughly bored stiff with the human body and its functions . . . we've gone past the kitchen sink drama haven't we, it's just sewage." What both these comments express is a marked refusal to have physical intimacies of human behaviour presented to them as a form of entertainment. The comment that such material was boring and tedious was raised many times during the course of our research:

"You see, I get sick and fed up with the plays, and one knows the thing. It's the usual thing, girl goes to London or boy goes to London, shacks up in a bed-sitter, everybody sleeps with everybody else, and this is so boring, it's simply appalling. All right people go to bed, but I don't want to look at them on TV. When you get sex rammed down your throat morning, noon and night, day in and day out, year in and year out, you can't stand any more of it. It's so boring."

She even went on to suggest that such programmes not only bored her but in fact had a quasi-physical effect on her. She continued:

"I had my father living with me for a time and I found a lot of stuff that was on television was terribly embarrassing. I do find this worries me if I'm with young people or with older people. This is what I felt so I used to squirm. In fact, some of the things I've seen make me squirm on my own."

To consider this response to more or less explicit sex as somehow a commentary on her own private sex life, though perhaps psychologically appealing, is in fact inappropriate. The fact that the Association members we interviewed were embarrassed by publicly available sex, or even made to feel physically uncomfortable by it, does not *necessarily* imply anything about their own sexuality. What we feel it demonstrates is a totally different set of attitudes, interpretations and judgements to those individuals who in fact enjoy such material. What then are the contrasting attitudes?

Rather than dealing in abstracts, one can more readily tease out the contrasting assumptions and values by examining Whitehouse's attitudes to the whole question of sex education. To be blunt, there is quite simply no way in which Whitehouse will countenance pre-marital or extra-marital sex, and therefore there is no way in which she can countenance the type of sex education which, for example, sections of the Family Planning Association now offers—that is, basically a form of trying to make sex safe for young people. At one level it is precisely because she feels that one cannot make sex safe in any sense by offering the sheath to teenage lovers that she is opposed to the orientation of this type of sex education. Hence the frequent references in books, articles and lectures to rising VD rates, illegitimacy etc. At another, for her more important, level, it is because such sex, outside the institutions of marriage, transgresses moral law that she is opposed to it. Thus, for example, she will argue that the solutions the Family Planning Association offer are an illusion and that the real solution lies in changing not just the whole physical environment, but the whole psychic environment within which prevalent attitudes towards sexual behaviour are defined. The difference between them is the difference between Elastoplast and major surgery.

In her autobiography Whitehouse makes it very clear that she feels that childhood and schools, as much as television, are the battleground upon which they are fighting trends within modern society (Whitehouse, 1972). She refers to the inalienable right of the child "to mystery, to dreams, to tenderness and to love". Of the sex instruction film, *Growing Up*, she says, "This brought out into the open, in no uncertain fashion, the nature of the contemporary assault upon the young and upon the ethical structure that would support them" (Whitehouse, 1972). Thus even though in one sense NVALA is campaigning for the restoration of parental rights, at another it clearly hopes that through the medium of the parent the child will not learn only about the physiology of sex, but about the total ethical structure within which the Association prefers to place sex. Though she recommended to the BBC's former Chairman, Lord Hill, that rather than making programmes for the young, the BBC could have produced programmes aimed at enabling parents to talk freely to their own children, what she is also concerned with is what they would be talking about. It is not just a transfer of texts from the programmes into the privacy of the home; it is a change in the nature and content of the text. The family therefore becomes the medium for the transmission of information not simply because, in a utilitarian sense it is the most suitable means for making sure that the message is learned and that therefore any adverse social problems do not arise, but also because there is a God-given right for instruction to take place there.

In a letter by a member of the Association which was subsequently reproduced and distributed by them, schools were likened to potential "moral gas chambers" and sex education as "more horrid than pornography, more evil than vice". What had brought this condemnation was an FPA-backed pamphlet which included such comments as:

"We no longer believe in telling the young what to do but if we were asked for advice on this topic (moral Rules) we would say something like this: Make love if you both feel like it. But first make sure that you are safe. If you cannot be satisfied without reaching orgasm, there are many ways of doing this without danger of conception, such as manual stimulation, or oral or anal intercourse . . . (referring to girls), your masturbation is no-one's business but your own, so privacy is appropriate. Make the most of it. . . ."

The pamphlet he was referring to was *Sex Education* by Maurice Hill and Michael Lloyd–Jones and published by the National Secular Society (1970), with a foreword by Brigid Brophy. When a complaint was made to Swann, chairman of the BBC, about a reference to this in a programme, he commented:

"We recommend parents to search diligently for suitable books and pointed out the pamphlet as one which was helpful in underlining some of the sillier and more gross scientific and biological errors which sex education manuals are prone to."

The NVALA member also pointed to the campaigning zeal of the Gay Lib movement, the film, *Growing Up*, and a Health Education Council 'Casanova' leaflet (for sixth formers), on the cover of which is a picture of the famous gentleman kneeling before a bare-breasted young woman under the title "Casanova never got anyone into trouble". His own conclusion is that "the best instruction we can give the young is to cleanse ourselves and keep ourselves from the filthiness of the Permissive Society". He summons up the image of a man, horrified by his own vileness hanging his head in shame and wishing that:

"he might be a little child again and that his teacher would teach him that his body was the Temple of God, the Holy Spirit, and that he should never defile that temple, but shun the very thought of impurity and all that is improper and unclean."

What is actually being discussed, then, is not sex education but moral education, and their feeling about the moral neutrality of schools' television. Thus Whitehouse described one BBC series for 8- to 9-year-olds as ill-conceived, dangerous and 'totally amoral'. This does not mean that they are unconcerned with the physiological and emotional aspects; merely that they do not separate these out from a total view of life and a concept of the existence of God. The philosophical assumption of perfectability and a commitment to the belief that man can control his own destiny, both of which do seem to be important themes within the repertoire of arguments for sex education, are clearly incompatible with the view that human nature is of itself incapable of moral perfection. Sex education is therefore seen as part of the ideology of secular optimism, the fashionable view that man's salvation lies in material, as opposed to spiritual, progress. Thus the Association reverses the equation and argues that even in sexual matters man can only achieve his destiny through his spirituality.

When Two Worlds Collide: Empirical v. Religious

On July 1975, BBC Radio 4 broadcast a programme called *Homosex-*

uality: The Years of Change. The programme looked at the reactions to the Wolfenden reforms and interviewed numerous people including a number of homosexuals and Lord Wolfenden himself. On listening to the programme one active NVALA member, a senior teacher of music in a large Midlands school, wrote to the Chairman of the BBC, Sir Michael Swann:

> "I wish to complain most strongly about the programme which I can only describe as propagandist in favour of the notion that homosexuality is a perfectly acceptable pursuit between adults who consent so to behave and in favour of lowering the age of consent for such behaviour."

He complained that one participant, a voluntary worker:

> "regarded homosexuality as merely an incidence in a family pattern, like dark hair or left handedness"

and then continued by objecting that:

> "Nowhere in the programme did we hear from men who had overcome their homosexuality, whether through Christian faith or by other means."

The notion of overcoming homosexuality, as if it were a mere sexual stammer rather than an expression of an individual's sexual being, part of his personality and identity, is of itself interesting and common to the members' thinking. Sex itself tends to be seen not as a collectivity of expressions, but more in terms of a fixed point of human behaviour, departure from which constitutes a *fall* and not an extension of human sexuality. For the moment, though, there is a much more important strain in the above letter than a particular view of homosexuality; namely, the objection to a naturalistic treatment of sex and which therefore might be said to run counter to recent social and legislative thought.

By understanding the relationship between the process of secularization and the group's formation, one begins to understand this *opposition to the age.* In the ceaseless battle with broadcasters, they were confronting that which they felt to be the most immediate and most prominent manifestations of the secular world. They complain that man's sexuality is increasingly treated as no more than a secular biological fact. Thus, for example, in the autumn of 1970 the NVALA carried out a "limited monitoring project of Schools Broadcasting". Commenting on a programme entitled *Monkeys, Apes and Man,* the report observes, with echoes of William Jenning Bryan and the Monkey Trial, that:

"1. This programme was factual where it stuck to facts, but contained the inference that men were developed from monkeys.
2. Despite the continual reference to the differences between primate humans and primate apes the general impression was that man is only a glorified ape.
3. The implication throughout was that man is merely a superior ape."

To treat the world in an empirical or matter-of-fact way, to examine sex from a physiological basis alone, to see human relationships as pure social arrangements, to treat knowledge itself as relative to situations, epochs and ages is, so far as NVALA is concerned, to fall in line with the drift of present day thought which is fundamentally wrong, and wrong to the extent of being socially dangerous. It is wrong because it transcends biblical truth, and dangerous because to transcend biblical truth is to misunderstand that which holds the world together. Social scientists, then, with their tradition of empirical enquiry not only mistake the nature of the world, but in a sense create their own employment by the problems generated through empirical interpretation and redefining the world in terms of human construction. Thus, homosexuality is not something to be understood as an academic exercise in human sexual response, and neither do statistical demonstrations of its prevalence, even if it were the norm, make it any less wrong and ultimately destructive.

Essentially, Whitehouse and her supporters' view of sexual relations is something akin to a mystical experience and, for them, the tragedy of the modern world is that it is treated as no more than a physical experience. With Malcolm Muggeridge they would say, "The orgasm has replaced the Cross as the focus of longing". For them sex is about a human essence, and thus, for example, their opposition to pornography cannot simply be rooted in a kind of prurience, but rather a deep-seated theologically based conviction that pornography dehumanizes its participants and therefore distorts that essence. Sex must always take place within the context of religious feeling, if not always emotionally, then at least ideologically. Anything which threatens this state is therefore decried as wrong. Thus, for example, oral sex is prohibited even within marriage because it invokes the danger of standing apart from religious truth. Free from the central meaning of sex it becomes sex *per se*, and as sex *per se* can locate itself on any number of partners. Thus Whitehouse once described the impersonality of pornography as "a travesty of sex", by which she meant that as simple physical arousal it was not bounded by religious feeling, it had no focal point of expression and, therefore, by its very generality involved the danger of promiscuity. Whitehouse therefore was outraged when the fashion designer, Mary Quant, stated that her clothes were deliberately made to draw attention to the female crutch. This localization of sex, its abstraction from content, leads to promiscuity since there is nothing behind it, or above it, by which to anchor it in any more meaningful whole than that of carnal arousal.

In so far as the members are concerned then, there is a refusal to recognize intellectually much that passes for sex in our society. Consequently, 'High Street sex', televized sex, in fact any sexual behaviour falling outside spiritual communication, is seen as a sickness. The outcome of this view is that there tends to be within NVALA a somewhat unselective cultural criticism whereby films such as *Danish Dentist on the Job* or *Can you Keep it Up For a Week* are lumped together as being abhorrent along with Granada's prize winning serialization of H. E. Bates' *Country Matters*. Aesthetically and contexturally, the sex portrayed is totally different, but aesthetic finesse or contextural necessity cannot protect against the basic fact that each is an abstraction from the 'correct' relationship within which sex takes on its true purpose and meaning—spiritual enrichment. Indeed, in understanding this it is easier to understand the apparent 'cultural Philistinism' which many perceive in the movement. In fact, what Whitehouse specifically dislikes, for example, is the use of expert witnesses in such cases as the *Lady Chatterley's Lover* trial, because she believes that the moral issue is reduced to a debate on artistic merit. In private conversation Whitehouse did not deny the artistic integrity of *Country Matters*, yet still found it objectionable and wrong that explicit sex scenes were portrayed. No matter how sensitively done, they still broke the canons of proper behaviour.

Defending the Faith and Defying the Profane

In the final analysis we can only conclude that the basic nature of NVALA's concern with sex in the modern world is that such activity amounts to the most profound encroachment by a modern secular world which they dislike. To accept the biological imperative, to acknowledge the importance within human behaviour of gratification, to indulge in practices long forbidden, is to rid sex of its sacred connotation. It is *this* process which they claim 'permissiveness' has engendered, and to accept such a view of sexuality would be to accept that the profane infests *every* facet of life right down to the most personal and most human. What one begins to detect then, is just as television was opposed by NVALA because they saw it as the carrier of profane culture into the home, so the opposition to contemporary patterns of sexuality rests on a deep fear of bearing the profane within the soul. A culture that treats the most personal of acts as it does, secularizes the sacred, is one they must reject in the name of God.

Owing largely to organizational weakness NVALA at the moment is relatively small, but this ought not to disguise the very real possibility that Whitehouse speaks for many thousands of individuals who find themselves in a similar structural and ideological position. The movement shows no signs of lessening in tempo; in fact, quite the reverse. Whitehouse's recent success in invoking the old law of blasphemy to successfully prosecute *Gay News* for publishing a poem characterizing Jesus Christ as a homosexual ought to make it abundantly clear that, should the movement become an influential mass movement, then their success would definitely alter the contours of existing sexual experience. Their protest is an attempt to define not only how man shall live, not only how man shall behave, but all importantly how man shall be judged. Kinsey may have told us how man *does* behave, Whitehouse is telling us how man *should* behave.

References

Berger, P. L. (1973). *The Social Reality of Religion*, p. 58. Harmondsworth, Middlesex: Penguin Books.

Cox, H. (1965). *The Secular City*. London: Macmillan.

Gusfield, J. R. (1972). *Symbolic Crusade: Status Politics and the American Temperance Movement*. Urbana: University of Illinois Press.

Hill, M. and Lloyd-Jones, M. (1970). *Sex Education*. London: National Secular Society.

Tracey, M. (1976). *The Production of Political Television*. London: Routledge and Kegan Paul.

Tracey, M. (forthcoming). *Hugh Greene: A Biography*. London: Bodley Head.

Whitehouse, Mary (1972). *Who Does She Think She Is?* London: New English Library.

Wilson, B. R. (1966). *Religion in Secular Society*. London: C. A. Watts (Pitman).

Zurcher *et al.* (1971). The anti-pornography campaign: a symbolic crusade. *Social Problems*, **19**, No. 2 (Fall).

Moralists, Causalists, Sex, Law and Morality

CHRISTIE DAVIES

Department of Sociology, University of Reading,
Reading, England

During the decade 1959–69 the British Parliament passed four important Private Members' Bills having a direct relevance to sexual behaviour and sexual conduct. These bills became the Legitimacy Act of 1959, the Sexual Offences Act of 1967,the Abortion Act of 1967 and the Divorce Act of 1969. In addition, Parliament passed a number of other Private Members' Bills relating to the censorship of obscenity which clearly is also a part of the legal framework which helps to influence and determine sexual morality and behaviour. These bills became the Obscene Publications Act 1959 and the Theatres Act 1968, and I have analysed them elsewhere (Davies, 1978) in terms similar to those employed here in discussing abortion, divorce, homosexuality, illegitimacy and the law.

The essence of my argument is that the law in each of these subjects traditionally embraced a particular moral outlook which I have termed 'moralism' and that this was also the moral creed of those who opposed reform of these laws. By contrast, the successful law reformers held to a very different set of moral assumptions that I have termed 'causalism'. The history of law reform in these areas consists of the defeat of the previously dominant 'moralists', by the new, rising group of 'causalists', though neither group was either conscious of itself or organized in these terms. Moralism and causalism are simply analytical categories designed to provide a coherent structure within which to place the diverse confusion of arguments put forward in Parliament on a wide variety of issues.

For the moralist it is sufficient reason to forbid an activity (e.g. homosexual behaviour or abortion) and to punish those detected in it, if the activity can be represented as wrong *a priori*, immoral or wicked. The purpose of the law in matters such as divorce, abortion or illegitimacy is to identify the guilty and the innocent, to penalize the

13

guilty, to protect the innocent and to reward the virtuous. It is not necessarily a purely restrictive moral tradition for there are also libertarian moralists who assert a man's basic right to be free and to order his own life on equally absolute grounds, even if the consequences of his behaviour are harmful to himself or a nuisance to others.

By contrast, causalists are not primarily concerned with individual virtue or even motives but with considerations of cause and consequence. If it turns out that more harm is done by legally forbidding an activity than by allowing it, then causalists will argue that it should be permitted, even if they consider the activity to be wrong or immoral. On the other hand, causalists are willing to forbid by law actions which no one considers wrong in themselves if, through no fault of those indulging in them, they constitute an intolerable nuisance. Whereas the aim of the moralist is always to distribute benefits and penalties according to the moral deserts of the parties involved in a situation (e.g. in divorce cases), the causalists seek to minimize the overall harm and suffering experienced by the various people involved regardless of their moral status or past behaviour. The moralist seeks justice, the causalist seeks welfare.

The causalists are essentially short-term negative utilitarians. A causalist differs from other utilitarians in that he chooses to enact or to repeal or to support a law so as to minimize suffering, and not in order to maximize happiness nor to minimize the excess of suffering over happiness. The causalists are in no sense hedonists or epicureans—they are only concerned with 'disutility' or 'negative utility'; with the avoidance of harm, distress, suffering or conflict. Furthermore they seek to minimize suffering *now* in the particular observable and measurable situations with which they are confronted. They thus tend to consider only the short-term consequence of their decision to enforce or to repeal or to enact a particular law, and to assume that people's moral attitudes are not affected by their (the causalists) decisions. They are concerned only with the immediate and tangible consequences of the law, with things that can be measured or easily demonstrated.

These definitions and descriptions of moralism and causalism are derived and constructed from an analysis of the arguments to be found in parliamentary debates and reports. It is to these debates that we should now turn for an examination of the profound change that occurred in parliamentary thinking on the law and moral issues and in relation to moral issues involving or impinging on sexual conduct in particular.

Divorce

Prior to the 1969 Divorce Act, the law relating to divorce clearly embodied moralist thinking about the circumstances under which a divorce should or should not be granted. By contrast, the new law is largely based on moral principles of a causalist kind. Under the old law divorce was possible only if either husband or wife had committed a 'matrimonial offence', the standard offences being adultery, cruelty or desertion. In each and every divorce there had to be an 'innocent' and a 'guilty' party. A divorce action had as its core an accusation by one spouse that the other was guilty of one of these key offences. The accused spouse could either allow the divorce to go through undefended, thus in effect admitting they were guilty of the matrimonial offence, or could contest the divorce. Davies (1975, 15–16) described the process thus:

"If the divorce was contested then the courts settled the issue by a process in many ways similar to a criminal trial. Indeed the person accused of a matrimonial offence was described as defending the action. The accusatorial procedure with its two clearly separated and opposing sides, the ruthless cross-examination of witnesses by counsel, the angry recriminations, the accusations and counter-accusations, the giving of evidence by detectives and inquiry agents, all reminded the participants in a contested divorce action that the purpose and function of the court was to determine guilt and innocence. The petitioner sought to prove to the court and to the world that his or her spouse was guilty of a matrimonial offence. The spouse sought to deny this, to assert his or her innocence and even to show that it was the petitioner who was really the guilty party. A divorce became a prize that was awarded to the innocent party, a penalty imposed on the guilty spouse. The divorce procedure aimed at attaching the correct moral labels to the two parties. If no offence had been committed or at any rate if there was no evidence before the court that proved such an offence to the court's satisfaction then no divorce would be awarded, however clear it was that the marriage had broken down. In order for there to be a divorce somone had to be found to take the blame and usually the whole blame. In theory there could be no divorce by consent of the parties. Where a matrimonial offence had occurred the initiator of a divorce action had, of course, to be the innocent party. Unless the innocent party was willing to take such action, then the guilty person could do nothing to end the marriage and was unable to remarry, however pressing his or her need or wish to do so. In such a case the guilty person was felt to have received his or her deserts and it was felt proper that the innocent party should have the right to withhold consent to the legal severing of the marriage tie.

Fairness was seen as the distribution of rights and penalties according to the moral worthiness of the parties."

By contrast the new procedures for divorce laid down in the 1969 act do not seek primarily to determine guilt or innocence, but are concerned rather to ascertain whether or not a marriage has irretrievably broken down. The new law, its differences from and continuities with the old law and its causalist justification were summed up during the third reading of the bill in the House of Commons by one of its supporters, Dr Hugh Gray (Hansard, 1969), in these terms:

"It is true the Bill introduces the irretrievable breakdown of marriage as the basic reason for divorce and this should be welcomed but at the same time it retains the doctrine of the matrimonial offence despite its two principal innovations, namely divorce by consent in a civilised way after two years and divorce after five years against the wish of one party. Although one has to recognise that this last provision will be a source of grievance and suffering for many, one should also recognise that it will be a cause of great rejoicing to thousands more in this country, who have lived in stable relationships (i.e. with partners whom they are not free to remarry) for many years and the one hundred and eighty thousand illegitimate children in this country who will become legitimate. These people will be brought formally within society and surely this is a good thing."

The matrimonial offences are still part of the law but they are now neither necessary nor sufficient criteria for the granting of a divorce. The issue of guilt or innocence is no longer the crucial one but rather the weighing up of the alternative consequences for the various parties involved. The law no longer asks the question "who is to blame?" but asks rather "what is the best course of action to take in the given situation?" An unwilling 'innocent' party may feel aggrieved at being divorced against his or her will but in the view of a predominantly causalist legislature this may be outweighed by benefits to other persons.

The causalist supporters of the new act were careful to stress their dislike of divorce and support for the institution of marriage. However, in keeping with their causalist principles, they accepted that divorce was inevitable and sought to minimize the amount of harm and pain involved in the process of divorce itself. As Daniel Awdry, MP for Chippenham, put it:

"I believe the Bill will remove . . . . from the divorce courts a great deal of the distress, humiliation and bitterness which surrounds them today. I speak with some feeling here, as one who has practised a certain amount in a minor way in the divorce courts." (Hansard, 1969.)

The causalist supporters of the new act rejected entirely the moralist view that human interaction could and should be viewed in terms of the moral guilt of one party and the moral innocence of the other. Peter Emery (Hansard, 1969) stressed:

"It is necessary to repeat time and time again that the concept that in divorce there is only one guilty party is just not the case. I do not believe that there is one case in 5,000 where the blame can be placed on only one spouse. Therefore, there is the sharing of the problem of the breakdown. This should be analysed and proof of absolute breakdown should be a reason for final divorce. That seems a major step forward which today even the Church is willing to accept."

Mrs Lena Jeger (Hansard, 1969), who undermined the moralist assumptions about guilt and innocence even more radically, said:

"I am glad that we are getting away from the hypocrisy of the guilty or innocent party. This has always been a most artificial polarisation. We cannot indicate guilt on one side and innocence on the other when we are dealing with the strongest forms of human emotions, thought and relationships. We none of us know what are the strains and tensions which produce certain marital situations".

Here she argues not merely that it is impossible to allocate blame between the two partners in a way that would clearly discriminate between them, but that the whole concept of blame, of guilt and innocence, is irrelevant to divorce legislation. The explanation of 'certain marital situations' is to be sought not in terms of the consciously willed marital offences of one or other partner, but in terms of impersonal causes, of 'strains and tensions'.

These causalist views of divorce were of course anathema to the moralist opponents of the changes in the law. For many of them divorce was an absolute evil, marriage being an indissoluble sacrament. They saw people who indulged in divorce as wicked and had little sympathy for legislation that sought to spare such people grief or pain. Peter Mahon (Hansard, 1969) fulminated:

"Divorce has been known as the sacrament of adultery but with the passing of the Bill those days are over. Now we are legislating for divorce without shame and without guilt. Divorce is now to be a respectable sacrament . . ." . . . . "What of the hard cases as they are called? Those of us who are men and women of the world and feel that we have our feet on the ground say that in human affairs there are inevitably bound to be hard cases."

Even where the moralists conceded that a divorce, though wrong in itself, might be granted to an innocent person as a kind of consolation prize for virtue, they could not accept that the guilty party should be able to get a divorce against the wishes of the innocent. In their eyes to reward bad behaviour in this way was unethical even if it caused less anguish than the earlier moralist legislation. Sir Tufton Beamish (Hansard, 1969), though acknowledging that there was some merit in the causalist case against 'guilt' and 'innocence', felt strongly that the causalists had gone too far:

"The Bill also reflects the great anxiety that most of us have to remove the elements of guilt and innocence which sometimes bedevil our present divorce system but not as much as is sometimes pretended. The Bill seems to swing much too far the other way. A man or a woman would be able as a result of the Bill to extricate himself or herself from a solemn contract of which he or she was a willing party by committing an offence—by unilaterally breaking that contract to enable him or her to gain the support of the law in having it annulled. The matter is as straightforward that and I do not like it one bit."

Sir Tufton Beamish's sober repudiation of the rewarding of contract breaking is matched by Peter Mahon's anger at the rewarding of moral wickedness:

"With the passing of the Bill this House is proposing for the first time in English law that a defaulter can benefit from wrong doing. He can walk out on his wife and demand as in law some sort of freedom. He can walk out with somebody else's wife and still with the reform make his own bid for freedom. This is not freedom. This is licence. This is legislation for marital pandemonium or if we prefer it the law of the jungle." (Hansard, 1969.)

Even the clause permitting divorce by mutual consent after the marriage partners have lived apart for two years came under moralist criticism because it awarded a divorce to two people both of whom might be guilty parties, and neither of them innocent. Here there was no injustice to an aggrieved innocent party but nonetheless it was seen as a crime against morality that two guilty people should not somehow be penalized for their wickedness by being forbidden to remarry (other persons). Quintin Hogg (Hansard, 1969), though a supporter of the new law, saw on this issue some merit in the old law of divorce:

> "Let me explain the present (i.e. old) law when quite irrespective of the demonstration of matrimonial offence both parties thoroughly despise the institution of marriage so as to show by their conduct that they hold it in contempt" . . . "I have known many bilateral examples in which both parties have played fast and loose with the institution of marriage. The law at the moment is that they forfeit their right, even if their marriage breaks down, and irrespective of matrimonial offence, to have their marriage wound up by the courts" . . . "in other words it is said that their behaviour brings marriage into contempt and they are not free to undertake it again. We are abolishing that safeguard for the institution of marriage and I have considerable reservations whether that is wise. I do not think that this by itself would lead me to condemn the Bill but it is an issue which requires a little further consideration."

Abortion

The supporters of the Medical Termination of Pregnancy Bill 1966, which in an amended form became the Abortion Act 1967, put forward a predominantly causalist case, stressing the alternative sets of consequences stemming from the law if reformed and if left as it was. They did not press for individual freedom, or women's liberation or an extension of the permissive society. They simply insisted that legalized abortion was the lesser of two evils. In moving the second reading of his (Private Member's) Bill in July 1966, David Steel declared "We want to stamp out the back-street abortions, but it is not the intention of the Promoters of the Bill to leave a wide-open door for abortion on request." He went on to say "We have to avoid in the Bill wording which is so restrictive as not to have the effect we are seeking, namely the ending of back-street abortions." (Hansard, 1966.)

A year later in July 1967, in moving the Third Reading, David Steel still took essentially the same causalist line:

> "Anyone advancing the Bill has in no way been advocating abortion. I must make this clear because I detect from some of the mountain of correspondence I have received over the last year a belief that some who advance the Bill think that abortion should be encouraged and more widely practised. I must say that this is not so" . . . . . "So often this is not understood by those outside the House who believe that those advancing

the Bill have done so on quite spurious grounds, that we are advocating abortion as something to be encouraged. The main case for the Bill and for clarifying the law rests on the grounds that we are hopeful that the scourge of criminal abortion will be substantially removed from our land." (Hansard, 1967.)

The essentially causalist nature of the reformers' arguments was noted at an early stage by one of the reform's principal opponents, Dr Norman St John-Stevas (Hansard, 1966): "The case for the Bill has rested partly on utilitarian considerations—that there is a high number of illegal abortions and that this Bill would reduce them." The reformers' case was consistently presented in terms of the need to clarify the law relating to abortion and to extend it in such a way as to replace the unsafe procedures of unqualified abortionists by medically supervised operations, even if this meant permitting and condoning an action regarded by many people as utterly abhorrent. Always the stress was placed on specific issues and the limited number of alternative outcomes of particular situations. Wider moral and philosophical issues were played down. Cause and consequence lay at the centre of their arguments, not the assertion of rights and values.

The opponents of the Bill replied in moralist terms. They tabled an amendment (Simms and Hindell, 161–2) asserting that the bill "threatens the independence of the medical profession, contains no adequate safeguard against the destruction of potentially healthy babies and undermines respect for the sanctity of human life." Simms and Hindell (1971, 162) comment on this moralist strategy in a causalist legislature: "Perhaps it was the most honourable if not the most shrewd decision to oppose the whole Bill on principle". The moralist objection that abortion was essentially morally wicked was later advanced even against the reformers' main aim of seeking to eliminate the back-street abortionist. Peter Mahon (Hansard, 1967) declared rhetorically:

"How do we abolish the back-street abortionist—by substituting front-street killing of the innocent unborn on the National Health? Is that the way we are to do it? Herod's was no greater crime than this" ...
"Back-street abortionists are rightly abhorred but whatever the harm done to the women the first and greatest injustice is the taking of the unborn child's life. This injustice is by no means abated by having the abortion carried out by doctors in the best aseptic conditions." (See also Wells, 1966.)

The moralist objections to abortion were strongly advanced in opposition to two clauses of the original bill, the social clause which permitted abortion in the interests of the well-being of the mother and her existing children and the eugenic clause which permitted abortion if there was a risk "that if the child were born it would suffer from such physical or mental abnormalities as to be seriously handicapped." The former clause was especially objectionable to the moralist because it weighed up the life of the foetus not against the life or health of the mother, which might be expected to arouse equal moral sympathy, but against the apparently material criterion of social well-being. The latter was seen as the thin end of the wedge to infanticide and euthanasia, and thus as raising further absolute moral objections. Dr Norman St John Stevas (Hansard, 1966) argued that it "introduces quite a new principle into the law, namely that one human being can make a judgement about another as to whether that human being's life is worth living."

The moralist's position on the taking of life was a curious one, since many of those who were opposed to abortion were, however, in favour of capital punishment. Equally many of the supporters of the abortion act had earlier voted to abolish capital punishment. Mrs Jill Knight (Hansard, 1966) found this paradoxical when seen from a moralist point of view:

"Once we accept that it is lawful to kill a human being because it causes inconvenience where do we end? Society or at any rate the majority in this house has already conceded that the life of a convicted murder shall be preserved. How can we possibly agree to that and yet kill the most innocent of things, an unborn baby? It just does not seem to be logical."

There is of course a logical consistency to the position of those causalists who supported the abortion bill and opposed capital punishment, but their moral premises are very different from those of the moralists. (I have outlined the differences on capital punishment in detail elsewhere; see Davies, 1975, 37–44.) They are primarily concerned to avoid harm and pain regardless of moral status. The foetus can be sacrificed but not the murderer simply because its capacity for suffering is less. It cannot anticipate the moment of its demise, it has no plans, expectations, relationships that would be suddenly, finally and irreversibly disrupted. It cannot know the sufferings that spring from human self-consciousness and awareness. The real problem implicit in this position was the one pointed out by Norman St John Stevas in the debate on the eugenic clause: "If it is desirable to blot out deformity, it would be much more logical and sensible to let the child be born and then to destroy it" (**Simms and**

Hindell, 1971, 164). However, these causalist considerations were not seen as relevant by the stalwart moralist Mrs Knight, for whom the key moral criteria were the moral guilt of the murderer who deserved to be punished and the moral innocence of the foetus that deserved to be preserved. Her bafflement was shared by those who were against both abortion and capital punishment on moralist grounds. Peter Mahon (Hansard, 1967) declaimed:

> "Not long ago I voted with pride as did the vast majority of Hon. Members against judicial murder. Basically we voted that way because we believed it wrong to take a human life *irrespective of the measure of accountability* involved. Is the House now about to turn turtle by accepting as a general principle that it would be right to destroy a potential human life? How can the nation which has abolished the legal killing of murderers and ended judicial murder sanction the killing of an unborn child?"

When the question of whether a woman should automatically be granted an abortion if she 'became pregnant as a result of rape' the moralists were split decisively into two groups, rather as they had been on the question of divorce. Some regarded abortion as so abhorrent that it could not be granted under any circumstances, just as there were some members of Parliament who believed that divorce should never be allowed (as was the case until recently in Italy). Others felt that a divorce or an abortion could be granted to *innocent* persons to extricate them from the consequences of other people's crimes. Just as adultery could justify divorce in the eyes of these moralists, so could rape justify abortion.

In the view of this category of moralists the Abortion Bill threatened to give abortions to the wrong people—to sinful, feckless, promiscuous people who did not deserve an abortion. In their view an abortion ought to be granted according to the moral deserts of the mother. The special moral status of the *innocent* foetus can be disregarded if the mother is more innocent and sinned against than the embryo. The chief exponent of this view was Mrs Jill Knight, who found abortion abhorrent but was prepared to allow this abhorrence to be overridden by her even greater abhorrence of rape (Hansard, 1967):

> "When I outlined the method of operation required for this horrible abortion I said that one must have good reason for it. I said that it was not enough that the child was not wanted. An act of rape completely changes the character of this ordeal. If the Right Honorable Lady reads my speeches she will see that I have said consistently that rape must be

regarded as a horrible experience and that it was quite unfair to ask a woman to carry through a pregnancy resulting from rape."

Mrs Knight was arguing here against the causalist view of Miss Alice Bacon that the victim of a rape could get an abortion anyway on the grounds that to bear the rapist's child would damage her health or well-being (Clause 1a of the Act—see below). Mrs Knight did not accept this and declared (Hansard, 1967) "I regard these circumstances as meriting special consideration. I want to see rape spelled out clearly as a particular reason for abortion." The implication of her argument is that a woman who has been raped deserves an abortion not because she is liable to suffer most but because she is free of all blame. Rape was an involuntary act from her point of view. She did not will it. She is indeed in one of the most deserving of all the moralist's categories—she is a victim. This view curiously was shared by Mr Aleck Bourne who has been quite wrongly attacked (Shaw, 1969, 46) as "the patron saint of the movement for easier abortion" as a result of his prosecution in 1938 for performing an abortion on a 14-year-old girl who was pregnant as a result of having been raped by a group of guardsmen. Mr Bourne, however, belonged to an even more curious category of moralists than Mrs Knight. The worthy doctor sought to discriminate morally between worthy and unworthy rape victims.

Simms and Hindell (1971, 70) describe how Bourne's attitude to the rape victim was determined by her moral standing:

"Dr. Joan Malleson . . . wrote to Mr. Bourne at St. Mary's Hospital where he was Consultant Obstetrician, strongly recommending that the child's pregnancy be terminated and this Mr. Bourne agreed to do—though not immediately. There is a curious and disquieting passage in his autobiography *A Doctor's Creed*, in which he says of his young patient: 'I admitted her on June 6th, 1938. I kept her in bed in the ward for eight days to be sure of the type of girl I was dealing with . . . both I and the ward sister watched my patient very carefully during the eight days.' Then Bourne took a swab for pathological examination. 'The occasion caused a complete breakdown of her morale. All her assumed cheerfulness disappeared as she wept beyond control. This decided me at once that she had to be relieved of her pregnancy. In her there was nothing of the cold indifference of the prostitute.' For her innocence and good morals Bourne rewarded her with an abortion. Had she remained 'normally cheerful' to use Bourne's description of her when she was first admitted to hospital, she would have been punished by being made to continue with a pregnancy resulting from multiple rape. Bourne was a hero to the public of his time because he challenged the law and risked his career for the sake of a young girl. But the hero had the moral outlook of a high-minded albeit Victorian governess and later turned out to have feet of clay."

This view that abortion should be reserved for the virtuous was a common one among the opponents of abortion reform enlisted in SPUC, the Society for the Protection of the Unborn Child. Simms and Hindell (1971, 99) write:

"The Rev. K. Ward, Rector of Daventry . . . told (his congregation) that as Christians they must be certain that abortion was not 'made available for all and sundry who behave promiscuously and irresponsibly'. This notion that abortion if it was to be tolerated at all should be a reward for virtue, whereas the wicked and irresponsible should be punished with unwanted babies was a recurrent theme throughout the SPUC campaign and was probably the attitude most often voiced in the campaign against reform.'

The view that abortion could be granted to the virtuous and especially to the innocent was, however, anathema to other moralists who were infuriated at the injustice of punishing the innocent foetus for the misdeeds of the guilty rapist. Dr Norman St. John Stevas (Hansard, 1967) declared:

"There is an ethical point involved here. Although naturally we all agree that rape is an unjust and highly immoral action, the child conceived as a result of that unjust and immoral action is completely innocent."

and Peter Mahon (Hansard, 1967) proclaimed that:

"No one suggests today that terrible crime though it be, the person responsible for raping a woman or child should be put to death, yet that is precisely what is being done to the innocent unborn child who is by no means responsible. If our conscience is not outraged at the thought of this being done, what in heaven's name has happened to us?"

These divisions in the moralist camp were probably irrelevant in that the dominant causalists would have triumphed anyway. David Steel, whose original bill contained a clause permitting abortion after rape, withdrew the clause in the face of causalist criticism and opposed its reintroduction:

"I hope that the Hon. Member will not press the Amendment because I believe that the cases of genuine sexual assault and unlawful carnal knowledge are catered for by the discretion given to the medical profession to consider these two matters regarding the total environment of the patient and her mental health." (Hansard, 1967.)

On behalf of the Home Office, Miss Alice Bacon (Hansard, 1967) spelt out the orthodox causalist view of the matter in detail:

"The Clause (i.e. 1a) as amended, provides that it shall not be an offence if the doctor is of the opinion 'that the continuance of the pregnancy would involve risk to the life of or injury to the physical or mental health of the pregnant woman or any existing children of her family and in determining whether or not there is such a risk of injury to life account may be taken of the patient's total environment actual or reasonably foreseeable.' I cannot think of anything that would affect the mental health of a woman or a girl more than having to bear a child as a result of rape or sexual assault . . . .

". . . I hope that the mover of the Amendment will ask leave to withdraw it, because it would put us in a difficult position if we were driven to vote on this issue when practically everybody in the House would not want a woman to bear a child as a result of rape. It is not so much a question of what we want in the end; it is a question of the way to go about providing for it. My advice is that subsection (1a) covers the circumstances for which the Amendment seeks to provide."

It was this speech that so infuriated the moralist Mrs Knight earlier, and goaded her to reply so angrily to Miss Bacon. Mrs Knight's arguments failed to convince the causalists on the subject of rape just as they had earlier when she was rebuked by the arch-causalist Roy Jenkins (Hansard, 1967):

"(Abortion) is a very nasty business which should be resorted to only in certain circumstances but one does not necessarily take the easy view that she (Mrs Knight) does that an abortion may be for a good or a bad reason".

These causalist views prevailed throughout the abortion act and largely determined its final clauses as I have indicated in detail elsewhere (Davies, 1975).

Homosexuality

Until the Sexual Offences Act 1967, males indulging in any kind of homosexual behaviour, even if by mutual consent and out of public view, were liable to criminal prosecution and punishment. The reasons for the original enactment of such laws persecuting male homosexuals are complex and tied in with Britain's military and religious traditions (Davies, 1975, 1979). The Members of Parliament who successfully sought to overthrow these well-entrenched legal prohibitions mainly argued their case along causalist lines. They did not attack the view that homosexuality was wrong or sinful, nor did they radically assert the right of homosexuals to follow their sexual inclinations with the same freedom as heterosexuals, regardless of the censorious views of others.

Indeed, the supporters of law reform went out of their way to stress their lack of approval of homosexuality (see below). Rather they emphasized the harm and suffering that was caused by the law and the unhappiness of homosexuals generally. Typical of this position was the speech of Dr David Owen (Hansard, 1966) which began with the qualified libertarian moralism of an oft-quoted paragraph from the Wolfenden Report, but which shifted very rapidly to a curious mixture of moral condemnation of homosexuality and causalist sympathy for their plight in being harassed not merely by public opinion but by the criminal law:

"It was said in the Wolfenden Report, which most of us feel to be one of the best Reports ever to come out on this subject, that, the decisive argument which made the Wolfenden Committee take the stand it did was:

'. . . . the importance which society and the law ought to give to individual freedom of choice and action in matters of private morality.'

The quotation goes on:

'Unless a deliberate attempt is to be made by society, acting through the agency of the law to equate the sphere of crime with that of sin, there must remain a realm of private morality and immorality which is, in brief and crude terms, not the law's business. To say this is not to condone or to encourage private immorality.'

This, to me, is the nub of the problem, which this Bill tackles, and tackles most courageously. These people, suffering from what I would prefer to call a symptom of homosexuality, already suffer very deeply from social ostracism. They are to a great extent alone in the world. But, because of the present law, a law which the Hon. Member for Ilford North himself dislikes, they live in perpetual fear. Much has been made of the possibility of blackmail, and this is very important, but it is not the only fear. The real fear these people have is fear of prosecution. They know that they can be prosecuted. These are people who often, for other reasons, are mentally unstable in that they are anxious and nervous, and the threat of prosecution is very real . . . Those of us who have seen these people know how tortured they are. They come from all walks of life. We are not talking of the stage picture of the 'queer', the 'nancy boy'. Often, these people go through life with those in closest contact with them not having the slightest knowledge that they live this tortured existence. My Hon. Friend the Member for Rochester and Chatham (Mrs. Anne Kerr) told us of the difficulties for them when they are forced by society's pressures to marry. These can be very severe, too. But so often they live in loneliness and fear. We cannot stop their loneliness. Society, I submit, will always condemn homosexual practice, and it would not be my wish that the House should be seen to condone it. But I ask the House to vote to remove the fear from those men who so order their lives that they do not inflict themselves and their ailment on society, and to allow them in the privacy of their own homes to pursue their lives as they are driven to do."

Dr Owen began as if he were going to argue that the law should not curtail "individual freedom of choice and action" but rapidly moved to the position that the law should not cause fear and suffering. The arguments are not incompatible but it is significant that he choses to stress the latter.

As usual however the classic statement of the causalist case for law reform came from Mr Roy Jenkins (Hansard, 1967):

"It would be a mistake to think—my Hon. Friend the Member for Preston South (Mr. Peter Mahon) has some curious views on this—that by what we are doing tonight we are giving a vote of confidence or congratulation to homosexuality. Those who suffer from this disability carry a great weight of loneliness, guilt and shame. The crucial question, which we are nearly at the end of answering decisively, is, should we add to those disadvantages the full rigour of the criminal law? By its overwhelming decisions, the House has given a fairly clear answer, and I hope that the Bill will now make rapid progress towards the Statute Book. It will be an important and civilising Measure."

The moralists who sought to retain criminal sanctions against homosexuality argued with very varying degrees of sophistication. Often they simply saw the criminal law as providing a suitable vehicle for the expression of personal or popular disgust. Mr Ian Percival said of one type of homosexual behaviour (Hansard, 1967):

"Every jury which is directed by a judge is told in simple terms what that offence is, because people do not know what it is and they will not ask about it. I would tell this House what it is, if it were not for the fact that there are young people in the Gallery. The reason why I will not tell the House what it is when there are young people in the Gallery is that one offence is so utterly disgusting and degrading that I do not wish to give details of it in public, here or anywhere else. Let nobody be in any doubt, however, on that offence, which comes within the category of homosexuality, of the disgusting nature of . . . ." (interrupted).

Mr W. R. Rees-Davies (Hansard, 1967) saw homosexual behaviour as unnatural and shocking to Englishmen and Indians alike:

"I am delighted that the Leader of the House has woken up after that delightful speech. I do not dissent from the observations of the Hon. Member for Westhoughton (Mr. J. T. Price) when he says we want a rather less sophisticated approach.

"I had lunch with the Secretary of the Congress Party of India who expressed horror that the Government could have extra time for this Bill in the present circumstances . . ."

". . . The suggestion that those of 21 years of age should be given complete freedom to engage in acts of buggery without any kind of control or criminal sanction whatsoever is one which is completely contrary to nature. It has been far too frequently overlooked, particularly by the Press, that what we are concerned with first and foremost in this debate and on the Amendment is the basic fact that we are seeking to offer a complete right to do as one pleases on matters that are contrary to the normal nature of mankind. This is violently objected to by many of the countries in the Commonwealth as contravening the ordinary laws of nature."

The moralists opposed to the bill feared that the abolition of legal penalties would lead to an increase in homosexual behaviour. Sir Cyril Osborne quoted approvingly from a letter a doctor had written to him (Hansard, 1967) "Just a line to wish you success in your efforts to get Leo Abse's Bill for spreading filth chucked out tomorrow". Accordingly he sought unsuccessfully to move an amendment to the bill that:

"Anyone who indulges in activities tending to promote acts of homosexuality between consenting adults through the publication of lists of names and addresses of known homosexuals, or otherwise, shall be guilty of a criminal offence and shall be liable on conviction to imprisonment for a term of five years or to a fine of £5,000."

In support of his own amendment he declared that:

"The Hon. and Learned Gentleman also said that the Clause would punish people who ran clubs that incidentally brought homos together. Punishment is deserved by any association that brings homos together and encourages these acts that I think are repulsive. I read all the debates on the subject in the past two years last weekend and I did not find one Hon. Member who defended the practice of homosexuality. Everybody said that it was a degrading and disgusting habit. Therefore, if a club incidentally or partially operates so as to bring homos together and encourage this degrading and demoralising activity, I say that it should be punished. The Clause wants that to be done, but the Home Office says, 'No', and on this we shall have to oppose it."

More sophisticated moralists, stressing the function of the law as an expression of common moral standards, tried to refute the causalist utilitarianism of the reformers by appealing to a kind of Durkheimian mechanical solidarity. Thomas Iremonger was perhaps the best exponent of this point of view (Hansard, 1966):

"If we could have life and history all over again and could go back to that moment in the 1880s when the House was considering that Measure and Labouchère popped in that Amendment, (which has been the basis for the persecution and punishment of most minor homosexual acts) there would be Hon. Members here today who—if they could have been there—would have said, 'Let us not do this. It won't work out. This Measure will give rise to greater evils that it will cure.'

"I will concede that. But the trouble is that the law is the law and is accepted by the community, rightly or wrongly, as representing moral standards and the strength of the social fabric. This House cannot right a wrong just by changing the law. It has to consider the psychological implications on society of this House coming forward, as the public will see it—(Interruption)—With respect, many men and women whom I know will see this House coming forward as 'Authority', as Parliament, as the legislature, and saying, 'We are giving our blessing to sexual licence and to practices which you regard as abominable.'"

Here we have an attempt to meet the arguments of the causalists directly and to blend moralism with a long-term view of social change. Iremonger concluded (Hansard, 1966):

"What I am concerned with is the health and strength of society and the structure of life, the relationships between human beings that make society sane, healthy and beautiful. That is something which can only be ensured in respect of future generations. I do not think it can be ensured in respect of people who are already mature."

However, crude or subtle, the moralists were bound to lose. The short-term negative utilitarianism of the causalist prevailed once again on the issue of homosexuality, though perhaps not so decisively as in the case of divorce or abortion. The causalists successfully reformed the law, but they had to employ a wider range of arguments and to make significant verbal and substantive concessions to the moralists.

Legitimacy

A further Private Member's Bill involving sexual morality which succeeded in changing the law was the Legitimacy Bill which received its second reading in January 1959. The bill sought to enable parents to legitimize a child born out of wedlock by subsequent marriage, *even though* one of the parents had been married to a third party at the time the child was born. The supporters of the bill pressed the causalist point that changing the law would reduce the harm done to those who would otherwise suffer the stigma of illegitimacy. Mr John Howard (Hansard, 1959) who had previously tried and failed to get Parliament to accept such a reform noted that:

"It is apparent that real grievous hardship and mental suffering are being experienced by a wide range of people at all social levels by virtue of the stigma of illegitimacy. If we pass the Bill we shall make a very material contribution towards the contentment of mind of this class of person."

Sir Robert Cary (Hansard, 1959), fearful of moralist opposition to the Bill, urged Parliament to concentrate on the causalist aspects of the legislation:

"I ask Hon. Members in considering the Bill to keep in the foreground not so much the religious and social aspects of the matter which touch upon provocative subjects concerned with the divorce but primarily to regard this as a Children's Bill to benefit a minority of children, who have to drag socially one of the worst crucifixes in life which can be imposed upon a young child."

However, the moral climate in Parliament in 1959 differed significantly from the mood of triumphant causalism that prevailed in the middle and late sixties when abortion, divorce and homosexuality were debated. John Parker (Hansard, 1959) in introducing the legitimacy bill was careful to stress the moralist aspect of the case for the illegitimate child and quoted The British Medical Association report that stressed the fact that "It is not yet universally recognised that whatever the guilt of the parents of the illegitimate child no moral blame can rest on the child itself."

John Parker (Hansard, 1959) in a historical survey of previous Legitimacy Bills cited the moralist arguments that had defeated a similar measure to his in 1926:

"The most common argument first put forward was that 'justice could be done to the child but only by lowering the standard of public morality' . . .
"The second most common argument put forward in this discussion was that it would encourage divorce. It was said that people would not think twice before committing adultery if the resulting child would be legitimate" . . .
"the other most interesting argument was that put forward by Douglas Hacking then the Under-Secretary at the Home Office. His main point was that this was necessary to protect the wife from undue pressure for divorce when her husband had had an illegitimate child by another woman and wanted to marry its mother."

Against these arguments, which foreshadow the moralist objections to divorce law reform cited earlier, Parker pressed a moralist argument of his own which stressed the *innocence* of the children involved:

"It is worth while considering how far these various arguments of over thrity years ago stand up today. The most interesting thing about all these arguments is that underlying all of them is the evil, wicked doctrine that the end justifies the means, that one should discourage divorce, protect the woman, maintain public morality or tidy up the law so as to bring it into line with that of Scotland by condemning innocent children to suffer a stigma for life. The underlying doctrine that the end justifies the means we have seen underlying much of Nazi and Communist propaganda in recent years, but it is a serious reflection that it was so generally advanced in this British Parliament more than thirty years ago, without shame apparently.

"One should look at these different arguments in detail. First, I find it very difficult to understand the value of a public morality which in order to be maintained demands that guiltless children should go through life with a stigma just because one of the parents was married to a third party when the child was born."

This enabled him to gain the support of moralists such as Mr W. A. Wilkins who wanted to blame someone but agreed that it should not be the child:

"We are dealing here with a helpless and unfortunate section of the community who can do nothing for themselves and who rely absolutely upon us to rectify injustices as we see them. The children with whom we are concerned are the legitimate outcome of illegitimate association. If we want to place responsibility or blame or a stigma on someone, we should place it where it rightly belongs—on the people originally guilty of the offence of bringing an illegitimate child into the world." (Hansard, 1959.)

The moralist critics of the bill were not entirely convinced and David Renton (Hansard, 1959) described the debate as a "conflict between morality and compassion," . . . "between the sanctity of marriage and compassion towards children" though he conceded that the children had "not . . . chosen their parents".

Sir John Hobson one of the few members to vote against the second reading put forward the moralist argument that:

"Therefore, what we now have to decide is whether this Measure will, to some extent, cause a breach in the idea of the sanctity of marriage and, if so, whether the benefit that will be conferred on the few children whom it may concern in the future ought to outweigh that consideration. The Royal Commission on Marriage and Divorce majority put the argument in this way, that one of the fundamental moral bases of marriage in this country is that a man cannot during the subsistence of that marriage beget lawful children by another woman, and that if in accordance with this Measure adultery and bastards could be legitimised subsequently, an essential distinction between lawful marriages and illicit unions would disappear." (Hansard, 1959.)

Philip Bell (Hansard, 1959) agreed with this moralist argument but was clearly uncomfortable about the equally moralist argument that it was unjust to penalize the guiltless children. He put forward the extraordinary view that no stigma was attached to being a bastard and that the stigma was really directed only at the parents!

"People in England these days do not like being called a bastard. Why? Because they do not like their parents being insulted. It is the reflection on the family to which they object. It is the fact that a slur has been cast upon their parents to which they object. History . . . has never really been hard upon bastards themselves . . . bastards have played their part in history and nobody thought the worse of them. Therefore the stigma is directed strictly to the parents and when people object to it they object to the insult to their parents which implies that they broke the marriage vow . . .

"It is idle to think that by a law one can or should remove from the view of the world the fact that a married person has committed one of the most dishonourable acts he can, that while he is pledged by everything that is decent to one woman he should not even wait for a divorce but has to associate with another woman. There should be no excuse. . . .

"There are around people who are known as illegitimate, who themselves are not blamed but stand as witnesses to the consequences that happen, to the dislocation and sometimes the pain and embarrassment that happens not merely to the person concerned but to collaterals and other people. They are living witnesses to the fact that legitimacy and keeping one's word and being true are one thing, and no legislation and no retrospective legitimation alters the fact. We should face facts and not try, no matter how good the reasons, to disguise from ourselves that sin is sin."

This peculiar argument brought a mixed causalist-and-moralist rebuke from George Isaacs (Hansard, 1959):

"The Hon. and Learned Gentleman completely forgot that we are not talking about marriage, we are talking about the welfare of little children. . . . a man does not like being told that he is illegitimate and was born out of wedlock. It is not such a man's fault. He could not help it. He did not ask to be brought into the world. Why should people continue to suffer for this reason?"

Because of their ability to bring both moralist and causalist arguments to bear in support of the bill at a point in time when causalism was beginning to replace moralism as the dominant mode of argument, the supporters of reform of the law relating to legitimacy were in general successful. The pure moralism of the opposition was overborne.

However, one clause suggested by John Parker at a later stage had to be withdrawn. Parker had suggested that:

"Any child born to a married woman and accepted as one of the family by her husband shall be deemed to be the child of her husband provided she was married at the time of the child's birth and upon acceptance by the husband the birth certificate shall be amended to provide that the said child is the legitimate child of the marriage." (Hansard, 1959.)

This piece of benevolent chicanery was supported on causalist grounds by David Weitzman (Hansard, 1959) who argued:

"The deed has been done. The child has been born. I do not think that anybody would suggest that any of these children could have been prevented from being born merely because some one would have had a discussion about the responsibilities and the holiness of family life. We are dealing with actual cases, and consideration of the child's position goes to the heart of everybody. That is the real consideration. If there is the slightest chance of unhappiness in family life, if there is likely to be discord between children because in a family there are illegitimate children living with children that are legitimate, it should be the object of Parliament to alter that state. The tendency nowadays is to look at these matters realistically . . .

"I do not mind if it is a legalised forgery, assuming that it is possible for such a thing to exist. Let us have something in the register correcting it. Surely there is no objection to that.

"I return to the one simple point with which I am concerned. If this Clause does anything to remove unhappiness from a child, let us accept it."

On this occasion, however, it was the moralist harangues of Mr Philip Bell that prevailed. Here we see a classic statement of the old-fashioned moralist case:

"The real point behind our discussions is not the happiness or welfare of an individual but how far it contributes to the solidarity of family life. The point is whether it makes the family a better unit. The point is not whether it makes it easier or more comfortable for people to live together but whether it makes the family with its vow of faithfulness and honour a better unit. Does it encourage people to carry out their vows? . . . In our affairs there is often a desire prompted by hard cases and by irritation to take short cuts. We see it in all forms of legislation. It is attractive in that it remedies a particular pain . . . these are short cuts. The real answer is not to remove every restraint there should be upon a mother or upon a father by saying, 'Even if you have an illegitimate child nothing will happen to the child. It can be put into a position equivalent to that of your lawful children. There is still, and there should be, some restraint on people giving way to their passions, and one restraint is the consequences on other people . . . It is true, as the Hon. Gentleman said, that it would be—or could be—very nasty in family life to have some legitimate and some illegitimate children. The answer is for husbands and wives to remember that before they indulge their passions.

"To change the name from illegitimacy to legitimacy is not the answer—it is only changing the name. The wife or husband remains dishonoured. It is no good their saying that the child is legitimate—in the circumstances foreseen someone has been dishonourable, and no change in name can change what was an act of dishonour into an act of honour". (Hansard, 1959.)

The clause was withdrawn. This (May 1959) was one of the last victories the moralists were to enjoy. Over the next ten years, they were to doomed to lose heavily to the rising causalists as has already been shown in the analyses of divorce, abortion and homosexuality.

The Nature and Roots of Causalism

At this point it is necessary to analyse the sociological reasons for the rise of the causalists and the way in which they emerged from the interaction of (a) the general social changes that have affected most industrial societies, (b) the distinctive lack of a coherent shared secular ideology in Britain and (c) the changing situation and experiences of members of Parliament. It would be a mistake to view causalism in terms of general secularization or creeping egalitarianism, though these changes certainly undermined the position of the moralists. Such a view is unhelpful in that it provides no explanation of why British secularization and creeping egalitarianism took the particular form that they did. The merit of concentrating on the particular nature of causalism itself is that it can direct our attention to the different forms secularization can take and to the structural factors that determined its course in Britain due to the absence of strong secular ideological constraints.

It is significant that in Britain it was causalism that filled the vacuum left by the collapse of religious morality. There are after all at least three secular alternatives that might have competed with causalism but which were nothing like as significant features of the Parliamentary debates, viz. (i) libertarian moralism—the assertion of individual freedom and rights; (ii) hedonism or at least a happiness-based utilitarianism; and (iii) a long-run secular view of what constitutes a good or a happy society or at any rate a more sophisticated view of social evolution set within a longer time-span than that considered by the causalists.

Although arguments concerning the rights of homosexuals or women seeking abortion clearly excited the members of pressure groups seeking to influence Parliament, these arguments were rarely advanced in Parliament itself. Appeals to the principle of individual liberty were not a central feature of the reformers' arguments and the moralist defenders of the *status quo* sometimes found themselves refuting a libertarianism that no one was putting forward. It was the moralists who saw the world in terms of a tension between morality and liberty and they found the causalists' moral universe difficult to comprehend. Hugh Fraser ended up complaining that: "It is a sad commentary—sad perhaps but accurate that after 1,000 days of this Government there has been no extension of freedom save to the bugger and the abortioner." (Hansard, 1967.)

The absence of libertarianism is particularly striking if we consider the contrast with the United States where both restrictive and libertarian moralism are much stronger than in Britain. In America attempts to regulate sexual behaviour by law have been far more determined and ferocious than anything that has been seen in Britain. Secularization is undermining these restrictions but the mechanism of change is different simply because America has an official secular ideology embodied in the American constitution. For this reason American abortion reformers fought their case in the courts rather than in the legislatures and on the grounds that anti-abortion laws constituted "an invalid abridgment of women's constitutional rights" (Simms and Hindell, 1971). It was the United States Supreme Court that legalized abortions in 1972 and the law now firmly gives women the right to choose. By contrast the libertarian moralists in Britain, despite the reform in the abortion laws, feel somehow betrayed by the causalists. Simms and Hindell complained at one stage that "David Steel, the medical profession and the Government were propounding the view that the law must not be made too clear lest the public read it and begin to demand their rights." (Simms and Hindell, 1971, 185.)

The American *opponents* of abortion similarly put forward distinctively American arguments grounded in the American Constitutional guarantees of individual rights. Russell Shaw (1969) argued that:

"The unborn child threatened with abortion, though he is guilty of no crime and is charged with none, does not enjoy such elementary protections as a defender, a hearing, specifications to support the demand for his destruction and the right of appeal . . . Violation of due process and equal protection of the laws: though the unborn child is a person with an inalienable right to life, he could under the proposed statute (i.e. of the American Law Institute's model penal code) be condemned to death in secret and summary proceedings and without representation . . . the statute would leave the determination of life or death to secret proceedings conducted by medical practitioners rather than judicial authorities . . ."

The moralist argument about innocence is familar from the British moralist objections to abortion and so is the overall legal philosophy. However, only an American appealing to the official liberal ideology of the American Constitution could press questions of individual rights and due process in such a legalistic fashion. In America the stripping away of religious moralism merely reveals a different kind of moralism, a secular libertarian and legalistic moralism which is very different from British causalism.

The second point of view that was absent from the British debates was hedonistic utilitarianism. No one dared to argue, for instance, that freeing homosexuals from legal constraints was a good thing because it would enable them to have more frequent and satisfying sexual encounters or that the legalization of abortion as a back-stop to possible contraceptive failure would make for greater heterosexual sexual enjoyment. The merely farcical and jocular nature of Parliamentary hedonism may be illustrated from a speech by Mr W. Rees-Davies (Hansard, 1967) during the report stage of the Sexual Offences Bill:

"The Hon. Member for Smethwick (Mr Faulds) is not here. Being a man who, like me, makes no shame of the fact that he likes the ladies, he raised the point 'I think it is a bit hard on 'queers' if they cannot have their pleasures without being bullied'."

Even in the most liberal view, sex was merely viewed as a 'compulsive' drive and the difficulties and pains of abstinence were stressed rather than the potential pleasure of perverts. Leo Abse in introducing the Sex Offences Bill declared:

"In fact, the law gives them a brutal choice. It offers them either celibacy or criminality, and nothing in between. And since homosexual behaviour, it is to be assumed, is no less compulsive, though lamentably different in direction, than heterosexuality, we are demanding a code of behaviour from them which the heterosexualists among us know that we could not possibly sustain. I ask those of us who are blessed with the emotional security of a heterosexual life, those who are blessed with a good wife and with a family, those who have the blessing of children, have we the right to demand this code of behaviour from those whose terrible fate it is to be a homosexual? I do not think that we have, and in any event it is an unreal demand, and it is impossible for it to be met." (Hansard, 1966.)

Finally there was a lack of sophisticated consideration in the debates of long-run social changes. The dominant causalists were, with a few honourable exceptions, not interested in such problems and the moralists found it difficult to adapt their arguments, outlook and vocabulary in such a way as to grapple with them effectively. The causalists often failed to see that the problem of changing attitudes to law and morality even existed while the moralists saw the problem but lacked the intellectual flexibility to deal with it adequately.

The decline of moralism and the rise and particular characteristics of causalism may be related to the evolution of British society into a *non-ideological bureaucratic welfare state* by the 1960s. Causalism was the natural moral outlook of such a society. The causalists' central obsession with minimizing harm and suffering regardless of people's moral deserts paralleled the explicit aims of the welfare-bureaucracy and the politicians who had created it. The absence of hedonism and of libertarian moralism reflect the welfare bureaucracy's faith in paternalistic social controls. The short-run outlook of the causalists on moral issues was equally that of the politicians and bureaucrats on social and economic problems. The politicians lived from election to election, the bureaucrats from crisis to crisis.

The lack of ideological agreement in British society and politics also contributed to the rise of causalism. Causalism is the lowest common denominator of morality, the only possible language of communication between the diverse ideological groups to be found in Parliament. Anyone seeking to reform the law on a moral issue by Private Member's Bill, will seek to maximize the support he receives by capturing the middle ground (cf. Simms and Hindell, 1971, 157). In a secular society without an official ideology that middle ground is necessarily a causalist area. The British cannot agree on what are the central political principles of their society or its long-term goals. The only basis for discussion and agreement is the proposition that it would be a good idea to minimize the harm and suffering that some group of citizens will undergo in the immediate future.

The social changes involved in the bureaucratization of British society and the way in which, in the absence of any countervailing ideology, this has led to a causalist moral outlook among the bureaucratic and political élite can be analysed at two levels. First let us consider the question at an institutional level. The causalist mode of tackling moral questions is one that developed originally because it was the most convenient method of governing the relationship between large bureaucratic organizations. The moralist world outlook which had evolved in small communities as a means of regulating the relationships of individuals proved unsuitable in this new context. One cannot describe British Petroleum or Courtaulds or the Post Office or the Prudential Assurance Company or the Department of Education and Science or the Union of Shop, Distributive and Allied Workers as 'good' or 'bad', 'praiseworthy' or 'blameworthy' in exactly the same sense as one can apply such terms to particular persons. They are not persons and the relationships between such institutions are more usefully seen in terms of cause and effect than in terms of praise and blame, reward and punishment. The legal relations between such institutions are necessarily increasingly causalist in nature. The emergence of Devlin's category of quasi-criminal laws is a good example of this which he describes thus:

"The distinction between the real criminal law and the quasi-criminal in their relationship to morals is that in the former a moral idea shapes the content of the law and in the latter it provides a base upon which a legal structure can be erected. In the former the law adopts a particular moral idea usually taken from a divine commandment. In the latter no more is required of the law than that it should maintain contact more or less remote with the general moral idea that a man, if he cannot reach the perfection of loving his neighbours, should at least take care not to injure them and should not unfairly snatch an advantage for himself at their expense . . . The distinguishing mark between the criminal and the quasi-criminal lies not in the use of a special statutory provision but in the presence or absence of moral content in the statutory provision containing the offence . . . The first distinguishing mark of the quasi-criminal law then is that a breach of it does not mean that the offender has done anything morally wrong. The second distinguishing mark is that the law frequently does not care whether it catches the actual offender or not. Owners of goods are frequently made absolutely liable for what happens to the goods while they are under their control even if they are in no way responsible for the interferences; an example is when food is contaminated or adulterated. Likewise, they may be made liable for the acts of their agents even if they have expressly forbidden the acts which caused the offence. This sort of measure can be justified by the argument that it induces persons in charge of an organization to take steps to see that the law is enforced in respect of things under their control . . . The majority of quasi-criminal offences are committed in the course of trade or commerce and the fines imposed in respect of them fall upon the shareholders of a limited company or the proprietors of the business." (Devlin, 1965, 27–30.)

A similar point can be inferred from Devlin's description of the law of tort which is clearly based on causalist rather than moralist principles:

"But that is not the way in which the law of tort has grown up nor is it the function which it now performs. Normally the relevant question in this branch of the law is not 'who is to blame?' but 'who is to pay if things go wrong?'; and the judgement is expressed as a sum fixed not as punishment for blameworthiness but as compensation for damage done. I do not think that a branch of the law whose object is to provide compensation for damage can be used directly to serve a moral purpose. The reason put shortly is that while liability can be made to depend upon moral guilt, full compensation for injury done cannot be made to depend on the degree of moral guilt; guilt depends upon a state of mind but damage done does not." (Devlin, 1965, 34.)

These features have been part of the law for a long time but in recent years the quasi-criminal law has been extended and the number of strict liability offences has increased as large impersonal institutions have become more important and their relationships more complex. Members of Parliament are more and more involved in making laws and rules of the kind which govern and regulate large bureaucratic institutions. Their thinking on social and economic issues is less concerned with the moral guilt of individuals and seeing that each man gets his deserts and more with the causalist regulation of corporations so as to avoid harm and to provide 'compensation for damage' regardless of 'blameworthiness'. It seems plausible to argue that men who habitually argue about corporations and bureaucracies in this way may well come to regard the behaviour of individuals in sexual and allied matters in similar terms. Causalism is the application of the ethos of the law regulating bureaucracies to questions of individual morality.

There is a second level at which it is possible to link the shift from moralism to causalism to the bureaucratization of society—the level of individual experience and socialization. Miller and Swanson (1958, 40, 50–1) discuss the effect that a shift from "individuated-entrepreneurial' to 'welfare bureaucratic' organization has had on morality and child training among middle-class families. The key theme emerging from the life experiences of the older entrepreneurial middle classes is that the child must be taught "self-denial, rationality and a firm control over his current impulses". But they note that:

"the whole development of welfare bureaucracy changes the world for the middle-class citizens who join its ranks. No longer need they struggle and strive so hard . . . Large organisations keep their employees by providing them with tenure and pension plans and by guaranteeing them advancement on the basis of seniority." . . . "Even though entrepreneurial and bureaucratic organisations make some similar demands of their personnel they also differ in critical ways. In particular bureaucratic organisations find unnecessary or undesirable the rather extreme self-control and self-denial and the active, manipulative ambition that entrepreneurial organisations exalt."

Miller and Swanson (1958, 56) says of the entrepreneurial parents:

"they needed to train their youngsters by means which would ensure that strong consciences were acquired". By contrast when parents feel that their children will not need to be so self-reliant as they will be members of great organizations that will provide external control and supervision then "there is less need for fathers and mothers to provide the child with a stern self-propelling conscience".

The entrepreneurial middle class with its strong emphasis on self-control, self-denial and the acquisition of a stern self-propelling conscience seems likely to be the source of the moral outlook I have called 'moralism'. With the decline of this class and the rise of a new middle-class whose world is that of 'welfare bureaucracy' the moralist approach to moral issues has become redundant. The second genera- tion of the new middle-class whose parents were part of the welfare bureaucracy and whose upbringing has lacked any entrepreneurial element are especially likely to discard moralist principles.

The Parliament of 1966–70 was particularly likely to contain persons drawn from this second generation of the welfare bureau- cracy. The heavy Conservative defeat at the 1966 election consider- ably reduced the number of old entrepreneurial middle-class MPs. Meanwhile, working-class Labour MPs who had retired or lost their seats in the successively greater Conservative victories of 1951, 1955 and 1959 were replaced in 1964 and 1966 by members of the new middle-class. Analyses of voting by individual members (Richards, 1970) show that MPs who had been in 'business' prior to the election were the least likely to support reform of the laws relating to abortion, divorce and homosexuality and those with a professional background most likely. The working-class MPs came somewhere in between but were notably reluctant to support homosexual law reform. These middle-class categories do not coincide precisely with those of the 'new' and 'old' middle classes but the findings are at least congruent with the basic thesis.

The social changes here described have, of course, profound implications for more general changes in sexual morality and atti- tudes than simply those of Members of Parliament. However, the attitudes and moral outlook of Members of Parliament are particu- larly important because they are the people who have had the power to determine the legal framework within which ordinary citizens' sexual behaviour takes place. Furthermore, in so far as the law has an effect on the moral thinking of those subject to it, the shift in moral outlook of Members of Parliament in turn affects the moral outlook of the people. Other social changes may well have had a more profound effect on sexual attitudes and behaviour than parliamentary and legislative change but the role of legislation cannot be ignored. In any case, the changes in legislation impinging on sexual behaviour are important in their own right and no overall study of social and sexual change that does not incorporate these can claim to be complete.

References

(All references to Hansard are to "Hansard Official Reports of Parliamentary Debates 5th Series, House of Commons".)

Abse, L. (1966). *Hansard*. Vol. 738, Col. 1070.
Awdry, D. (1969). *Hansard*. Vol. 784, Col. 2037.
Bacon, A. (1967). *Hansard*. Vol. 750, Cols 1176–7.
Beamish, T. (1969). *Hansard*. Vol. 784, Col. 2050.
Bell, P. (1959). *Hansard*. Vol. 598, Cols 1440–1–2.
Bell, P. (1959). *Hansard*. Vol. 605, Col. 768.
Bell, P. (1959). *Hansard*. Vol. 605, Col. 770.
Bell, P. (1959). *Hansard*. Vol. 605, Col. 771.
Cary, Sir R. (1959). *Hansard*. Vol. 598, Col. 1412.
Davies, C. (1975). *Permissive Britain. Social Change in the Sixties and Seventies*. London: Pitman.
Davies, C. (1978). How our rulers argue about censorship. In *Censorship and Obscenity*. Edited by R. Dhavan and C. Davies. London: Martin Robertson.
Davies, C. (1979). The social origins of some sexual taboos. In *Love and Attraction*. Edited by M. Cook and G. Wilson. London: Pergamon.
Devlin, Lord (1965). *The Enforcement of Morals*. London: Oxford University Press.
Emery, P. (1969). *Hansard*. Vol. 784, Col. 2056.
Fraser, H. (1967). *Hansard*. Vol. 750, Col. 1362.
Gray, H. (1969). *Hansard*. Vol. 784, Cols 2037–8.
Hobson, J. (1959). *Hansard*. Vol. 598, Col. 1419.
Hogg, Q. (1969). *Hansard*. Vol. 784, Cols 2047–8.
Howard, J. (1959). *Hansard*. Vol. 598, Cols 1426–7.
Iremonger, T. (1966). *Hansard*. Vol. 738, Col. 1103.
Iremonger, T. (1966). *Hansard*. Vol. 738, Col. 1107.
Isaacs, G. (1959). *Hansard*. Vol. 598, Cols 1442–3.
Jeger, L. (1969). *Hansard*. Vol. 784, Cols 2055.
Jenkins, R. (1967). *Hansard*. Vol. 749, Col. 934.
Jenkins, R. (1967). *Hansard*. Vol. 749, Col. 1511.
Knight, J. (1966). *Hansard*. Vol. 732, Col. 1101.
Knight, J. (1967). *Hansard*. Vol. 750, Col. 1180.
Knight, J. (1967). *Hansard*. Vol. 750, Col. 1181.
Mahon, P. (1967). *Hansard*, Vol. 750, Col. 1353.
Mahon, P. (1967). *Hansard*. Vol. 750, Col. 1354.
Mahon, P. (1967). *Hansard*. Vol. 750, Col. 1357.
Mahon, P. (1969). *Hansard*. Vol. 784, Cols 2034–5.

Miller, D. and Swanson, G. (1958). *The Changing American Parent*. London: Chapman and Hall.
Osborne, Sir C. (1967). *Hansard*. Vol. 748, Col. 2115.
Osborne, Sir. C. (1967). *Hansard*. Vol. 748, Col. 2119.
Osborne, Sir C. (1967). *Hansard*. Vol. 748, Col. 2150.
Owen, D. (1966). *Hansard*. Vol. 738, Cols 1110–1.
Parker, J. (1959). *Hansard*. Vol. 605, Col. 760.
Percival, I. (1967). *Hansard*. Vol. 748, Cols 2136–7.
Rees-Davies, W. R. (1967). *Hansard*. Vol. 749. Cols 1421–2.
Rees-Davies, W. R. (1967). *Hansard*. Vol. 749, Col. 1435.
Renton, D. (1959). *Hansard*. Vol. 749, Cols 1463–4.
Richards, P. (1970). *Parliament and Conscience*. London: Allen and Unwin.
St. John Stevas, N. (1966). *Hansard*. Vol. 732, Col. 1154.
St. John-Stevas, N. (1966). *Hansard*. Vol. 732, Col. 1156.
St. John-Stevas, N. (1967). *Hansard*. Vol. 750, Col. 1175.
Shaw, R. (1969). *Abortion on Trial*. London: Robert Hale.
Simms, M. and Hindell, K. (1971). *Abortion Law Reformed*. London: Peter Owen.
Steel, D. (1966). *Hansard*. Vol. 732, Col. 1075.
Steel, D. (1967). *Hansard*. Vol. 750, Col. 1166.
Steel, D. (1967). *Hansard* Vol. 750, Cols 1347–8.
Weitzman, D. (1959). *Hansard*. Vol. 605, Cols 772–3.
Wells, W. (1966). *Hansard*. Vol. 732, Col. 1080.
Wilkins, W. A. (1959). *Hansard*. Vol. 598, Col. 1437.

Sexuality in the
Post-Kinsey Era

PAUL H. GEBHARD

*Institute for Sex Research, Indiana University,
Bloomington, Indiana, USA*

I initially chose this broad title for my presentation with the idea of leaving myself a wide latitude of choice of topic. Time passed, procrastination continued, and when I finally addressed myself to the preparation of this lecture I realized I had irrevocably committed myself to an impossibly vast subject. The only solution to this dilemma is to speak in generalities rather than specifics and to try to present a synthesis and overview. You will probably welcome this solution to my problem because it means I will not be burdening you with only the statistics of the numerous surveys and research projects which have proliferated at an exponential rate since it has become safe, if not wholly respectable, to indulge in sexology. The quality of research in sexual behaviour and attitudes ranges from good to adequate to execrable and regrettably some of the latter have received wide publicity. The commonest defect is that of sampling. For example, surveys conducted by two popular magazines, *Redbook* (Levin and Levin, 1975) and *Psychology Today* (Athanasiou *et al.*, 1970) consisted of questionnaires printed in these magazines with an exhortation to fill them out and mail them in. While the roughly 100,000 returns received by *Redbook* seems mightily impressive, one must realize this constitutes a return of less than 5 per cent of the magazines distributed that month. Moreover, the 100,000 question-naires proved too much to process, and so only 10,000—one in ten—were utilized to form the basis of the report. This constitutes one-half of one per cent of those who received the questionnaire. Similarly, the *Hite Report* (Hite, 1976) on women, and the male counterpart produced by Dr Pietropinto and Ms Simenauer (1977) depended wholly on self-selection: only those who were motivated by who knows what reasons responded to the questionnaires which were handed out at supermarkets and other gathering places or which were simply mailed to an unknown population of respondents. Some of the Swedish studies were excellent in this respect; for example, Zetterberg (1969) used census data to select 2,156 persons aged 18 to 60 to constitute a representative cross-section of Sweden, and all but 153 responded. In the USA, the studies of Zelnik and Kantner on young people (1977) and Westoff's study of married persons (Westoff and Ryder, 1977) approach this ideal. At the risk of seeming vain, I will cite the Institute for Sex Research studies as examples of good research. The bitter fact is that there is no cheap and easy way to obtain good data on human sexuality.

At this juncture let me confess to a strong bias in favour of interviewing rather than self-administered questionnaires. If a question, no matter how carefully written, can be misconstrued, it will be. Kinsey learned this early in his career when he experimented with a questionnaire (Kinsey et al., 1948). One of his questions to college males was "Are both of your testicles descended?" To his profound amazement a substantial percentage replied "No". When he inquired personally, he received the reply, "Well, one seems to be descended, but the other hasn't come down as far." A similar case resulted in Dr Schmidt's questionnaire given to West German college students. He asked males what percentage of their premarital coitus resulted in ejaculation, and was taken aback to learn that about one-fifth of the young men suffered from ejaculatory impotence—that is, they had coitus, but did not ejaculate. Interviews with these young men revealed that they were in universities far from their usual female partners and on those rare occasions when they were reunited they tried to make up for lost time. Consequently in the first night of reunion, they would ejaculate during the first and second coitus, but run dry by the third or fourth. This scarcely constitutes impotence!

Taking the good studies along with the bad and attempting to discern general proportions and trends, one finds enough agreement to permit one to make the following generalizations.

Masturbation evidently has changed little in prevalence and frequency over the past few decades except that it is becoming more common in females now that they are increasingly recognizing that they are entitled to have sexual desires and needs. While the ever–never incidence of masturbation in males approaches 100 per cent (as it always has) and while there has been an increase in females to at least the two-thirds level, masturbation still suffers from taboo. While all educated people will stoutly maintain that it will not cause insanity and that it is a normal and natural function, no one wants their spouse or sexual partner to know of it.

Orgasm during sleep suffers not from taboo, but from almost total neglect. So few researchers have inquired about this subject one can make no 'guesstimate' as to whether it is increasing or decreasing. I find this neglect fascinating: it suggests that an involuntary act has no moral or ethical significance and hence does not merit our consideration. This, I believe, reflects our obsession with sin. Note that in the realm of sexual behaviour the public is primarily interested in fornication and adultery, our primary sources of sin and gossip.

There is little to say regarding trends in premarital petting. A phenomenon so near to being universal cannot change appreciably unless it were to decrease, which is close to an impossibility in European–American society. However, there have been changes in petting techniques. Larger numbers of persons at ever younger ages are experiencing (or should I say, enjoying) manual and oral stimulation of the genitalia. These more sophisticated techniques have naturally caused an increase in the number of persons who reach orgasm in petting. For example, about a quarter of the unmarried college females interviewed during the Kinsey era had reached orgasm in petting by age 20, whereas an Institute survey in 1967 revealed that about half had done so. The percentage of unmarried persons having mouth–genital contact has risen steadily from under 20 per cent in Kinsey's time to nearly one-third in the late 1960s, and the *Playboy* survey (Hunt, 1974) reported over 80 per cent. This increase is in keeping with the suggestions, or even commands, found in current marriage manuals and magazines.

Premarital coitus has always been the focus of attention in our twentieth century western society obsessed with penile penetration. We deem a female virginal despite digital or lingual penetration of the vagina, but a partial penile penetration of a few seconds is sufficient to put the female in a totally new category: that of non-virgin. Note that the legal definition of rape in the USA is always a matter of penile penetration no matter how slight or brief.

In examining the various studies, nearly all being of college populations, it is clear that there has been a progressive increase in premarital coitus in the USA and in northern and western Europe. This has not been a sexual revolution, but simply the continuation of a trend visible since the beginning of this century. For example, the Kinsey data reveal that 8 per cent of the females born before 1900 had had premarital coitus by age 20 (Kinsey *et al.*, 1948, 1953), and this percentage gradually rose until among women born between 1910–19 some 23 per cent had had premarital coitus by age 20. Both Packard's 1968 study entitled *The Sexual Wilderness* and our own 1967 college study showed that at that date 33 per cent of the unmarried college females were no longer virgins by age 20. The slightly later *Psychology Today* survey reported 78 per cent of their female readers had had premarital coitus. Finally the *Playboy* survey in the early 1970s offers some more useful data. Taking only those who had married and hence ended their premarital life, the investigators found that 31 per cent of their oldest group of females (55 or older) had had premarital coitus, but each younger cohort had higher figures until their youngest group reported 81 per cent. The *Redbook* survey gave somewhat higher percentages and again found the behaviour most common among the younger generations. Figures for males are higher than those for females, but the differences are decreasing with each generation. Ultimately we shall arrive at the point now reached in Sweden where roughly 95 per cent of both males and females have experienced coitus before marriage (Zetterberg, 1969).

It is clear that as a part of the general emancipation of women they have gradually become recognized as humans with their own sexual needs and rights. Beyond this, many women are now striving for the same degree of sexual freedom previously accorded only to males. This trend toward egalitarianism when coupled with the continual exhortations of magazines and marriage manuals has caused females to demand sexual satisfaction from their husbands and lovers. This feminine expectation of sexual competence in males has made many males feel an uncomfortable sense of obligation. For them coitus has become a test of competence and manhood, and this in some cases has engendered worry and impotence. It is one thing to have coitus with a virgin or near virgin; it is quite different to have sex with an experienced woman who not only has high expectations, but is in a position to make invidious comparisons. Comparisons can now be made almost instantaneously in certain situations thanks to a recent change in law or at least in law enforcement. In a number of places such as Sandstone Lodge in Los Angeles and Plato's Retreat in New York the members can enjoy coitus in full view of anyone who cares to watch.

The increase in premarital coitus has several beneficial aspects: it is biologically and psychologically healthy in the sense that we are all sexual beings whose imperative needs cannot be postponed with impunity for up to a decade between puberty and the legal age of adulthood. Moreover, we tend to forget that some people marry late or never, and we cannot expect chastity from them. We are always guilty of thinking of premarital coitus as being confined to the teens and early twenties. Premarital coitus causes marriages to be contracted on bases other than just sexual accessibility: in the past there was an unfortunate custom of bartering one's body for a wedding ring. Now young people marry for other and more rational reasons. True, divorce rates are higher, but this is not because of premarital coitus, but of higher expectations of marriage and the removal of the condemnation which formerly applied to divorcees.

On the other hand, the increase in premarital coitus has brought with it an increase in premarital pregnancies and venereal disease. Zelnik and Kantner's non-college white females had a 22 per cent incidence of pregnancy by age 19, and of Sorenson's sample of non-virgins aged 13–19 essentially the same percentage had conceived before wedlock. While a fair number of these pregnancies terminate in marriage, many of these marriages forced early in life result in unhappiness and educational and occupational disability. Most of these unwanted pregnancies are not the result of contraceptive failure, but of failure to use contraception. In the aforementioned Zelnik and Kantner study, only 20 per cent of the girls used contraception regularly and fewer than half had used any in their most recent coitus. It seems incredibly irrational not to use the extremely effective and readily available contraceptives—and that is precisely the problem. The girls are emotional rather than logical: they do not wish to acknowledge to themselves or to others that they want or at least expect coitus; they fear that by using contraceptives they will make the male think they are promiscuous; and many of them complain that premeditated contraception spoils what they would like to believe is romantic spontaneity. Still others think that not having contraceptives available will prevent them from yielding to temptation. Lastly, there is always the thought that just this one time won't make me pregnant. The males are also remiss in assuming that contraception is the female's responsibility. To add to the problem are the numerous myths about the time of fertility, the idea that female orgasm is a prerequisite for conception, etc.

While venereal disease is not the devastating plague it was before antibiotics, it is common for two reasons. One reason is simply the increase in the number of sexually active persons. The second reason is the recognition of many diseases not previously considered venereal. The commonest sexually transmitted disease is now non-gonorrhoeal urethritis. Venereal warts and herpes genitalis vie for second place. Syphilis is no longer considered by venereal disease specialists as important: it is easily cured and many people inadvertantly cure themselves by taking antibiotics for colds and other infections. The big concern of the venereal disease specialists is gonorrhoea. We know now that as much as half of the disease is without symptoms in females and the same may be true for 10 or 15 per cent of the males. This great reservoir of undetected cases will keep the disease common until a vaccine is developed or until some totalitarian government forces everyone simultaneously to receive a massive dose of antibiotic.

I will devote little time to the subject of marital coitus since it has been remarkably stable in both incidence and frequency. The only consequential change appears to be a higher rate of female orgasm and the use of a greater variety of foreplay techniques and coital positions. The male-above female-supine position is no longer the only position suitable for decent folk, and mouth–genital and anal contact are no longer considered the monopoly of the French or of deviants. The *Psychology Today* and *Redbook* surveys found 80 to 90 per cent of their married females reporting mouth–genital contact. The incidence of anal coitus given by the *Playboy* survey was 25 per cent among couples under age 35, and *Redbook* reported an unbelievable 47 per cent. While I mistrust these figures, I believe that an increase has occurred since the Kinsey era in these techniques, possibly as single experimental trials.

Like other forms of heterosexual activity, extramarital coitus (adultery) has increased among females. The Kinsey figure of 26 per cent (Kinsey *et al.*, 1953) has now risen to 30 per cent according to *Redbook*, or 36 per cent according to *Psychology Today*. The male figure seems to have changed but little, hovering between 40 and 50 per cent. The number of extramarital partners for females seems to have remained constant: nearly half of the women confined themselves to one partner and an equal proportion limited themselves to between two to five men. Lastly, while no one has good data, it is my impression that extramarital petting has also increased and in its milder forms has become standard procedure at parties.

Homosexual activity, despite the great publicity accorded it in recent decades, does not seem to have increased. This is what one should have anticipated, for with the exception of a few females who try lesbianism as a political gesture of independence from men and except for a few male prostitutes, no one chooses to be homosexual. One's sexual orientation is beyond one's volition and the die seems to have been cast in childhood or early adolescence. Consequently, homosexuality seems little influenced by fads, fashions, and changing morality.

Similarly the paraphilias such as fetishism and sadomasochism seem largely independent of social change, and what little evidence we have does not indicate any real increase. There may be more temporary experimentation motivated by curiosity or a desire for novelty, but paraphilias as regular behaviour seem not to have become more prevalent despite their greater exposure in the mass media.

Now let us turn from behaviour and examine the changes in attitudes and *mores*. Here there have been changes worthy of the term 'revolution' for they have been vast and rapid.

Cohabitation is one such change. In my young adult years only lower socio-economic level couples lived together without benefit of clergy; married or divorced young people were excluded from high schools and colleges; college women had to return to their segregated quarters by specified times; and coitus constituted grounds for dismissal. Now unmarried couples of any social class live together with little censure, and some of our most famous actresses and models not only cohabit, but unabashedly reproduce. I must add that many of these cohabitations eventually metamorphose into conventional legal marriages, and they represent the trial marriages advocated many years ago by free-thinkers.

Sex education in the schools, although delayed and impeded, is another change. Society has in the main grudgingly accepted the need for some sexual instruction prior to marriage. The term 'grudgingly' is apt: in my own state of Indiana until last year the State Board of Education specified that in sex education courses in grammar and high schools there should be no mention of masturbation, homosexuality, sexual techniques, abortion, or contraception. There was and still is great resistance to sex education below the college level. Many otherwise reasonable people cling to the idea that children are sexless innocents who would never have a sexual thought or impulse unless some adult had spoiled their purity with premature knowledge.

Gay liberation certainly represents a great change and a sudden one. Rather than leading secretive and hypocritical lives, many homosexuals are now revealing themselves and some are politically active, marching with placards, holding public meetings, forming openly gay organizations, and publishing their own magazines and newspapers. Famous and/or respected people are proclaiming their sexual orientation. Some gay groups have established a continuing meeting and dialogue with the police and clergy. In colleges we now have Gay Liberation groups conducting meetings in college buildings. In Kinsey's day a known homosexual student was immediately expelled and a gay faculty member was forced to resign quietly at the end of the semester.

With the change toward a permissive society, a host of previously hidden persons have emerged into public view and are publishing their own specialized magazines and advertisements. Swingers, spouse traders, transvestites, sadomasochists, and others are now in the open. Even in the highly taboo area of paedophilia there are organizations which hold public meetings and publish. The prostitutes have formed an organization named 'Coyote', an acronym for 'call off your old tired ethics', and are politically active in some areas. Accompanying this outburst of freedom have come some publications so highly specialized as to be almost humorous. Recently there appeared a magazine devoted entirely to 'fist fucking': the insertion of the hand or even arm into the rectum. Or, to be accurate, I should say into the colon. We researchers presumed this technique to be an innovation until it was drawn to my attention that this act was depicted by Michaelangelo and still graces the ceiling of the Sistine Chapel. The emergence of all these hithertofore hidden deviations has profoundly shocked many people.

Perhaps the greatest change of all has been the rapid collapse of censorship. In the United States today there is no censorship of the written word, theatre, photography, graphic art, or cinema. The only media retaining strict control are radio and television, and even here control is weakening during the late hours of the night. Change has been so rapid that we at the Institute for Sex Research are in the absurd position of having locked away in steel cabinets books and magazines which are on open display in the local reputable bookstores. The degree of change is illustrated equally dramatically by my clear recollection that in 1948 a newspaper man who visited us following the publication of our first volume regretfully stated that he could not write about our work because he represented a family newspaper in which a word such as 'masturbation' could not appear. Some enterprising businessmen have produced sales catalogues of not only sadomasochistic apparatus, but sadomasochistic jewellery: rings for pierced foreskins and pierced labia. This conjures up the fantasy of someone saying, "Excuse me dear, but you forgot to take off your ring." While foreskin rings have a respectable antiquity, going back to Roman times, their appearance in publicly available catalogues strikes me as a change if not an innovation.

All of the changes in behaviour and attitude have necessarily had repercussions in the fields of ethics and religion. Theologians are now being forced to re-examine previously unquestioned tenets. Is fornication or adultery always a sin? Can a homosexual be a good Christian? Are contraception and abortion sins against God and nature? Pandora's box has been opened on the altar.

Medicine, too, has had to revise its thinking. Many medical men are debating if the things we thought were sexual pathologies might not really be unusual adaptations or perhaps only the extremes of the range of normalcy. The American Psychiatric Association has removed homosexuality from its list of disorders. In transsexual operations surgeons now perform the previously forbidden act of removing healthy tissue. Contraceptives and abortions are now not only freely available, but available to minors without parental consent. At present there is heated debate over the ethics of using surrogate partners (or even the therapist) in treating sexual dysfunction. Ethical problems hithertofore unimagined have arisen in the past few decades; for example, should a male infant with a microphallus be raised as a deficient male or given an operation and raised as a functional, albeit sterile, female?

Law, usually the slowest to respond to social change, has changed markedly and rather rapidly in regard to sex. I have already mentioned the collapse of censorship and the making of abortion legal. In addition, in the USA nineteen states have changed their sex laws so that what consenting adults do sexually in private is no longer subject to legal sanctions. Various municipalities have enacted ordinances prohibiting discrimination against homosexuals even though homosexual activity was a felony a few years ago. Mouth–genital contact, once included in the sodomy statutes, is currently protected by a Supreme Court ruling that marriage brings an aura of sexual privacy which the law cannot invade. The changes in our laws were not instigated by young radicals, but by respected older persons in impeccable organizations such as the American Law Institute and, in Britain, the Wolfenden Committee. A number of model penal codes have been devised which are refreshingly rational in their sexual aspects. For example, no longer do they observe the old dichotomy of adult and minor, but have graduated crimes and punishments depending not upon some absolute age, but upon the age discrepancy between the individuals involved. Another welcome development is the abolition of ancient, vague, and poorly defined sex offences which could be interpreted so as to indict almost anyone. There were until recently some fantastic examples. One state defined sodomy as the insertion, however slight, of the penis into any 'unnatural orifice' of the body. Setting aside the problem of what bodily orifice is unnatural, a strict interpretation of that law would mean that a man who, in impetuous haste, missed the vulva and struck the navel would be guilty of sodomy. One of the broadest and most common of these vague laws was the one against contributing to the delinquency of a minor, under which in some states a male aged 21 could be convicted for petting with his 20-year-old fiancée. A number of legal scholars have suggested that there need be only three sex laws: one to forbid acts involving force, duress, or trickery; one to forbid the sexual exploitation of children by adults; and one to prevent offensive public behaviour.

Our advances in law since Kinsey's day have given rise to some knotty problems. Allow me a series of rhetorical questions. Does the 'consenting adults in private' law legalize prostitution? Does it allow consenting sadomasochists to inflict substantial physical damage? Does it negate adultery as grounds for divorce? And what of incest between consenting adults? If homosexuality is no longer a crime, can it be brought up in divorces where there is a battle over child custody? Lastly, the legal problems resulting from the transsexual operations boggle the mind. Our society has been based on a male–female dichotomy, and any gender reversal utterly confounds our sacrosanct record system. Does a divorced man escape alimony by becoming a divorced woman? Can a female-to-male transsexual marry a woman? Would an adoption agency give them children? The possibilities of confusion are endless until society accepts some new definition of genders.

In concluding this section on law, I believe law is slowly being forced to face a major question: is physical sexual expression a natural human right? If so, does this right extend to children, the mentally deficient or insane, and to prisoners? Beyond this is an even more difficult question to which I am sure you have devoted much thought: is reproduction a natural human right? Ultimately I feel this question must be answered in the negative, for irresponsible procreation infringes upon the well-being of others (Gebhard *et al.*, 1965).

Up to this point I have concerned myself with change in the sense of the modification or abandonment of previously normative behaviours and attitudes. Now let us examine reverse change, that is, rejection of recent changes and a return to former *mores*. It is an anthropological axiom that changes which are too drastic and/or rapid cannot be accommodated by a society, and there will be a backlash response. We are now seeing this clearly in the United States. Numerous local and some national anti-pornography groups have been formed and are vigorously seeking the re-establishment of censorship. They have been rather successful, particularly since some greedy pornographers ventured into the field of child–adult sex ('kiddie porn') and caused a violent revulsion even in those with liberal viewpoints. Our Supreme Court has reversed its erosion of censorship and has in essence made censorship a matter of local option. In consequence, the producers of and actors in explicitly sexual motion pictures have been successfully prosecuted in a number of cities, and even theatre owners and projectionists have not been immune. At the risk of seeming paranoid, I must say that everywhere I look I see evidence of a renaissance of sexual repression. The Supreme Court has refused to review a federal District Court's ruling in Virginia which upheld a sodomy statute. New York modified its 'consenting adult' law to make homosexuality a misdemeanour, and Idaho revoked its 'consenting adult' law entirely. Anita Bryant has launched her anti-homosexual campaign labelled 'Save Our Children' and has received the enthusiastic support of religious fundamentalists and right-wing conservatives. Recent referenda in Wichita, Kansas; Eugene, Oregon; St. Paul, Minnesota; Moscow, Idaho; and Dade County, Florida have abolished the ordinances designed to prevent discrimination against homosexuals. The Roman Catholic Church has reaffirmed its stand against abortion and most contraception, and stressed its condemnation of any orgasm-producing act save for marital coitus and orgasm while sleeping. Resistance to sex education persists. Our federal government has made abortion difficult for the poor, and Louisiana has surrounded abortion with almost insuperable restrictions. Senator Proxmire and his staff, in ferreting out the waste of taxpayers's money, has attacked a number of sex research projects, and an Illinois politician followed his example and succeeded in terminating a federally funded sex research project in the southern part of that state. Even we at the Institute have been receiving ominous inquiries as to the sources of our grants and the amounts of money involved. Johns Hopkins Hospital has evidently ceased, or greatly curtailed, transsexual operations. The Equal Rights Amendment faces defeat in no small measure due to the sexual liberality of its proponents. I predict a protracted period of strife and litigation which will be exacerbated as politicians seize upon sexual issues to win votes. The Institute for Sex Research has conducted a national survey of attitudes which reveals that the majority of adults are strongly opposed to homosexuality and adultery, and do not accept premarital coitus even between adults. Politicians sense this conservatism and make use of it. The battles I predict will involve not only the conservative traditionalists and the ultra-liberals, but will engage many sincere and thoughtful citizens who hold strongly opposing views. We can hope that ultimately tolerance and rationality will prevail though the cost be Churchillian blood, sweat and tears.

Since I am addressing a eugenics society, it is fitting that I conclude on an appropriate note: the proper relationship between sexuality and population. I think it is obvious that any objective and intelligent person who is not hampered by religious or nationalistic constraints must conclude that the greatest danger facing mankind is overpopulation. Uncontrolled reproduction must rapidly deplete our finite resources and pollute our environment. It will negate many of our efforts toward the betterment of the human condition. It will lead to struggle and possibly warfare between the 'haves' and the 'have-nots'. Uncontrolled reproduction, like uncontrolled cellular growth, is ultimately lethal. Advances in science and technology can only delay the inevitable. Even nuclear war cannot be viewed as a horrible solution to the problem for it will simply reduce the habitable space for the survivors. We must abandon our age-old goal and biological imperative to be fruitful and multiply freely. Distasteful as the idea is, we cannot rely upon the voluntary co-operation of humans to hold constant or reduce population. While the intelligent persons with consciousness of the problem will co-operate, these persons are far outnumbered by the uneducated, less intelligent, and selfish. I doubt if we have the time to educate and persuade this majority which will grow larger as those who appreciate the problem reproduce less. Reproduction must become a privilege and not a right, and birth limitation must be imposed by adjustments in taxation policy, the rewarding of minimal reproduction, delaying marriage, and devising ways to appeal to self-interest. We must, as someone succinctly put it, make sex more recreational and less procreational.

What of our chances of waging a successful campaign against overpopulation before we are all living in a crowded polluted world on a subsistence economy? I am somewhat pessimistic since I agree with the neurophysiologists who point out that our newly evolved neocortex has not yet established control over our primitive brain. We remain more creatures of emotion and habit than of logic, and this is especially true of sex, for it is an inherent genetically determined phenomenon. On the other hand, evolution holds some hope. While most other life forms have their sexual behaviour rigorously programmed, the higher life forms are progressively emancipated from the control of hormones, pheromones, and patterned behaviour. The human female, for example, is the only mammalian female without an oestrus cycle: she can be sexually aroused and functional at any time. We are freer than any other animal to determine our sexual lives. This shift from problem-free machine-like sexual functioning determined by chemical substances to the myriad options available to us through learning and conditioning, holds the possibility of our modifying our attitudes and behaviour to insure our survival and well-being.

References

Athanasiou, R., Shaver, P. and Tavris, C. (1970). Sex. *Psychology Today*, **4**, 39–52.
Gebhard, P. H., Pomeroy, W. B., Martin, C. E. and Christenson, C. V. (1958). *Pregnancy, Birth and Abortion*. New York: Harper–Hoeber. London: William Heinemann (Medical Books).
Gebhard, P. H., Gagnon, J. H., Pomeroy, W. B. and Christenson, C. V. (1965). *Sex Offenders: An Analysis of Types*. New York: Harper–Hoeber.
Hite, S. D. (1976). *The Hite Report: A Nationwide Study on Female Sexuality*. New York: Macmillan.
Hunt, M. M. (1974). *Sexual Behavior in the 1970s*. Chicago: Playboy Press.
Kinsey, A. C., Pomeroy, W. B. and Martin, C. E. (1948). *Sexual Behavior in the Human Male*. Philadelphia and London: W. B. Saunders.
Kinsey, A. C., Pomeroy, W. B., Martin, C. E. and Gebhard, P. H. (1953). *Sexual Behavior in the Human Female*. Philadelphia and London: W. B. Saunders.
Levin, R. J. and Levin, A. (1975). Sexual pleasure: the surprising preferences of 100,000 women. *Redbook*, **145**, 51–58.
Packard, V. O. (1968). *The Sexual Wilderness; the Contemporary Upheaval in Male–Female Relationships*. New York: D. McKay. London: Longmans.
Pietropinto, A. and Simenauer, J. (1977). *Beyond the Male Myth: What Women Want to Know About Men's Sexuality: A Nationwide Survey*. New York: Times Books.
Westoff, C. F. and Ryder, N. B. (1977). *The Contraceptive Revolution*. Princeton, New Jersey: Princeton University Press.
Zelnik, M. and Kantner, J. F. (1977). Sexual and contraceptive experience of young unmarried women in the United States, 1976 and 1971. *Family Planning Perspectives*, **9**, 55–71.
Zetterberg, H. L. (1969). *Om Sexuallivet i Sverige*. Stockholm: Nordiska Bokhandeln.

Sexual Attitudes and Behaviour of Young People

CHRISTINE FARRELL

Department of Applied Social Studies,
The North London Polytechnic, London, England

It seems platitudinous to begin a talk on teenage attitudes to sex by saying, as Bob Dylan did, "The times-they-are-a-changing". But compared with the pre- and post-war years, and certainly compared with the Victorian era, the last decade might well be called the permissive age. The evidence of increasingly permissive attitudes and behaviour appears to be all around us. The media are constantly extending the limits of acceptability; the newspapers are full of stories which apparently indicate greater sexual freedom within and outside marriage and most people, both young and old, appear to be able to talk about sex and related topics much more openly than before. But in spite of these observable trends, there is very little hard evidence, in this country at least, about how much or in which direction sexual attitudes and behaviour have changed over time. Michael Schofield (1965) published the first national survey of teenage sexual behaviour and since then, apart from one or two small non-representative studies, there have been no attempts to study the changes which were taking place. But in 1974–75 we carried out a survey at the Institute for Social Studies in Medical Care which did allow comparisons over time to be made. The purpose of our study was mainly to look at ways in which young people learned about sex and birth control and how this affected their attitudes and behaviour (Farrell, 1978). Questions were asked, therefore, about sexual and contraceptive behaviour and attitudes to premarital sex, abortion, contraception and venereal disease. The findings show that there have been substantial changes in behaviour over the twelve-year period, but that the attitudes and behaviour of the majority of teenagers are far from being as permissive and free-thinking as most newspapers and Bob Dylan would have us believe. In many respects the young people we studied were more conservative in their attitudes and behaviour than most people would expect.

The research was based on interviews with over 1,500 young people aged 16–19, together with more than 300 of their parents. The sample was selected with probability proportional to population in twelve areas of England and Wales. Details of the methods used will not be discussed here because of the limited time available. It should just be said that the sample of young people was representative of the age group as a whole on all the characteristics with which it was possible to compare. The sample population matched the national age group on age, male/female ratio, social class and nationality.

Attitudes to Sex Before Marriage

The attitudes of the young people in our study were mainly in favour of sex before marriage. Nearly half of them said outright that they approved of it; less than one in ten said they definitely disapproved, and the rest said they had mixed feelings about the question. More of those who had mixed feelings were inclined towards approval than disapproval, but a fifth said they were unable to sort out their feelings sufficiently to decide whether they were inclined to approve or disapprove. Girls were less likely to say they approved, but their lack of approval was made up for by mixed feelings rather than disapproval, as Table I shows.

Table I
Young peoples' attitudes to sex before marriage

	Male (%)	Female (%)	Both sexes (%)
Approved	60	37	49
Disapproved	7	10	8
Mixed feelings	32	52	42
Don't know/can't say	1	1	1
Number (= 100%)	779	771	1550[a]

[a] Six excluded because replies inadequate.

The people who disapproved gave a variety of reasons for their disapproval; some were religious: "It's contrary to the Bible . . . because of the sacred state of marriage"; some were social:

"Mainly I disapprove from what I've seen of people having to get married and the conditions they live in." . . .

"Don't think it should be allowed because of over-population."

and some were linked to personal experience:

> "Now I don't really believe in it because it doesn't work out. If you fall and have to get married as we did and it didn't work out. Since I've had the experience I feel it's worse on the woman really."

However, amongst those who expressed additional comments to this question (they were asked "Do you have any views on sex before marriage? Could you say whether you approve, disapprove or have mixed feelings about it?" If they had mixed feelings they were asked "Would you say you are more inclined to approve or disapprove or are you equally balanced?" Additional comments were given (though not asked for) by 48 per cent), the widespread view was that premarital sex was acceptable if it happened as part of a stable relationship and care was taken to avoid unwanted pregnancy:

> "I think sex before marriage is alright as long as you don't just sleep around with anyone. I think if you're going steady with someone for a long time—but just to sleep with anyone I think is wrong."

and:

> "I believe that when one feels one is mature enough to lead a healthy spiritual relationship then one is also mature enough to lead a healthy sex relationship if the right precautions are taken."

The next most common view was that it was a decision which should be left to the individuals concerned:

> "I think it's entirely up to the couple concerned, as long as they're sort of . . . kids, that's ridiculous, 12, 13, they're at it now, but the over-age couple they know what they're doing—if they don't they shouldn't be doing it."

Outright approval without qualification was not common and some young people mentioned that they disapproved strongly of sleeping around with anyone (9 per cent):

> "Well, I think if you really do love a bloke I don't see why you should wait

till you're married, but you have to be careful or you might end up
sleeping around and that's not good."

A few (4 per cent) made the point spontaneously that sex before
marriage was necessary as a precaution against an unhappy marriage:

> "It's nice to know what you're going to live with instead of waiting until
> you're married to know what the bloke's like. Even though it's against my
> religion, I think it's good because you know what you're going to live
> with."

and more succinctly: "You have to try your shoes on before you buy
them."

Two trends were suggested by the data: the first showed the older
age groups more likely to say they approved of premarital sex (56 per
cent of 19-year-olds approved compared with 38 per cent of 16-year-
olds); the second suggests that middle-class children are less likely to
say they approve than working-class teenagers. This can be explained
by a movement to greater congruence between attitudes and behaviour since subsequent data show that 19-year-olds and boys from
working-class families are more likely to be sexually experienced.

There is little doubt that attitudes to sex in western societies have
changed, and that discussions of sex are more open now than they
were a hundred years ago. Whether these changes in attitudes affect
sexual behaviour or simply reflect the changes in behaviour which are
taking place, is a question discussed in an article by Osofsky (1971).
He suggests that attitudes to sex may change as a result of changes in
sexual behaviour, or alternatively that behavioural changes in sexual
habits take place because attitudes have changed. He goes on to say
that:

> "Alterations in patterns of sexual behaviour which occurred during the
> early part of this century, together with the recognition of these alterations
> as a result of scientific investigations, may have preceded and contributed
> to present-day thinking. Attitudes may merely have caught up with
> existent behaviour."

He then introduces evidence from two recent American studies which
suggest, he thinks, that attitudes have not only caught up with
reported sexual behaviour but "may have passed beyond them"
(398–9).

Another of our findings was that a higher proportion of girls said that all or most of their peers had sex before marriage, and reported they themselves had not, which suggests that their attitudes or beliefs about others outstrip, in time at least, their own sexual involvement. Osofsky concludes his article by saying that changes in adolescent sexual behaviour could occur in either direction; that is, that rates of change in both behaviour and attitude may begin to decline. On the other hand, he says: "Recent data, while obviously not conclusive, suggest the possibility of quantitative increments in adolescent female sexual behaviour, and qualitative changes for both sexes". These 'intuitions' are untestable from our data, but the reference to qualitative changes for both sexes is important. If there are to be 'qualitative' changes in adolescent sexual behaviour for both males and females, the information on which they make their individual decisions about when and how they become sexually involved will itself need to be of an appropriate and relevant quality. Other evidence from our survey suggested that for many young people, whether they had learned from parents, school or, particularly, if they had learned from friends, neither quantitative nor qualitative information is always being provided.

This qualitative information is particularly important with regard to birth control. Experience will always be an important factor in learning about sex and, however much information is given, it can never prepare fully the individual for their physical and emotional reactions.

Sexual Experience

In 1965, 16 per cent of Schofield's sample of 15- to 19-year-olds said that they had had sexual intercourse at least once. In our sample of 16- to 19-year-olds ten years later, 51 per cent said they were sexually experienced, 45 per cent said they had not had any sexual experience and 4 per cent refused to answer the question ("Could you tell me if you have had sexual intercourse?" If they said "Yes", or were uncertain, they were asked "Does that mean you have 'gone all the way'?"). The comparison is not a direct one because Schofield included 15-year-olds in his sample, but there has obviously been an increase in the number of teenagers saying that they have had sexual intercourse. The proportion of boys in the 1974 sample who said they were experienced was 55 per cent and the proportion of girls 46 per cent. This bears out Schofield's findings of ten years ago, that boys become sexually experienced at an earlier age than girls (in 1964, 20 per cent of boys aged 15–19 and 12 per cent of girls in the same age group said they were sexually experienced (Schofield, 1965, 39–40). If the married young people are excluded from our sample, as they were from Schofield's, 54 per cent of all single males in the sample said they were sexually experienced and 42 per cent of the girls, an overall average of 48 per cent for unmarried teenagers aged 16–19.

AGE OF FIRST SEXUAL EXPERIENCE

Nearly half of those who said they were sexually experienced said that they had had their first experience before they were 16. This means that a fifth (21 per cent) of the whole sample had had at least one sexual experience by the time they were 16; three-quarters of them were boys. Twelve per cent of all the girls in the sample said they had had intercourse by that age and 31 per cent of all the boys. Although this is a question to which young people may be tempted to give an exaggerated answer, the possibility that over a third of all teenagers in the sample had had some sexual experience before or by the age of 16 has important implications for sex educationists and medical services offering contraceptive advice.

Table II shows the proportion of boys and girls who said that they had had sexual intercourse by their current age and the age they were when they had their first experience.

Four   years   is   usually   too   short   a   time   for   significant

Table II
Age of first experience by current age and sex

Age of first sexual experience (years)	Females				Males				All
	Age at time of interview				Age at time of interview				
	16	17	18	19	16	17	18	19	
	%	%	%	%	%	%	%	%	%
Before 16	26	32	32	33	13	13	14	10	22
16	5	16	17	24	9	17	12	16	15
17	—	2	12	12	—	9	21	19	10
18	—	—	4	4	—	—	5	14	3
19	—	—	—	1	—	—	—	8	1
Refused	5	2	4	3	3	5	5	6	4
No experience	64	48	31	23	75	56	43	27	45
Number (= 100%)	181	211	186	198	170	189	216	190	1541

trends to emerge and there is no real evidence from these figures that there is a trend to earlier experience for either boys or girls. In a recent American study of 4240 teenage girls, the authors point to a "dramatic change in teenage sexual activity" in recent years. They say that:

> "For those currently aged 19, 97 per cent were still virgins when they reached age 15, whereas only 91 per cent of those now aged 15 reached the age in the virginal state" (Kantner and Zelnik, 1972a, 339).

However, a better comparison for our sample is with Schofield's figures. Unfortunately the only age breakdown given there is for those under 15. In 1964, 6 per cent of 15-year-old boys and 2 per cent of 15-year-old girls reported that they were sexually experienced (Schofield, 1965, 59). If we compare the 16-year-olds in our sample who said they had had their first sexual experience before they were 16, the proportions are 26 per cent of the boys and 12 per cent of the girls. Some of this increase could be accounted for by the difference in the age at which they were asked the question, but it is unlikely that all of it can be explained in this way. It is difficult to begin to offer explanations as to why some teenagers have early sexual experience and some do not. We know that in the past, in Western Society at least, fear of pregnancy, social stigma and economic factors, often prevented it. To a large extent these barriers no longer exist, and in some ways it is more appropriate now to ask why any teenagers wait until they are married. It was possible to examine a number of variables within our study to look for explanations.

Religion Most religions aim to act as a brake to physical expressions of desire or emotion before marriage, but people no longer seem to accept this. Except in the case of those who belonged to non-conformist churches, there was no difference in stated sexual experience between those who said they were not religious and those who said they were (54 per cent were sexually experienced compared with 51 per cent of those who identified themselves as belonging to a particular religion; but 40 per cent of those who said they were Methodists or belonged to other non-conformist churches said they were sexually experienced).

Social class Although Schofield reported no differences between social class groups and sexual experience, other studies have observed class differences. Kanter and Zelnik's findings (1972b) are complicated by racial mix, but there was a correlation between socio-economic status and sexual experience in the 'expected' direction (i.e. more working-class teenagers said they had had sexual experience). Venner's study (1972) also suggested a relationship between higher levels of sexual experience and the lower socio-economic groups. At age 16, 7 per cent of professional and managerial groups said they were experienced, compared with 21 per cent of daughters of blue-collar workers. Our findings are more in line with these more recent American findings than with Schofield's. His data suggest the same pattern although the differences were not statistically significant. The main class differences in our study were between working-class boys and the rest. Analysis of middle-class boys and girls and working-class girls showed similar proportions saying they were sexually experienced (49 per cent of middle-class boys, 47 per cent of middle-class girls, and 46 per cent of working-class girls), whereas 60 per cent of working-class boys said they were sexually experienced. This finding is not unexpected but seems important in beginning to unravel the web of factors which account for early sexual experience. Working-class boys are more likely to have sexual intercourse because they are boys and society half expects it; their parents are more likely to approve of sex before marriage; they are more likely to be economically self-supporting and therefore to qualify for adult status (Reiss, 1970; Musgrove, 1964); and they have nothing to fear in terms of becoming pregnant.

Also peer group influences are likely to encourage it, as Schofield (1965) and Willmott (1966) pointed out. Middle-class boys are subject to some of these influences, but in this study they were more likely to be in full-time higher education (28 per cent compared with 8 per cent of working-class boys) which means that they are not usually economically independent and have 'more to lose' if a girl with whom they have sex gets pregnant and they have to support a family. Girls of both classes have the most to lose (or gain) if they have sex and become pregnant. The lack of social class differences between the girls is surprising. Initially we had taken the traditional view that working-class girls would be more attracted to early marriage as a way out of dull jobs, and would therefore be more likely to be sexually experienced. It is possible that the desire not to have children at an early age is uniting women of all classes in more effective use of contraception.

Combining results from our own study and Schofield's, there has been an increase of 250 per cent in the proportion of girls reporting experience of sexual intercourse since 1964, compared with a corresponding increase of 170 per cent for boys (Schofield, 1965, 39–40). Whilst this evidence supports Osofsky's general findings that male adolescent rates of sexual activity are not increasing as fast as female adolescent rates of premarital sexual activity, the only evidence we have about behaviour overtaking attitudes would not confirm his suggestions. The fact that more girls in our study said that they approved of sex before marriage than were sexually experienced is an indication that their attitudes were, at this point in time, more liberal than their actions (30 per cent of the non-experienced girls said they approved of sex before marriage).

Although we were able to demonstrate substantial changes in teenage attitudes and sexual behaviour over time, on a number of other issues, such as abortion, their attitudes were less than permissive.

Attitudes to Abortion

The majority of young people expressed strong feelings about abortion and, contrary to what might have been expected, a greater proportion disapproved than approved. When they were asked to say whether they approved, disapproved, or had mixed feelings about abortion, 38 per cent said that on the whole they approved, 49 per cent disapproved, and the remaining 13 per cent had mixed feelings which were equally balanced for and against. Most young people expressed strong views about abortion. When asked, "What do you think of abortion?" over one-third (36 per cent) made comments which could be classified as strong disapproval, half of them mentioning the word 'murder' or 'killing'. Others felt it was wrong except in specific circumstances, 11 per cent mentioning rape or medical reasons as justifications. Some (13 per cent) said it was preferable to producing unwanted children and a small proportion (3 per cent) mentioned that it should be allowed only if the mother were very young.

Over a half of those who approved of abortion explained their views mostly in terms of avoiding human misery:

"It's good thing. Having a baby can lead to a great deal of unhappiness for a girl or boy—him if he's forced to marry her, and the child when it grows up."

A further 23 per cent made comments which revealed a mixture of feelings:

"I don't really agree with it but it's an easy way out for the mother—too easy sometimes. I think I'd say I was mixed really, I can't make my mind up."

Finally, a small group (5 per cent) avoided making moral judgements, saying that it was neither right nor wrong, but necessary: "It's a positive method of solving a problem if you can afford it." Girls, for whom abortion is a more directly practical problem, were less likely to say they approved than boys. Table III shows the differences between them and the class differences.

Table III
Attitudes to abortion by social class and sex

Attitudes	Females		Males		All
	Middle class	Working class	Middle class	Working class	
	%	%	%	%	%
Approved	22	11	34	25	22
Mixed—more to approve	11	7	11	11	16
Mixed—equally balanced	18	18	15	11	13
Mixed—more to disapprove	18	14	10	11	9
Disapproved	31	50	30	42	40
Number (= 100%)	286[a]	425[a]	308[a]	422[a]	1540[b]

[a] These figures exclude 16 young people whose answers were inadequate.
[b] Including 99 young people whose fathers' occupations were not classified as either middle class or working class, but excluding inadequate answers.

The girls were asked a more specific question to discover, in personal terms, under what circumstances they might consider having an abortion, and 29 per cent said that they would never consider it in any circumstances. Another 29 per cent said they would consider it only if there were strong medical reasons. Typical comments were:

"If the doctor says there is something going to be really wrong with the baby I would have an abortion, otherwise I would have the baby."

"If it was going to endanger my life or the baby wasn't going to be normal."

Altogether over half (58 per cent) of the girls could not see themselves having abortions unless there was a risk to life or health.

About one-third (36 per cent) described what might be called social reasons for considering an abortion. Within this group financial support was mentioned as a consideration by 9 per cent, the baby being unwanted by either the girl or the father or her parents by 7 per cent, and lack of family support and not wanting to marry the father by 21 per cent.

Finally, 11 per cent said they would think seriously about abortion if it looked as if their future would be ruined, and 7 per cent felt uncertain what they would do. (Percentages here do not add up to 100 because some gave more than one circumstance; but the 58 and 36 per cent are exclusive.)

The fact that over half the girls and over 40 per cent of the boys expressed disapproval (and often horror) of abortion is an indication that young people are not encouraged to have sex because abortion is more easily available now. The evidence on contraceptive use from another part of the study suggests that the majority of girls and boys use birth control methods, and girls certainly do not regard abortion as an alternative to contraception.

To summarize the changes in adolescent attitudes and sexual behaviour, it is clear that more young people have sex before marriage and that more of them have sexual intercourse at an earlier age than they did in the early 60s. However, there is no evidence that they are more promiscuous and their attitudes to premarital sex are in line with the widespread view in this country that it is acceptable if it takes place within the context of a stable relationship and precautions are taken to avoid unwanted pregnancy.

References

Farrell, C. (1978). *My Mother Said. . . .: The Way Young People Learned About Sex and Birth Control*. London: Routledge and Kegan Paul.

Kanter, J. F. and Zelnik, M. (1972a). The probability of premarital intercourse. *Social Science Research*, **1**, 335–341.

Kanter, J. F. and Zelnik, M. (1972b). Sexual experience of young unmarried women in the United States. *Family Planning Perspectives*, **4**, No. 4.

Musgrove, F. (1964). *Youth and the Social Order*. London: Routledge and Kegan Paul.

Osofsky, H. J. (1971). Adolescent sexual behaviour: current status and anticipated trends for the future. *Clinical Obstetrics and Gynaecology*, **14**, 393–408.

Reiss, I. L. (1970). Premarital sex and deviant behaviour. *American Sociological Review*, **35**, 78–87.

Schofield, M. (1965). *The Sexual Behaviour of Young People*. London: Longman.

Venner, A. M. (1972). The sexual behavior of adolescents in Middle America. *Marriage and the Family*, **34**, 696–705.

Willmott, P. (1966). *Adolescent Boys of East London*. London: Routledge and Kegan Paul.

Sexual Experience and Attitudes of British Women

ROBERT CHESTER and CHRISTOPHER WALKER

Department of Social Administration, University of Hull, Hull, England

Introduction

We cannot be sure what changes there may have been in the sexuality of women during recent generations, although clearly there have been great changes in the way in which it is regarded and discussed. So far as documentation goes, at least, Freud's description of the sexual life of women as a 'dark continent' still holds good in Britain. In the USA there has been some considerable volume of sex research, with a bias towards the investigation of female sexuality and an emphasis on the female orgasm. In this country the pioneer work of Chesser (1956) has not been developed by others, although there is material relevant to the sexuality of women in certain more widely focused studies (Schofield, 1965, 1973; Eysenck, 1978). Certainly the British woman's experience of sex is not well mapped. The aim of this paper is to provide a primarily descriptive account of some results from a recent survey based upon magazine readership.

Following upon interest generated by the publication in England of *The Hite Report* (Hite, 1977) opportunity was taken to print a forty-item questionnaire in *Woman's Own*, a general-interest women's magazine with a readership in excess of six million. Over 10,000 questionnaires were returned, many of them accompanied by amplifying comments which varied from brief notes to lengthy letters, and of this total 2,289 were drawn at random for analysis. It is not proposed to justify at length the use of materials derived from such a sample, the problems of which are well-recognized here. It is obvious, for example, that because of self-selection the representativeness of the sample cannot be known, so that distributional data in particular must be treated with great caution. However, there has not yet been (and perhaps cannot be) a truly 'representative' sample in a survey of sexual practice and experience, and attempts to achieve one have been vitiated by high rates of non-response. Furthermore, the objective of the present research was not to establish general population parameters but to examine relationships between variables and to elicit patterns of experience. As Eysenck (1978) has pointed out in countering the methodological strictures of Cochrane and Duffy (1974), for such purposes randomness of selection is not essential, so long as the sample contains a range of respondent types and is not selected by reference to the variables of interest. The merit of the material reported here is that it contains unique data for this country, elicited from a sample which is both diversified and very large.

As with all survey materials there are problems besides those of representativeness, such as veracity of response and the fact that some desired information may never have existed in the minds of the respondents in the form in which it was sought. No guarantees can be given in these regards, but from correspondence there was ample evidence of a positive and co-operative attitude from respondents. Abusive and spoof letters were conspicuously absent, and there was no evidence of exhibitionism or extremist display. There were numerous thoughtful comments on the form of the questionaire and the wording of questions, etc. and the general tone of the letters was of helpfulness and sincerity, even though some found it hard to reveal things which had hitherto been secret. The letters contained little explicit sign of 'women's lib' attitudes, although some contained an unarticulated liberationist perspective (e.g. objections to feeling sexually 'used'). There was also a widespread expression of trust in the sponsoring magazine, which doubtless helped in eliciting honesty and co-operation. Many correspondents praised the idea of the survey, mostly from the point of view of 'helping women'. The theme of reassurance about 'normality' often came up, with women either having a secret concern that they might be unusual, or not knowing how to know what was usual. Three quotations will illustrate:

"Until a few years ago I had never read of oral sex and thought this was something only myself and husband did, resulting in a feeling of shame about it."

"I'm glad you included the question on 'faking' orgasms. I must admit I thought I was the only one."

"I try to convince myself about the 'myth' of the female orgasm, but I know that many women do have orgasm frequently. I read facts and figures as in the Hite Report, but still the media in general make me doubt my own sexuality by showing ladies of immense orgasmic prowess (or so it seems to me)."

Co-operative attitudes cannot ensure veridical responses, of course, but they do indicate goodwill, and since the questionnaire was anonymous the respondents had little to gain from giving deliberately misleading answers. Despite its necessary limitations, therefore, it seems probable that the materials are worthy of some respect in an area where little other information exists.

As an addendum to the above it can be noted that some 200 volunteers have provided extensive accounts of some aspects of their sexual experience in response to guide notes drawn up subsequently to the main survey. This qualitative material will form the basis of future papers but has been gathered too recently to have been analysed yet. Impressions drawn from inspection of this material have, however, informed some of the comment in this paper.

Some Characteristics of the Sample

Of the respondents sample, 63 per cent were married and living with their husbands, while 11·3 per cent were cohabiting without marriage, and for some purposes these will be added together and called the cohabiting group. In addition, 20·5 per cent were unmarried and not living with a sex partner, while 4·8 per cent were previously married women, and these together are referred to as the non-cohabiting group. These groupings are made because for some purposes interest centres on sexual situation rather than on civil status *per se*. Provision was made for the category 'living with a female sex partner', but so few respondents fell into this category that they have been ignored in the analysis.

Part A of Table I shows that the sample was weighted towards the younger age groups, with two-thirds under 30 years old and most of the remainder aged between 30 and 40 years. As would be expected from this age distribution, those in the cohabiting group tended to have relatively low duration of living together so far, and Part B of Table I indicates that this duration was under five years for approximately half of the respondents, and under ten years for about three-quarters of them. Most of the respondents, therefore, came from age groups which might be expected to be the most sexually active, and were in partnerships which might not have become stale through very lengthy duration. The young age groups and the inclusion of single women meant that a high proportion of the women had not had children (51·4 per cent). Among those cohabiting, the proportion without children was 41 per cent, while the figure was 83 per cent for the others (most of the mothers here being previously married women).

Table I
Age distribution of respondents and duration of cohabitation

A Age group ·	Both groups (%)	Cohabiting (%)	Non-cohabiting (%)
Under 20	9	3	29
20–29	59	59	58
30–39	22	26	11
40–49	7	9	2
50 or more	3	3	1
B Duration of cohabitation			
5 years or less	—	53	—
6–10 years	—	22	—
11–15 years	—	11	—
Over 15 years	—	14	—

As measured by terminal age of education, the sample was not unduly biased towards women with greater education, unlike the groups studied by Hite (1976) and Fisher (1973). Some 55 per cent had left school at 16 years or less, and 30 per cent at 17 to 19 years, while 11 per cent had continued their education to 20 years or more, and a few were still being educated. Employed women predominated among the respondents, with only one-third having no outside employment. As would be expected, the non-cohabiting women were most likely to have full-time jobs (30 hours per week or more), while the cohabiting women were more likely to have part-time jobs or no jobs at all.

Birth control practice was dominated by the oral contraceptive, which was the choice of 45 per cent of respondents overall. The non-cohabiting women well exceeded the cohabitees in the use of this method (64 *v.* 40 per cent); although some 10 per cent of the latter had been sterilized, this was uncommon amongst the others. Use of the diaphragm was uncommon in both groups, and the sheath was not all that common either (cohabiting 12 per cent, non-cohabiting 9 per cent). Some 16 per cent of cohabiting women were using no method, although some of these were specifically trying to become pregnant. About 12 per cent of the non-cohabiting were also using no method, a figure which might cause concern to some because presumably few of these women would be attempting to conceive.

Aspects of Sexual Practice

It has been noted above that it would be incautious to generalize distributional data from this sample to the general female population. Nevertheless, it is necessary to record some aspects of sexual practice before moving to the discussion of sexual satisfaction and orgasm. This section, therefore, briefly notes some appropriate data.

PARTNERS

Some 90 per cent overall claimed current sexual activities only with a regular or steady partner, and 7 per cent reported 'regular partner and others' (which from correspondence seems likely for most to mean one regular other). As could be expected, cohabiting women were particularly likely to report a regular partner only (94 per cent), while the others reported this somewhat less (80 per cent), together with 11 per cent 'regular plus others', 7 per cent 'short-term partners', and 3 per cent 'casual partners'.

FREQUENCY OF INTERCOURSE

The mean reported frequency of intercourse was 2·3 times per week, and the distributions are shown in Table II. The pattern indicated corresponds well with that found in national random samples (e.g. Gorer, 1971), and as in most such tabulations the greatest single frequency is two to three times per week. Not surprisingly, the cohabiting respondents claimed higher frequencies than the non-cohabiting, who often complained in correspondence about restricted opportunity, but even cohabiting women had complaints of external constraints on frequency, such as the presence of other people in the home being intrusive, incommoding work patterns, etc. Inevitably, of course, estimates of intercourse frequency are subject to error, because few people record their sexual activity and in any case frequencies are bound to fluctuate over time. Nevertheless, it is improbable that the answers given are without foundation, and it is of comfort that the figures shown are in alignment with those found by others.

Table II
Frequency of intercourse

Frequency	Both groups (%)	Cohabiting (%)	Non-cohabiting (%)
Daily or more	5	5	5
4–6 times per week	20	21	15
2–3 times per week	37	40	31
weekly	17	19	13
fortnightly	8	7	9
rarely	11	7	21
never	2	1	6

Some 56 per cent of the respondents claimed to feel that their intercourse frequency was 'about right' for them, although this was more often claimed by cohabiting women (63 per cent) than by the others (36 per cent). A point of interest here is that of those who did not endorse their frequency as about right virtually all said that their frequency was insufficient. In the traditional picture wives complain of over-sufficiency rather than insufficiency, but Bell (1964, 1966, 1967) found a progressive change in this respect, and this American phenomenon doubtless exists in Britain too. The finding noted here is thus congruent with the impression found in a number of studies that contemporary women have a more affirmative attitude towards intercourse than their predecessors, and are more willing to recognize and express sexual desire (Bell, 1964, 1966, 1967; Bell and Chasker, 1970; Sorensen, 1973; Hunt, 1974). Only 3 per cent of the respondents claimed that their frequency was too great, and these were particularly likely to be women who rarely or never achieve orgasm during intercourse. Frequency was also related in other ways to orgasm, and to masturbation, and these will be referred to later.

TIME AND PLACE

Questions were asked about when and where intercourse took place, primarily to elicit how far this was mainly in bed and mainly at night. Unfortunately these questions proved not to be good discriminators because 60 per cent of replies indicated 'sometimes' other than in bed and other than at night. However, the extreme categories ('often' and 'never') have some utility in eliciting patterns of sexuality, as will be seen.

POSITION OF INTERCOURSE

Respondents were asked how often they varied from the intercourse position with the man on top, again to elicit the extent of variation in sexual practice. About half of the women claimed 'often' to vary from this position, and most of the remainder claimed to 'sometimes'. Only 10 per cent claimed 'never' to vary from this position, and this answer, too, was related to a certain sexual pattern.

ORAL SEX

Approximately 40 per cent of respondents reported that they engaged in oral sex 'often', and a similar proportion said 'sometimes', leaving only a minority who claimed 'never'. Unfortunately the material does not permit inference about how much these answers referred to fellatio or cunnilingus or both, but it was evident from correspondence that women and their partners sometimes had asymmetrical attitudes, so that reciprocity was not necessarily involved. Qualitative material also suggests that women may have a greater desire for cunnilingus than their partners are apt to satisfy.

There were marked differences by age group in the extent of participation in oral sex. Of women aged under 30 years some 46 per cent reported 'often' and 12 per cent 'never', whereas for those aged 40 or more the corresponding figures were 20 and 42 per cent. The material does not permit conclusions about how far these differences reflect the effects of age *per se* on sexual practice, or the 'career pattern' of sexual relationship, or the influence of generation as distinct from age. This is, of course, characteristic of problems with a snap-shot survey, but various kinds of evidence suggest that generational factors are very influential here.

EROTIC AIDS

Questions were asked about the use of certain aids to stimulation in sexual episodes, namely special clothing, books or pictures, 'spanking', and playing games. These questions seem to have been found disturbing by some respondents, because whereas other questions (except those on masturbation) were rarely left unanswered by as many as 1 per cent, the items on erotic aids were left blank in 10 to 16 per cent of cases. The figures obtained are thus perhaps conservative; the distributions are shown in Table III. This indicates that none of these stimulatory aids are used by a majority, although approximately one-third make some use of erotic books or pictures, and a quarter use special clothing at least sometimes. From correspondence, special clothing seems to refer to such items as stockings, suspenders and provocative underwear, rather than to materials such as rubber or plastic. Correspondents were divided in their attitudes to erotic books and pictures. Some found them stimulating and recommended them, some were embarrassed by such material, and others again feared comparison with the women in the pictures. A very few complained that such pictures exploited women, but there was widespread condemnation of pornography involving children or animals.

Table III
Use of erotic aids

Type of aid	Often (%)	Sometimes (%)	Never (%)	No answer (%)
Clothing	3·3	18·2	68·4	10·1
Books/pictures	4·0	28·4	58·6	8·9
Spanking	1·5	6·4	75·4	16·6
Games	1·1	8·4	74·9	15·6

Sexual Satisfaction

In 1974 a sample similar to the present one was used to study marital satisfaction among British wives (Walker, 1977; Walker and Chester, 1977). That study measured self-rated satisfaction with seven individual aspects of marriage, as well as marriage in general, and concluded that dissatisfaction where it existed was very much concentrated onto the expressive as opposed to the instrumental aspects of married life. In rating their satisfaction with 'kissing and cuddling', the 'intimate side of marriage', and the comparative quality of their lovemaking, some one-third of wives expressed some measure of dissatisfaction (and one-third of these claimed to be very dissatisfied). The present study aimed to study the sexual component more explicitly, and produced closely comparable findings on satisfaction. The current sample also contains unmarried women, of course, although these differed from wives only in expressing themselves marginally more likely to be a bit dissatisfied, and (equally marginally) less likely to be very satisfied.

Even apart from the limitations of the questionnaire method it is obviously the case that measurement of satisfaction is a difficult and uncertain undertaking. Satisfaction is an entirely subjective feeling, and there is no way of knowing the criteria or parameters of evaluation employed by the respondents. Equally, however, only a handful of respondents declined to assess their feelings of satisfaction on a four-point scale, regarding both the quality of intercourse and current sex life more generally. The consequent ratings are shown in Table IV, and it is immediately apparent that, although the representativeness of the distributions cannot be known, at least the survey did not attract only respondents who wished to express dissatisfaction in the sexual sphere. In both the measures some two-thirds of respondents expressed themselves as either reasonably or very satisfied, and this corresponds with the proportion who, in a different question, disagreed with the proposition that "on the whole sex is rather a let-down for women". Ratings of satisfaction with quality of intercourse and with current sex life are obviously closely related, and the responses are highly correlated. The questions are not identical, however, so that respondents could answer each one somewhat differently without being inconsistent, and a proportion did so.

Table IV
Satisfaction with quality of intercourse and with sex life in general

	Very satisfied (%)	Reasonably satisfied (%)	Bit dissatisfied (%)	Very dissatisfied (%)
Intercourse	38	30	20	11
Sex life	34	34	20	12

Of this particular sample of women it can be seen that around one-third expressed themselves as less than reasonably satisfied in their sexual experience, and that one-third of these were very dissatisfied. If these proportions are at all representative (which, to repeat, is not known), then the numbers of women in Britain experiencing sexual dissatisfaction are very large. It must be remembered that in some cases dissatisfaction is caused by factors either external to the couple or external to their sexuality (e.g. ill health), but this is clearly not so in most cases, and it seems likely that investigation of the sources of lack of satisfaction could be an important endeavour. The present material has limitations for such an investigation, but, nevertheless, contains suggestive elements.

Chesser (1956) questioned his respondents about impediments to sexual enjoyment originating with the sexual style of the husband, and found these to centre on such matters as abruptness, lack of foreplay, lack of tenderness and absence of consideration for the wife's satisfaction. Such complaints were widely repeated in correspondence accompanying the present survey. There was frequent mention of what was termed 'the wham-bang approach', and typical comments were that men are: too ignorant of female anatomy and needs; too inclined to ignore or to cut short on arousal; too vigorous; too insistent, and too inclined to finish abruptly and turn away. There was evidently widespread inability to discuss such sources of dissatisfaction, sometimes attributed to the partner's attitude or refusal, but often also to mutual diffidence or the woman's own inability to broach the subject.

There was common mention of the need for verbal and physical expressions of love and affection as part of the sexual relationship. Some two-thirds of the women agreed (most strongly) with the proposition "you can't have good sex without love and affection", and intercourse unaccompanied by signs of love was said by some to lead to feelings of being used, of pointlessness, and of general disenchantment with sex. Among this sample women's traditional association of sex with love and affection has not been eroded away by developments in contemporary *mores* (although some were at pains to point out that this did not necessarily involve marriage). Many women mentioned the store which they set by physical signs of affection such as kissing and cuddling, hugs, hand-holding, etc. Sometimes this referred to the (as it were) pre-bed preliminaries to lovemaking—that it should begin downstairs. Often, however, the women wanted these physical demonstrations to be part of ordinary daily living, as tokens of loving feelings. From their words it is clear that such touching is important to many women, and that many men disappoint them by restricting embraces to the intercourse context, even then being sometimes rather perfunctory about it.

Other factors which Chesser found related to sexual satisfaction among his sample of wives were general happiness in their marriage and the kind of impression they had gained about sex when growing up. The present material does not address the first issue, which is anyway difficult to disentangle because sexual satisfaction may be both a symptom of a happy marriage and a contributory factor to it. However, there is some material on upbringing in the present survey. Chesser found that where a childhood impression had been gained that 'sex was unpleasant' this had a negative relationship with both frequency of orgasm and sexual satisfaction. The current sample was asked to agree or disagree with the proposition that "on the whole I was brought up to feel that sex is rather bad", and some 42 per cent expressed agreement (with generational differentials). In their letters many women claimed that their upbringing had to some extent impaired their capacity to enjoy their sexuality, and they often said explicitly that they were trying to bring up their own children differently. There is in the data a certain confirmation of this impairment (and of Chesser's point). Although the tendencies were only slight they were definite, and in comparison with those not brought up to feel that sex is bad, those who had been were more likely to feel very dissatisfied with their sex lives; more likely to feel that sex is a let-down for women; and more likely to never, or rarely, reach orgasm in intercourse while being less likely to always reach orgasm. There is at least a suggestion here that adverse impressions gained during upbringing can have durable effects, even when consciously rejected.

Sexual satisfaction is thus related to matters of diffuse emotional meaning, but from the data it seems also to be related to such specific matters as frequency of intercourse and orgasm during intercourse. Women who deemed their intercourse frequency to be insufficient, for instance, were more than twice as likely to express sexual dissatisfaction than were those who endorsed their frequency as adequate. There was also a positive relationship between the actually reported frequency rates and expression of satisfaction (or, conversely, the lower the reported intercourse frequency the greater the propensity to express dissatisfaction). What the data cannot show is the direction of causality in this relationship, or indeed, whether low frequency and high dissatisfaction are both the consequences of some other factor, such as a generally unsatisfactory relationship with the partner. Looking at a number of variables together there was evidently a pattern of sexuality which was associated with higher levels of expressed satisfaction, and this pattern included more frequent intercourse, more variation of position, more frequent participation in oral sex, more frequent use of stimulating aids, more frequent masturbation as a stimulus for the partner, and stronger disagreement that men should always take the lead in sexual matters. This was not so much a particular group of women as a pattern of sexuality which women approached to a greater or lesser extent, and it contained a generational component in that the pattern was more evident among younger than among older women.

One of the more striking aspects of expressed satisfaction was the impact of orgasm during intercourse. Orgasm is the subject of the next section, but here it may be noted that women who rarely or never attain orgasm during intercourse were more than three times as likely as those who do so frequently or always to express some sexual dissatisfaction (51 *v.* 16 per cent), and four times as likely to depict themselves as 'very dissatisfied' (21 *v.* 5 per cent). These relativities were reversed in the category of women who were 'very satisfied', and orgasm during intercourse is clearly an important aspect of sexual satisfaction for women, even if not its only source. Before examining further data on orgasm, however, it seems reasonable to summarize this section by reiterating that, for whatever reason, quite a high proportion of women probably do not achieve satisfaction in their sexual lives.

Orgasm

The main question on orgasm was worded thus: "In about what proportion of cases would you say that you reach orgasm (full climax or relief) actually *during* intercourse?" The qualification in the question is important because the aim was not to measure total experience of orgasm, but only orgasm produced by and during intromission and thrusting of the penis. So far as can be judged most respondents understood the question in this sense, although it is possible that some may have regarded direct manual stimulation of the clitoris during penetration as 'during intercourse', or even, perhaps, have interpreted the phrase to mean the whole sequence of action in a sexual encounter and thus including orgasm from manual or oral stimulation before and/or after intromission. If this should be the case then the figures shown later for lack of regular orgasm during intercourse are likely to be conservative, and even so only a minority of respondents claimed regularly to achieve orgasm as defined.

In this matter there is another problem than that of possible ambiguities in the meaning of 'during intercourse', and this concerns women's interpretation of their genital experiences. There are in the literature suggestions that women may sometimes be somewhat confused as to what constitutes orgasm, and that some may **mis-**

identify as orgasm the generalized excitement of aroused passionate feeling (Cuber and Harroff, 1965). This is, perhaps, unlikely to be a majority problem, but that it does exist can be shown by reference to some sample quotations from survey correspondence, such as:

"I don't have any doubt that I reach orgasm when I masturbate—but I'm not so sure that I have an orgasm during intercourse. What I do experience sometimes during intercourse is a feeling of release, pleasure and exultation, and when I experience this I have no desire afterwards for the sort of orgasm that results from masturbation."

"I enjoy sex very much but I can honestly say that I haven't known when or even if I have a climax."

"My problem is that I don't know exactly what an orgasm is. I am very satisfied with my lovemaking, but it does worry me when I read about other women having them."

"As regards orgasm—I'm still not entirely sure as to what it is exactly, although I'm told I would if I'd had one."

It is thus not unreasonable to believe that there may be in the case of some respondents a problem concerning the interpretation of sexual sensation. However, it is probable that this would more likely run in the direction of a women believing she has had an orgasm when she has not than in the contrary direction, in which case the effect on measures such as the one described here would be conservatizing (i.e. it will minimize the proportion claiming not always or frequently to experience orgasm during intercourse). Meanwhile it is important to note that for discussion here the meaning of orgasm is as defined above, and there is no measure of orgasm from all sources. However, from qualitative evidence it seems that at least most of the correspondents could experience orgasm through some means, and in so far as they were anorgasmic it was only in a special and restricted sense.

To judge from correspondence, the ability to achieve orgasm, particularly during intercourse, has acquired considerable symbolic importance for many women. In their letters they worry about the lack of it, express longing and striving for it, and have feelings of deprivation or inadequacy if they fail to achieve it. What many of them seem to be seeking is simultaneous intra-coital orgasm, which they feel they have been tutored by the media and by sex instruction manuals to see as an important aim and an achievable end. Certainly magazines and (increasingly) newspapers constantly exhort readers to be sexually active and competent, and manuals lay great stress on orgasmic satisfaction for wives. The evidence of this survey, however, which parallels the findings of other research, is that the majority of women do not readily achieve orgasm during intercourse. The figures are given in Table V, which shows that only a minority of the women always or nearly always achieve orgasm during intercourse, and that as many more never do or do so only rarely. Therefore, when a woman asks (as many correspondents did) "I wonder how many other women share this problem?", the answer is probably that millions do, and that the explanation cannot lie all that often in anatomical peculiarities or psychological flaws, even though the minds of some women turn in such directions.

Table V
Frequency of orgasm during intercourse

Always or nearly always (%)	Over half (%)	About half (%)	Under half (%)	Rarely (%)	Never (%)
36	8	15	5	17	19

To establish that the majority of women do not consistently achieve orgasm through intercourse would obviously be a finding of some significance, and so it is desirable to compare the findings here with those of other studies to test their generalizability. Unfortunately, however, comparisons are difficult and uncertain because investigators have used such different definitions and criteria, and some have based their work on clinical samples and psychiatric concepts. Bergler (1944), for instance, used the concept of *vaginal orgasm*, and concluded that probably only 30 per cent or less of women experience this, thus offering an estimate similar to that of Kroger and Freed (1950). If what they describe as vaginal orgasm refers at all to what is called here orgasm during intercourse, then the findings might be regarded as not contradictory (although the present authors should not be assumed to subscribe to the concept of vaginal orgasm in the traditional psycho-analytical sense). Clinical estimates, in fact, do not provide the best basis of comparison for the present findings, and there do exist certain other reports which might more appropriately be noted.

For the UK the main comparison must be with the findings two decades ago of Chesser (1956), although some slighter, more recent data is found in Eysenck (1978). Chesser did not place quite the same emphasis on orgasm *during* intercourse, and he used different response categories, but even so his findings seem to be not greatly out of alignment with those reported here. He found that 24 per cent claimed to achieve orgasm 'always' or 'nearly always', and that 35 per cent claimed 'frequently', as against 41 per cent who claimed 'sometimes', 'rarely' or 'never'. Direct matching with Table V is not possible, but if the categories from 'about half' upwards are taken to approximate to Chesser's 'always', 'nearly always' and 'frequently', then the result is 59 per cent in each sample. The legitimacy of this matching is uncertain because we cannot know what Chesser's respondents meant by 'frequently', but it is clear that only a quarter of them claimed always or nearly always to achieve orgasm in intercourse, and this fits into a range of approximately 25 to 40 per cent which can be taken or inferred from a number of studies. Eysenck is not reporting on frequency of orgasm, but it can be inferred from certain passages that, of a sample of female undergraduates, 49 per cent claimed to achieve orgasm during intercourse 'very often' or 'often', against 51 per cent who claimed 'middling', 'not very often', 'hardly ever' and 'never'. If 'very often' and 'often' can be equated with the 'over half', 'nearly always' and 'always' of Table V, then Eysenck's figure of 49 per cent is not far different from the 44 per cent of this table, and it is certainly clear that only a minority of the undergraduates consistently achieved orgasm during intercourse.

Some comparisons can also be made with three studies emanating from the USA, those of Hite (1976), Fisher (1973) and Kinsey *et al.* (1953). Hite's focus was very specifically on orgasm achieved via intercourse alone, and she reports that only 30 per cent of her respondents 'regularly' experienced this. Of Fisher's respondents, some 39 per cent claimed 'always' or 'nearly always' to achieve orgasm during intercourse, a figure very close to that found in the present study. Furthermore, it is clear that in Fisher's study 'during intercourse' included manual stimulation of the clitoris, for he also states that only 20 per cent of his respondents never required a final 'push' to orgasm from direct clitoral stimulation. Kinsey's figure for those 'always' or 'nearly always' achieving orgasm during intercourse is 42 per cent, which is slightly on the high side for the findings reviewed here. However, in Kinsey there is also some blurring of the meaning of 'during intercourse', since it can be inferred that his figures refer to orgasm achieved by any means during intercourse, and so clitoral stimulation is also a factor here. Kinsey's material also indicates that, of married women respondents, some 50 to 60 per cent achieve orgasm during intercourse 60 per cent or more of the time.

This can, perhaps, be compared with the 59 per cent of the present sample who are shown in Table VI to achieve orgasm half or more of the time.

Table VI
Frequency of orgasm during intercourse as found in several studies

Sample	Orgasm frequency				
	Always or nearly always	Over half	About half	Under half	Rarely or never
Present sample: cumulative (%)	36	44	59	64	100
Chesser	24	—	—	—	—
Fisher	39	—	—	—	—
Kinsey	42	—	—	—	—
Hite ('regularly')	30	—	—	—	—
Chesser ('always', 'nearly always', 'frequently'): cumulative (%)	—	—	59	—	—
Eysenck ('very often', 'often'): cumulative (%)	—	49	—	—	—

The findings of these various studies are compared as well as can be in Table VI, and despite the difficulties of comparison the overall consensus is quite striking. What is common to all the studies is that the majority of women do not consistently achieve orgasm from intercourse (in the sense of penetration plus the stimulation and traction developed by penile thrusting), and that a quite high proportion rarely or never do. This does not mean that most women are anorgasmic, of course, because many attain sexual climax before, during or after penetration through the use of other techniques, and virtually all women attain orgasm via masturbation. Penile thrusting alone, however, is an inadequate source of orgasm for most women, even though it may be the source of other pleasures and satisfactions.

It has, doubtless, long been part of both clinical knowledge and covert popular lore that the female orgasm is problematical, but this has usually led to the question "Why do these women fail to have orgasm during intercourse?" In view of the available data it may be that different questions should be asked, such as "why should intercourse be expected to stimulate women to orgasm?", or "why are women (and men) led to believe that orgasm should be readily and regularly achieved through intercourse?'' Such questions would raise considerable issues concerning both popular and professional assumptions and expectations about sexual experience, although these cannot be entered into here. What can be said is that many women have acquired a very considerable sense of the importance of achieving orgasm during intercourse, and experience varying degrees of anguish, self-doubt, disappointment and dissatisfaction when they do not do so. Whatever explanation might be offered for this widespread failure, it would almost certainly be of help and comfort if the knowledge of it were more generally distributed.

It was noted earlier that orgasm during intercourse was positively associated with expression of sexual satisfaction, and this was also found by Chesser. However, while coital orgasm may be the most satisfying outcome of sexual union it is by no means the only form that sexual pleasure takes, and it seems not to be *essential* to the achievement of satisfaction. Whereas only about one-third of the sample claimed consistent orgasm, some two-thirds expressed some measure of satisfaction with their sex lives, so that evidently they were finding alternative sources of satisfaction. From the correspondence these sources seemed to consist of more diffuse physical sensations than orgasm, and of psychological feelings concerning closeness, completeness, pleasuring the partner, etc. Not all of the respondents ascribed high importance to the achievement of orgasm actually during intercourse, the answers given being: 'very important', 21 per cent; 'fairly important', 34 per cent; 'not all that important', 36 per cent; and 'unimportant', 9 per cent. It needs to be reiterated that the question specified orgasm during intercourse, and not orgasm *per se*. Letters made it clear that for many who did not ascribe top importance to climaxing during intercourse it was nevertheless desirable to achieve orgasm at some point in a sexual encounter. To some extent the answers regarding the importance of orgasm during intercourse probably reflect some adjustment by the women to their actual experience. It was notable that those who always reach orgasm mostly ascribe importance to it, whereas those who never do are less likely to say 'very important' and more likely to say 'unimportant'.

As a final point in this section it might be noted that it is not only women to whom the female orgasm may be important. Many correspondents said that they did not mind not achieving orgasm during intercourse, particularly if they could do so before or after. However, many also felt great pressure from their partner to reach orgasm, and this can best be expressed by some sample quotations, such as:

"It is my husband who believes I should have an orgasm every time we make love. If I don't during intercourse he stimulates me after and I try so hard to give him *what he wants*, but it always ends up in a row because I can't. Then he believes that he is a failure in bed, and I can't seem to convince him that I don't always need it." (Italics not in original).

"I never feel frustrated because I have not reached an orgasm. I did, however, have to convince my boyfriend that there was nothing wrong with me."

"I have a terrible time trying to convince him that its not his fault I don't achieve orgasm. He thinks it is an insult to his manhood."

"The 'faking' is important because my husband needs to feel that he is a good lover."

Sometimes the male partner thinks that there is something wrong with *her*, sometimes with *himself*, and sometimes with their relationship, and the correspondence indicates that this can be felt by the woman as a pressure to 'perform'. This is related to the issue of faking orgasm, where the figures were: 'often', 9 per cent; 'sometimes', 17 per cent; 'rarely', 20 per cent; and 'never', 54 per cent. Thus just over half said they never fake, but clearly faking is not uncommon and is done to please or satisfy the man. This practice, once begun, can become a trap for the woman, since the correspondence indicates that it can cause personal strain and create distaste for intercourse. The longer it continues the more impossible does it become to confess, and even simply to stop requires an explanation. Some sexual relationships are thus based on a perpetual deception, initially undertaken to gratify the man, and while some women seem content to continue out of regard for their partner, for others it creates a burdensome situation where the woman's real needs and experiences cannot be discussed.

Material of this kind indicates that the public concept of coital orgasm has significance for men as well as for women, and that the study of female orgasm should include male perceptions and expectations. It would doubtless be an exaggeration and simplification to speak of male appropriation of the female orgasm, but there has nevertheless been a switch from under-concern to possible over-concern with the orgasm, and a change in popular imagery. The traditional myth of the passive and sexually anaesthetic woman permitting the man his rights is being displaced by the myth of the writhing, ecstatic woman being driven to orgasmic abandon and satisfaction so that the male may thereby prove his adequacy. Both myths are likely to place women in a strait-jacket and are unhelpful to sexual communication, which is why the male dimension needs to be brought into the consideration of female sexuality.

Masturbation

Among the women in the survey masturbation was very common. The questions related separately to masturbation after intercourse, by oneself, and in front of a partner, and only 36 per cent claimed never to masturbate in any of these contexts. However, it cannot be taken for granted that all the remaining 64 per cent did masturbate, because, interestingly, the respondents were considerably more likely to leave masturbation questions unanswered than was the case for other areas of questioning. The rates of non-response are shown in Table VII, and they suggest that the figures obtained for masturbation are probably conservative.

Table VII
Incidence of masturbation

	Total sample		Those answering
Masturbate	3·6	'often'	4·6
after inter-	14·6	'sometimes'	18·6
course (%)	60·2	'never'	76·8
	21·6	no answer	—
Masturbate by	12·8	'often'	14·2
oneself (%)	37·8	'sometimes'	41·7
	40·1	'never'	44·2
	9·3	no answer	—
Masturbate in	5·6	'often'	7·1
front of	15·1	'sometimes'	19·2
partner (%)	57·9	'never'	73·7
	21·4	no answer	—

It can be seen from the table that, of those who answered, more than half reported that they masturbate by themselves at least sometimes, and that this is much more common than the other two practices. As might be predicted, cohabiting women were less likely to report that they masturbated 'often' (12 v. 20 per cent of the non-cohabiting), but they also show a higher incidence of 'sometimes' masturbating, so that the proportions reporting 'never' in the two groups was very similar (45 v. 43 per cent). It should be noted that the question concerned *current* behaviour, so that there is no measure of the proportion of women who have *ever* masturbated. It is thus perhaps of interest to note that for more than half of women living with husbands or consorts, private masturbation was at least an occasional current practice, and its incidence seemed not to vary greatly by age. Women who report that they masturbate by themselves are found in this survey to have the following characteristics (*inter alia*):

i. lower intercourse frequencies, particularly frequencies of once a fortnight or less;

ii. feelings that their intercourse frequency (whatever it is) is insufficient for them;

iii. to fake orgasms with the partner (thus, presumably, making it more difficult to seek alternative avenues of relief with his co-operation);

iv. to be more dissatisfied both with the quality of intercourse and with sex life in general;

v. to be women who rarely or never reach orgasm during intercourse. Some two-thirds of such women say that they practice private masturbation (24 per cent 'often' and 40 per cent 'sometimes'), and they are also more likely to say that they masturbate after intercourse.

Not much was said about masturbation in spontaneous correspondence, but where it was mentioned a variety of attitudes were expressed. Some, for instance, felt resentment at the need for this practice as a course of gratification, although others were more matter-of-fact in attitude. A sense of guilt was mentioned by some, and there was frequent mention of shame. However, what was often expressed here was a feeling that it would be shameful and humiliating for the masturbation to be known about rather than actual feelings of shame or guilt. Little was written spontaneously about masturbatory techniques, although some impressions can be drawn from qualitative material collected later than the survey data. One such impression is that vaginal insertion is uncommon, as is the use of technological aids such as electrical vibrators. Most female masturbation thus seems to consist of direct or indirect manual stimulation of the clitoral region, typically accompanied by phantasy, and this suggests that the women concerned have, at minimum, an intuitive understanding of the mechanism which brings them to orgasm. It seems probable that female masturbation is largely undiscussed socially, so that many women have no idea how common it is. In view of its widespread occurrence, and the evidence it gives of orgasmic adequacy which is not always reproduced in intercourse, masturbation seems to play a not insignificant role in female sexuality which might repay greater study than it has received.

Conclusion

Inevitably this paper has indicated only some of the material that can be derived from the survey, and inevitably, too, the manner of its acquisition requires that it be treated with caution. Nevertheless, the material does cover ground where little other information exists, and many of its findings correspond in broad terms with what has been found in some studies made in the USA. Certainly, the nature of the material gathered suggests that in modern circumstances sexuality is an area of experience which can more readily be studied than some may have thought likely. Obviously there are peculiar difficulties involved in studying an area which is invested with so much social and personal significance and meaning, but the effort of overcoming these difficulties might be thought well worthwhile if the evidence is accepted that very large numbers of women (and doubtless men as well) experience dissatisfactions and problems in their sexual lives.

Such dissatisfactions and problems are commonly dealt with under the rubric of sexual dysfunction, but perhaps for many people this is to take a much too clinically oriented view. Undoubtedly there are those for whom the consulting room is most appropriate, and advances are being made in this sphere. However, it seems likely that much sexual disappointment finds its origin not in pathology of the psyche but rather in attitudes, expectations, assumptions and simple ignorance which might respond to action of a social or educational kind without the need for clinical attention. As a basic preliminary to any such action, however, it is necessary to have far more knowledge than currently exists about the sexual behaviour and experience of the general population. One of the most common research conclusions is the need for yet more research, but in the present case this is a call which is perhaps particularly apt.

References

Bell, R. R. (1964). Some factors related to the sexual satisfaction of the college educated wife. *Family Life Co-ordinator*, **13,** 43–47.

Bell, R. R. (1966). *Premarital Sex in a Changing Society*. Englewood Cliffs: Prentice-Hall.

Bell, R. R. (1967). Some emerging sexual expectations among women. *Medical Aspects of Human Sexuality*, **2,** October.

Bell, R. R. and Chasker, J. B. (1970). Premarital sexual experience among coeds: 1958 and 1968. *Journal of Marriage and the Family*, **32,** 81–84.

Bergler, E. (1944). The problem of frigidity. *Psychiatric Quarterly*, **18,** 374–390.

Chesser, E. (1956). *The Sexual, Marital and Family Relationships of the English Woman.* London: Hutchinson.

Cochrane, R. and Duffy, J. (1974). Psychology of scientific method. *Bulletin of the British Psychological Society*, **27,** 117–121.

Cuber, J. and Harroff, P. (1965). *The Significant Americans: A Study of Sexual Behavior Among the Affluent.* New York: Appleton-Century-Crofts.

Eysenck, H. J. (1978). *Sex and Personality.* London: Sphere Books.

Fisher, S. (1973). *The Female Orgasm.* Harmondsworth, Middlesex: Penguin Books.

Gorer, G. (1971). *Sex and Marriage in England Today.* London: Nelson.

Hite, S. (1976). *The Hite Report.* London: Talmy Franklin.

Hunt, M. (1974). *Sexual Behavior in the 1970s.* Chicago: Playboy Press.

Kinsey, A. C., Pomeroy, W. B., Martin, C. E. and Gebhard, P. H. (1953). *Sexual Behavior in the Human Female.* Philadelphia and London: W. B. Saunders.

Kroger, W. S. and Freed, S. C. (1950). Psychosomatic aspects of frigidity. *Journal of the American Medical Association*, **143,** 526–532.

Schofield, M. (1965). *The Sexual Behaviour of Young People.* London: Longman.

Schofield, M. (1973). *The Sexual Behaviour of Young Adults.* London: Allen Lane.

Sorensen, R. C. (1973). *Adolescent Sexuality in Contemporary America.* New York: Ward.

Walker, C. (1977). Some variations in marital satisfaction. In *Equalities and Inequalities in Family Life.* Edited by R. Chester and J. Peel. London and New York: Academic Press.

Walker, C. and Chester, R. (1977). Marital satisfaction amongst British wives. *Marriage Guidance*, **17,** 219–227.

The Orgasm:
A Sociological Consideration of the Interpretation of Physiologically Derived Response Norms

MICHAEL KINGHAM

Department of Health Studies, The Polytechnic,
Newcastle upon Tyne, England

What is the reality of the orgasm? Is it a simple somatic response with different degrees of intensity, and as Masters and Johnson (1966) showed, a definite excitation pattern with marked stages, or is it primarily a cognitive experience where the interpretation of the biological entity either enhances or detracts from the experience?

How should we begin to assess the varying social constructions made regarding such a deceptively simple 'biological event' and is this a task worth doing anyway? I contend that our current view of the orgasm is one still dominated by physiological interpretations and in which varying social constructions are made—there is no clarity concerning the differing theoretical and methodological levels of the studies. Thus, Hite (1976) seeks to interpret women's sexuality and in the last part of her book sketches out some ideas 'towards a new female sexuality'. But we are forced to consider her study in the feminist tradition and we need to look carefully at the value patterns concerning 'new behaviours', for there is within the work a prescriptive formula which is based on an articulate 'radical feminist's' view of sexuality. Since she also chose to 'throw out' traditional survey methods in her approach to classifying the response rates, debates concerning the typicality of the responses as related to other subcultural groups becomes even more problematic. As one of her respondents put it: "This is the most fascinating sex survey I have participated in, but I am baffled how you could compile an essay type of study in an accurate form." Hite responds "had I not written my Master's thesis on the methodology of the social sciences, undoubtedly it would be more difficult than it was."

This begs the question, for although there is a lot of interesting material in her book, the rules by which she makes abstractions, categorized respondents and highlighted aspects of orgasmic behaviour are not adequately represented. It seems to me that one of the academic roles that we should continue to play out, is to examine carefully the nature of the social theories held by various writers, just as we need to be alert to the reductionism of explanation that is characteristic of medical and psychological constructions. In the rest of this paper I want to try and characterize the varying interpretative levels of the orgasm.

The Medical Model

Medicine has played a major role in the characterization of the human sexual response. We derive our language for the orgasm from Masters and Johnson, and the technical characterization of specific stages of excitation from excitement up to plateau and then orgasmic and post-orgasmic phases, has had a marked impact on our cultural thinking. But medicine's interpretation of the sexual response needs to be set firmly in its historical setting.

Vincent (1967) argues that the fundamental change in knowledge and attitudes towards sexuality has been from a pathological model of sexuality to a 'normalization' of sexual behaviour. Where students in the nineteenth century would have been concerned with such things as the effect of too much masturbation, the need to contain childhood sexuality and the downward path that might be taken by men and women who indulged in many of the activities described in Krafft-Ebing's *Psychopathia Sexualis* (1894), the twentieth-century student will be concerned with aiding 'the management of the sexual drive' to the greater satisfaction of his patients, supported by data on the range of human sexual variations and responsiveness provided by Kinsey *et al.* (1948) and Masters and Johnson (1966). Medicine conceiving the body as a machine with various pleasure centres that can be cultivated has, it may be argued, become the secular authority that legitimizes various kinds of body-interaction. The medicalization of life thesis by Zola (1973) may be demonstrated in the field of sexuality; increased control over fertility via contraceptive dispensation and regulation; the great majority of popular writings on sexual interaction written by doctors and concentrating on physical response norms derived from Masters and Johnson, Kinsey and others; the enhancement of sexual pleasure by improved techniques often grounded in a better understanding of the physical functioning of the body and therefore a natural extension of the doctor's professional knowledge. As Comfort (1967) puts it, where in the last century many people would have asked the question "Am I pure?" (synonymous with sexual abstinence), today they might ask "Am I achieving complete satisfaction?"

The same thesis that considered masturbation as harmful because it channelled energy into sex and not into more creative activities, considered females 'without sexual feeling' for their duties were bound up with being 'good mothers, wives and managers of households.' Acton (1967) stated that:

> "I am ready to maintain that there are many females who never feel any sexual excitement whatever. Others, again immediately after each period, do become to a limited degree capable of experiencing it: but this capacity is often temporary and may entirely cease till the next menstrual period . . . many women know little or care little about sexual indulgences. Love of home, children and of domestic duties are the only passions they feel."

The logical conclusion for Acton of the above led him to suggest that if a woman gained sexual pleasure, "her clitoris could be removed to correct that abnormality." We have little evidence of the nature and range of symptoms presented as sexual problems in this period, but it is necessary to consider medical notions of pathology and thus interventions such as clitoredectomy, prepuce removal, masturbation restraint appliances and orificial surgery in relation to views about the social position of women, the consequences for society of displacing creative energies from work into sex, and the social beliefs about the evolutionary position of Victorian society.

In attempting to account for a shift from a pathological view of sex to a 'normal' one we can make the following two points. Firstly, that:

> "the convention of sexual privacy combined with the suppression of nearly all anecdotal literature left the doctor with only his own experience to go on, plus the occasional case history. The panic over masturbation and the conviction that his patient was ruining his health by attempting intercourse three times a week could hardly have survived frank conversation with a dozen assorted colleagues, given a genuine spirit of enquiry." (Comfort, 1967);

and second, in the context of modern practice:

> "one important factor in ending the type of anxiety making, has been the

great shift in cultural attitudes, within science, towards a concept of normality. A pre-statistical age paid little heed to human variation beyond the obvious, and with some justification it equated behavioural normality with acceptable behaviour. Not only has knowledge of other times and authors greatly complicated this definition, but the escape from straight line teleological thinking has made the intellectual difficulties of determining a norm too great for almost all those who none the less have to use one in daily practice." (Comfort, 1967.)

Since medicine operating in a tradition of western science has attempted to demonstrate empirically the nature of orgasmic responses, we may ask just how problematic is the interpretation of stages of response.

In the literature we find constant refinements in the analysis of the response; where Masters and Johnson establish four main phases of response, Diamond (1975) identifies six, namely resting, excitement, plateau, orgasmic, post-orgasmic and resolution phases. But a number of writers have pointed out that research training programmes at the Masters and Johnson clinic produce a high degree of inter-rater reliability in the assessment of orgasmic response. From a sociological point of view the differential perception of medical practitioners concerning orgasmic stages is problematic, and like the definitional problems related, for example, to the international classification of schizophrenia, or Bloor's (1976) article demonstrating that the regional variation in adenotonsillectomies was strikingly related to differential perception of symptoms, we therefore need to know more regarding medical 'standardization' in this area.

Just as evidence suggests poor 'standardization' in the recognition of orgasmic phases, Clark Vincent (1967) points out:

"that few couples have read the two books authored by Masters and Johnson, and sometimes their questions and discussion reflect some of the incomplete if not distorted ideas conveyed in magazine articles."

Gagnon and Simon (1974) are not surprised at the problematic interpretation of physiological sequences, for them:

"The doing of sex implies that there is some culmination to it, a moment of ecstasy or joy. Conventionally this has been identified with the moment of orgasm. . . . It is clear from much of their work that they know a good deal of the psychological components in this process, but their necessary focus is on the bounded character of the physical acts leading to orgasm, yet even here this social and psychological component is as crucial. No one comes to age in this society with a prepared set of socio-sexual repertoires that are immanent in their physical equipment. The capacity for erection or vaginal lubrication must be interpreted and linked to a suitable set of activities, people and situations that will lead to intromission and orgasm on the part of the male and the female. The feelings that occur in the interior of the body have no immanent meaning attached to them, and they must as surely be learned and managed as is the information that is processed from the exterior of the body. Indeed it may be that the confluence of internal sensations that is identified as orgasm, is so identified because of the situation within which it occurs rather than being a necessary connection between the sensory inputs and the central nervous system.''

Apart from interpretative issues related to physical response norms, medical practitioners have noted a number of special issues related to the orgasm; for example, Niles Newton (1973) has examined the similarity between the physiological processes related to stages of labour and argues that there is a striking parallelism with that of the orgasm. Her paper is interesting in the biological parallels that are drawn but, at the level of cognition, the interpretation of the two behaviour patterns is inadequate.

Goodlin (1971) has made interesting speculations, and has done some experimental work suggesting that coitus *per se* may not be related to premature labour, but orgasm may be. Goodlin reported on the foetal heart rates and uterine tension during maternal orgasm induced by masturbation in a gravida at term. Associated uterine contractions and deceleration of the foetal heart rate were noted in the single case. To my knowledge the issue is not yet resolved. A host of other issues relating various physiological disorders such as spinal chord injury have been reported in relation to orgasm attainment or loss.

We may also note that the output of findings on sexual responsiveness is of recent origin and the impact and effects of the dissemination of this knowledge has not yet been measured. The new wave of sexual therapies that have grown up in the wake of this knowledge have often been monopolized by a small number of specialist doctors who have limited their services to higher socio-economic groups. Gillan (1977) has argued that control over specialist knowledge and its dissemination in this field is, however, not limited because it is currently in the hands of a small exclusive group, but it is limited because in 'England the NHS (National Health Service) finds it difficult to invest' in these services. Currently little scientific evaluation has taken place in relation to the claimed effectiveness of many therapies. It is this situation that the medical student must contend with and, in the UK, few medical schools have incorporated 'sociological' teaching into the medical school curriculum, so that the curriculum in this area is still dominated by the biological and the psychological.

In 1976 the BMA (British Medical Association) published *Aspects of Sexual medicine* (Lock, 1976), in which it is argued that "few doctors in practice today have been given much instruction about human sexual behaviour—either normal or abnormal during their medical training." Yet changes in public attitudes have led patients to expect that they should be able to ask for help with their sexual problems. A content analysis of the book reveals that sexuality is dealt with at a biological level, often in terms of physiological dysfunction, with social factors excluded from the analysis. The social behaviour surrounding sexuality and the 'meaning' of sexuality as defined by Gagnon and Simon (1974) is not considered.

In 1973, the *British Journal of Sexual Medicine* was first published. This journal has been produced six times a year since that date, but a content analysis reveals that as yet no article on social aspects of sexuality has been included. The editorial board of the journal consists of general practitioners, specialist consultants (e.g. gynaecologists) and psychologists.

In the popular literature, doctors often have a monopoly on sexual guides. The 'How to Do It' books such as Comfort's *More Joys of Sex* (1974), are still primarily technique books. You can get books ranging from Lowen's *Love and Orgasm* (1968), to Dr Lee Rosenberg's book *Total Orgasm* (1973), which again draws a connection between the attainment of Kundalini Yoga skills (cultural emphasis) and the development of more intense orgasms (physical emphasis).

The Boston Women's Health Collective have made powerful arguments for the withdrawal of mass-circulation sexual books which they consider to be riddled with misinformation. A particular target recently was Lowen's *Love and Orgasm* (sub-titled: Against techniques towards maturity) which still contains outdated material on the Freudian vaginal/clitoral controversy.

What I am essentially documenting is that the medical model is a very powerful one and that physiological response norms have often come to dominate our thinking concerning human response. We have not time to look at the characteristics of psychodynamic analyses of the orgasm, but I would argue that, as with the medical model, sociological aspects that impinge on aetiology are implicit in most writings. For example Fisher's work *Understanding the Female Orgasm*, (Fisher, 1973) conceptualizes various kinds of loss event as they relate to orgasm capacity, and he, along with Kaplan (1974) and others, gives the reader no sense of the individual as an actor located in a specific social setting. But if one criticizes the reductionism in many medical and psychological analyses of the orgasm, we can turn the tables and ask what use anyway is some of the sociological data to the medical practitioner? For example, Reiss (1975) argues that the value of knowledge relating social class and sexual relationships for the doctor, might be seen in this way:

"It would be of value to a doctor when a woman presents the symptom of being non-orgasmic in much of her marital sex. For if the woman was from the lower classes this lack of orgasm would be more expected, for Rainwater's data support such a finding as common. But if the woman is college educated and reports orgasmic failure, then one knows that this is much rarer and more likely to reflect causes that are peculiar to that particular marriage or that particular person. The case that fits the social group's sexual pattern can be explained in good measure by the group's characteristics if one is familiar with the research literature."

Although I would not dispute this interpretation, I would argue that there is a closed conception of behaviour being utilized in the application of this knowledge to the clinical setting and that many surveys on sexuality are outdated. Thus, as Plummer (1975) noted: "No more detailed work than Kinsey's exists, yet it relates to a sample of experiences now at least forty years out of date."

So, if it is fair to characterize the medical situation thus, how should we characterize sociological conceptions of the orgasm? How do we move away from the power of physiology? I have broken the sociological literature down into the following categories: survey data; organizational perspectives; social system view and the interactionist perspective.

Survey Studies

Traditional survey methodology has produced a number of interesting correlations between social variables and orgasmic experience. Tolson (1977) and others made major criticisms of the Kinsey studies (1948, 1953) when they first appeared, arguing that complex behavioural issues were being reduced to a crude behaviourism. Gagnon and Simon (1974) noted that in Kinsey, "Here we have man in the decorticated state . . . the bodies arrange themselves, orgasm occurs, one counts it seeking a continuum of rates where normalcy is a function of location on a distribution scale." Thus in seeking the natural (innate) sources of behaviour. ". . . the meanings that the actors attribute to their own behaviour and that which the society collectively organises are left out," and Plummer (1975), in a critique of Kinsey's traditional survey methodology argues:

> "Rather the sociologist has set about his task assuming the everyday commonsense definitions of sex as given. In his social book-keeping he has assumed the meaning of sex, orgasm, love and the like: in his cross cultural comparisons he has assumed the comparability of masturbation, homosexuality and the like; in his metatheorising he has taken a series of biological assumptions about man's sexuality and used them as a basis for his theorising."

It might be argued that because Kinsey chose 'the orgasm' as a measure of sexual activity, and because his writings had such impact on the western world, we have witnessed a form of what sociologists call deviancy amplification of this phenomena over the last three decades. Where he was able to demonstrate that frequency rates for the orgasm had increased over the first two decades of this century and where he established patterns of orgasm rate in, for example, postmarital coitus among widows and divorcees and found correlations between the duration of marital relationships and orgasm increase, he established a strong investigative tradition which others followed. So Clark and Wallen (1971) investigating his data on orgasm and marital duration, tried to show that the key variable was not duration but quality of marriage. The establishment of the adequacy of measures in these studies has been much debated and continues. Other studies have indicated some of the following: Rainwater (1966) has highlighted the lower orgasm frequency rates among working class groups; Kinsey has highlighted differential petting to orgasm rates between rural and urban groups, as well as the correlations between heterosexual petting, class and orgasm rates, and the relationship between religious variables and orgasm. The survey method in this area may not be the most productive way of exploring dynamic behaviour, but in a historical sense we should not rule out some of the contributions that it has made. We may say that the survey is (when used well) a good instrument for identifying sexual trends, but since so many of these types of study lack an explicit sociological theory of behaviour, the critical problem of interpreting dynamic patterns of behaviour remains.

Organizational Perspectives

A number of writers have, both amusingly and in a more serious vein, interpreted the orgasm in particular organizational settings.

American historians noted examples of nineteenth century sewing machine shops in the USA where the shape of the seat and the action of the labourer's foot on the treadle could give ladies that 'far away look'. Naturally factory production was at risk and the owners actually employed supervisors to control the behaviour of the employees. Rosenzweig (1973) points out that the development of semen banks for frozen deposits are already doing business in New York, Minneapolis and elsewhere. While home collection is customary, at least one institution maintains an 'Ejaculatorium' where, with the aid of various kinds of erotic assistance, the semen may be conventionally produced by depositors. Some sociologist devoted to ethnomethodology, is almost sure to give us a range of accounts of the underlife of a vasectomy clinic.

Ward and Kassenbaum (1965), in a study of sexual behaviour in prisons, showed how a number of inmates who willingly manipulated other inmates to orgasm, would not allow reciprocal action from their fellows. The control of sexual behaviour in this setting, so argued these inmates, allowed them to retain autonomy and power over their fellows and also to obtain presents for themselves.

A new study which is exploring the characteristics of 'sex' industries is examining the relationship between social and medical theories of sexuality and the marketing and production of sexual wares. Thus in the nineteenth century medical theories with a strongly repressive element led to companies producing mechanical restraints such as anti-masturbation harnesses. In the 1960s, changing norms allowed for industries geared to orgasm increase and the market abounds with all manner of vibrators, etc.

Although these may appear trivial examples they do highlight one way of interpreting orgasm behaviour, and the getting away from an obsession with physiology and technique. One writer argues that examples like this are important because they extend our thinking away from physiology and focus it on the social scripts and sexual dramas that take place in everyday life. Gagnon and Simon (1974) share this view, that the power of commercialism and the nature of sexual taboos has meant that only a limited range of sexual scripts are known for:

"Until the 1960s it was only pornography that made available descriptions of some of the physical aspects of sexual behaviour. While limited in complexity and with a limited sensibility, the characters in pornography actually felt skin, smelled each others odours, tasted body fluids and did sexual things."

They regret the limited-role models that are available in popular and pornographic literature and, we may add, in other books such as the Hite report.

Social Systems and Human Sexuality

A number of writers have considered the nature of the orgasm from a systemic point of view. For Reich (1932), sexuality and 'orgastic' potential, as he called it, must be viewed in relation to the power of the state, thus:

"Although a powerful drive could be a means of creative self fulfillment, it can be twisted and repressed by an oppressive state for its own ends: the state regulates the powerful drive through the family in order to rigidify the personality system and render it subservient to the needs of the rulers."

In his book the *Invasion of Compulsory Sex Morality* (1975) Reich tries to demonstrate that orgasmic behaviour in sexual relationships is only part of a wider orgastic potential. The body has become enslaved to a whole range of neurotic reactions, and these can be related back to existing repressive social structures. This theme has been further developed in Tolson's book *The Limits of Masculinity* (1977) and the argument advanced by Hooker is that:

"The decrease in accentuated gender role differences in occupations has a number of potential sexual changes built into it. One of these is that the possibility . . . that males whose early rearing is in such a tradition will have lowered commitments . . . to the 'male alliance' during early adolescence. They may be less exclusively 'homosocial' in their relations during this period."

These altered gender relationships may have a number of consequences:

"Males may more easily relate to females, they could have lowered rates of early adolescent masturbation, a lowered level of genital focus, and have lessened commitments to aggressive fantasies as part of sexual arousal. For these males the experience of early adolescence and later adolescence will contain lowered levels of anxiety about sexual performance from the genital point of view, and a lowered pressure toward premarital coitus as part of a male achievement syndrome."

If this relationship between occupational structure, gender identity and sexual behaviour could be demonstrated, the new female sexuality that Hite argues for, particularly in relation to non-coital behaviour might be more possible.

As another example, masturbation may be analysed at a macro-social level and take on political implications. Strong (1974) has argued that: "the only active adult propagandists for masturbation in our culture are women, the very class (according to survey analysis) that have practised it least". Some of those who have campaigned for women's rights have seen the formulation of oneself as an active sexual being as one of those rights. They have therefore urged women to practice masturbation as a way of formulating themselves. The authors of *Our Bodies, Ourselves* (Boston Women's Health Collective, 1971), a book by women for women, write:

"It is hard to feel good about allowing time and space to give pleasure to ourselves, an affirmation by us of our sexuality. Masturbation is not something to do just when you don't have a partner. It is the first and easiest way to experiment with your body. It's a way to find out what feels good, with how much pressure, at what tempo, and how often. You don't have to worry about someone else's needs or their opinions of you. It is different from, not inferior to, sex for two."

As the quotation suggests there is a link between masturbation, personal well-being and political identity. Hite expresses almost the same view when she considers the structural characteristics of patriarchal organizations and the power of males to impose coital regimes, which she argues restrict major aspects of woman's sexuality.

These are only a few examples of systemic views of sexual expression as they relate to 'orgasmic' potential. We find examples in many other studies; Kinsey defended premature ejaculation in the male in relation to primate evolutionary theories; Newton argues that the orgasm is a form of operant conditioning which aids the 'pair bonding' of couples and reinforces and maintains family structures.

Contrasted with some of the 'physiological' views of the orgasm, many of these interpretations are quite bold, but they do attempt to situate the behaviour within an *explicit* social theory. However, there are dangers, as Stoller (1973) notes with regard to studies like these:

> "There is no need to summarise (but just ask that we continue to) diligently collect, examine and report data, and forgo the megalomania of premature unifying theory."

Interactionist Perspective

In the types of study and levels of analysis we have touched on so far, the social constructions related to the orgasm in different settings have not been treated as problematic from the 'interactionist' perspective (Plummer, 1975, opening chapters). Plummer, however, and Warren and Johnson (1972) take an interactionist approach to sexuality "which takes as one of its fundamental concerns the problematic and socially constructed nature of sexual meanings." Plummer criticizes, "the commonsense and research definitions", which frequently assume that "everyone knows what sex is", that "sex as we know it exists independently of its social construction", and that "when members talk about 'sex' the categories used are not problematic for the users".

At the present time, both Plummer, and Warren and Johnson have applied the interactionist perspective to the study of homosexuality; where Plummer analyses the emergent homosexual identity, Warren and Johnson emphasize the homosexual's reaction to various forms of labelling. However, there are no studies on a case-to-case basis examining the dynamic labelling processes that are used in relation to the orgasmic response. Medical accounts of orgasmic dysfunction in marriage, issues related to expectations between partners, factors contributing to the way women are 'triggered' into treatment-settings presenting symptoms of 'frigidity' are essentially dealt with as un-problematic; simple retrospective case histories are taken which are almost entirely asocial; biological and psychological analyses remain in the ascendancy.

In summary, we may note that the 'market' is full of attenuated accounts of people coming to climax—the commercial accounts situate this in a range of exotic settings and supply a range of stereotypical language. Medical accounts on the basis of therapeutic intervention are secular and technical; the body is a machine; questions about how medical- and lay-groups perceive the orgasm as part of sexual behaviour, how individuals are labelled and 'triggered' into treatment settings; how sexual response 'norms' are interpreted in different social settings, remains problematic. So, too, quasi-academic accounts similar to that of Hite have used formats which pose many problems, such as reliability checks, retrospective reporting, no explicit sampling frame, and feminist bias and political intent.

Sensitive studies of orgasmic behaviour, and its interpretation over time, is equally important for our understanding of how people live with a dynamic phenomena. And it is these accounts which are currently missing!

References

Acton, W. (1967). Cited in *The Anxiety Makers*. Sunbury-on-Thames: Thomas Nelson and Sons.

Bloor, M. (1976). Bishop Berkeley and the adenotonsillectomy enigma. *Sociology*, **10**, 43–61.

Boston Women's Health Collective (1971). *Our Bodies, Ourselves*. New York: Simon and Schuster.

Clark, A. L. and Wallen, P. (1971). Women's sexual responsiveness and the duration and quality of their marriages. In *Human Sexual Behaviour: A Book of Readings*. Edited by B. Lieberman. Chichester, Sussex and New York: John Wiley and Sons.

Comfort, A. (1967). *The Anxiety Makers*. Sunbury-on-Thames: Thomas Nelson and Sons.

Comfort, A. (1974). *More Joy: A Lovemaking Companion to 'The Joy of Sex'*. New York: Crown.

Diamond, M. (1975). Sexual anatomy and physiology: clinical aspects. In *Human Sexuality: A Health Practitioner's Text*. Edited by R. Green. Baltimore: Williams and Wilkins.

Fisher, S. (1973). *Understanding the Female Orgasm*. Harmondsworth, Middlesex: Penguin Books.

Gillan, P. (1977). Sexual therapy. *Psychology Today*, **3**, 18–23.

Gagnon, J. H. and Simon, W. (1974). *Sexual Conduct: The Social Sources of Human Sexuality*. London: Hutchinson.

Goodlin, R. C. (1971). Orgasm during late pregnancy; possible deleterious effects. *Obstetrics and Gynecology (USA)*, **38**, 916–920.

Hite, S. (1976). *The Hite Report*. London: Talmy Franklin.

Kaplan, H. S. (1974). *The New Sex Therapy*. London: Baillière Tindall.

Kinsey, A. C. Pomeroy, W. B. and Martin, C. E. (1948). *Sexual Bahavior in the Human Male*. Philadelphia and London: W. B. Saunders.

Kinsey, A. C., Pomeroy, W. B., Martin, C. E. and Gebhard, P. H. (1953). *Sexual Behavior in the Human Female*. Philadelphia and London: W. B. Saunders.

Krafft-Ebing, R. von (1894). *Psychopathia Sexualis*. Stuttgart: Verlag von Ferdinand Enke.

Lock, S. (1976). *Aspects of Sexual Medicine*. London: British Medical Association.

Lowen, A. (1968). *Love and Orgasm: Against Techniques Towards Maturity*. London: Mayflower.

Masters, W. H. and Johnson, V. E. (1966). *Human Sexual Response*. Boston: Little, Brown and Co.

Newton, N. (1973). Interrelationships between sexual responsiveness, birth and breastfeeding. In *Contemporary Sexual Behavior*. Edited by J. Zubin and J. Money. Baltimore: Johns Hopkins University Press.

Plummer, K. (1975). *Sexual Stigma: An Interactionist Perspective*. London: Routledge and Kegan Paul.

Rainwater, L. (1966). Some aspects of lower class sexual behaviour. *Journal of Social Issues*, **22**, 96–108.

Reich, W. (1932). The imposition of sexual morality. In *Sex-Pol. Essays 1929–1934*. Edited by L. Baxandall. New York: Brandon House.

Reich, W. (1975). *The Invasion of Compulsory Sex-Morality*. Harmondsworth, Middlesex: Penguin Books.

Reiss, I. L. (1975). Heterosexual relationships of patients: premarital, marital and extramarital. In *Human Sexuality: A Health Practitioner's Text*. Edited by R. Green. Baltimore: Williams and Wilkins.

Rosenberg, Lee, (1973). *Total Orgasm: Against Techniques Towards Maturity*. New York: Random House.

Rosenzweig, S. (1973). Human sexual autonomy as an evolutionary attainment, anticipating proceptive sex choice and idiodynamic bisexuality. In *Contemporary Sexual Behavior*. Edited by J. Zubin and J. Money. Baltimore: Johns Hopkins University Press.

Stoller, R. J. (1973). Psychoanalysis and physical intervention in the brain: the mind-body problem again. In *Contemporary Sexual Behavior*. Edited by J. Zubin and J. Money. Baltimore: Johns Hopkins University Press.

Strong, P. (1974). *Doing sex: some notes on the management of sexual action*. Unpublished manuscript presented at the British Sociological Association Conference, 1974, on *Sexual Divisions and Society*.

Tolson, A. (1977). *The Limits of Masculinity*. London: Tavistock Publications.

Vincent, C. E. (1967). *Human Sexuality in Medical Education and Practice*. Springfield, Illinois: Charles C. Thomas.

Ward, D. A. and Kassenbaum, G. G. (1965). *Women's Prison: Sex and Social Structure*. Chicago: Aldine.

Warren, C. and Johnson, J. (1972). A critique of labelling theory from the phenomenological perspective. In *Theoretical Perspectives on Deviance*. Edited by R. Scott and J. Douglas. New York: Basic Books.

Zola, K. (1973). Medicine as an institution of social control. *The Sociological Review*, **20**, 4.

Sex and the Handicapped: I
Changes in Attitudes

MICHAEL CRAFT

Bryn y Neuadd Hospital, Llanfairfechan, Wales

It is pleasant to be invited here to discuss the momentous changes that have taken place in society's attitudes to the handicapped over the last 100 years. Indeed one can say that there has almost been a reversal of attitude on the part of the public to sexuality and marriage of the handicapped in the course of this century. In this, the first half of our paper, I hope to outline the changes in public attitude that have taken place since the Eugenics Society itself was founded, and my wife and fellow research worker, Ann, will describe the results in practice of this change in attitude and the implications for the future care of the handicapped.

One must first define one's terms. In this and the following paper we are concerning ourselves with those physically and/or mentally handicapped from birth, or before puberty, most of whom would be congenitally handicapped from conceptual, uterine or traumatic causes at birth. We are not dealing here with the mounting tide of people permanently physically handicapped from road or work accidents or other disabilities occurring after puberty who are depressed at what they have lost. Our group of prepubertal handicapped can be enthused at what they have yet to gain, or rendered apathetic when shut away from all stimulation.

Many of the public attitudes prior to the turn of this century were formed by age-old theories and folk lore, only partly rooted in fact. It was known that physical handicaps such as those resulting from tuberculosis, and from syphilis could be passed on from parent to child, and it was also known that there was a strong tendency for the dull and feckless to have dull and feckless children, or for the bright and wealthy to hand on both brightness and wealth to their children. It was the rising science of genetics in the late nineteenth century which outlined one mechanism by which this occurred, whilst the

107

rising tide of imperialism on the continent formed a political back-drop. At the turn of the century the middle and upper classes noted with growing alarm that the decline in the natural birth-rate was not uniform across society. There were disturbing 'dysgenic' factors involved, with the largest families occurring in the lowest social classes. In 1904 that worthy lady, Beatrice Webb, was denouncing the Liberal Party for being "wholly blind to the ghastly tragedies of the mental and physical decrease of the mass of our race." (MacKenzie and MacKenzie, 1977). George Bernard Shaw had incorporated eugenic ideas into his latest play, *Man and Superman*, and the govern-mental Committee on Physical Deterioration was investigating the disquieting fact that in the decade prior to the Boer War, forty per cent of all recruits had been found to be unfit for active service. In 1913 the National Birth-Rate Commission was formed, in part the result of the public concern over the fall in births per thousand population from thirty-five in the 1870s to just over twenty in 1913, the Rev. James Marchant stating in his inaugural speech, "If it could be proved that only the weak and defective stock was ceasing to increase, there would be little cause for complaint." The evidence to hand, however, seemed to point in the opposite way. As a result there was segregation of the handicapped, with extensive provision of colonies for epileptic, for physically and, above all, the mentally handicapped. Subject to carefully defined limits, the unmarried mother on poor relief, the habitual inebriate, the recidivist and other mild defectives were swept away to colonies for the good of their souls and for the prevention of procreation. This process continued throughout the first half of this century with the 1929 Wood Commit-tee on Mental Deficiency declaring that if all the families containing mental defectives of the 'primary amentia type' were segregated, they would constitute:

"a most interesting social group. It would include, as everyone who has extensive practical experience of social services will readily admit, a much larger proportion of insane persons, epileptics, paupers, criminals (espe-cially recidivists), unemployables, habitual slum dwellers, prostitutes, inebriates, and other social inefficients than would a group of families not containing mental defectives. The overwhelming majority of the families thus collected would belong to that section of the community, which we propose to term the 'social problem' or 'sub-normal' group. This group comprises approximately the lowest 10 per cent in the social scale of most communities." (Board of Education and Board of Control, 1929.)

The 1934 Brock Committee on Sterilization reported:

"There is a concentration in the lowest social stratum of the physically and mentally defective, the chronic unemployable, the habitual recipients of relief and the delinquent element of a mentally subnormal type." (Departmental Committee on Sterilization, 1934.)

By 1949 the Board of Control of the Ministry of Health had slightly modified this policy to say "It is agreed that mentally defective persons are generally unfit for the responsibility of marriage and parenthood." (Ministry of Health, 1949.)

Even in the mid 1950s there was still a strong tendency to institutionalize the promiscuous, the handicapped and the epileptic. More colony beds were built and the number of inmates continued to rise.

Now, in 1978, the picture is quite different. The emphasis is on community care, the number of people in colonies and hospitals is decreasing, sheltered housing is being provided for the handicapped, and a comprehensive system of financial allowances with a fast-increasing profession of social workers to aid the handicapped to live in the community have transformed the situation. Indeed, there are some who say that the strong lead provided by the government in aiding people to be supported in community care is in advance of many communities themselves, especially when the community finds that a hostel or home for the handicapped is likely to be opened at the bottom of their street! Yet there is still much public and professional education to be done for there are still surgeons who sterilize mentally handicapped children from misplaced fear of the retarded children they may produce (*British Medical Journal*, 1976).

Our own research projects represent further stages in the factual accumulation of data which has helped to reverse attitudes this century, but more particularly over the last twenty years. It is extremely difficult to say which came first, whether pessimistic attitudes lie behind the accumulation of pessimistic data, or the reverse. I call your attention to those family studies of the Kallikaks and Jukes which were presented at the turn of the century, and some of the optimistic case histories we ourselves have presented (Craft and Craft, 1978). What I am trying to say is that case histories are essential to show the effect of dominant and recessive genetic inheritance, but that their interpretation often depends on the atmosphere of scientific inquiry of the day in question.

For instance, attitudes around 1900 were much influenced by the concept of damaged 'germ plasm', which was thought to be handed on from one generation to another, particularly by high-grade defectives. They were believed to be both the most promiscuous and therefore most reproductive in the community. To explain the submission that attitudes to a large extent shape the research that is engaged in, let me instance the Kallikak family. Martin Kallikak was a New England soldier who, at the time of the American Civil War, first had a child by a Boston prostitute and then, marrying into a wealthy New England family, had a second family. The descendants of both were followed. In the family table of the prostitute were many recidivists, murderers, thieves and so on, whilst from the wealthy New Englander came many professional men of superior social and economic status such as judges, lawyers and senators. It was concluded this showed faulty germ plasms in the prostitute's descendants, the reverse for the other. Nowadays, we would interpret this very same case study along the lines of the cycle of deprivation. Barbara Wootton puts it rather better:

"All that is needed to reduce the dimensions of the sub-normal group is a successful policy of full employment, or a welfare state which provides adequate protection against normal economic hazards, otherwise than through the Poor Law." (Wootton, 1959.)

Later she says of problem families that their only common characteristics are low income, the concomitant strains of management, and higher numbers of young children: "failure to cope adequately with [these] might well be a sign, not so much of their own sub-normality, as of their lack of supra-normal qualities which the situation demands."

The problems Barbara Wootton and others found contributing to the fear of sexuality and marriage among handicapped people in the community twenty years ago, have altered today:

a. the low income available to handicapped married couples, because they usually cannot work or are unemployed, has been supplemented by quite generous government allowances, together with the opportunity of either sheltered factory work or work within Training Centres;

b. contraception and family planning techniques allow the handicapped, like everyone else, to regulate the number of children they produce, so that a young handicapped mother does not have to cope with more children than she wants;

c. sheltered housing has now become the right of handicapped married couples, and as the result of Housing Trusts has now become widely available;

d. increasing numbers of professional social workers are available to explain to handicapped couples their entitlements and to counsel them before their problems accumulate;

e. there has been a start in sex education and marriage guidance for the handicapped as for the able-bodied, yet much needs to be done in:

f. the field of mental ill-health in relation to physical handicap and mental handicap, which in general has yet to be tackled;

g. the problem of day occupation and care for the handicapped as well as of the large group of unemployed in the community which is now with us, and likely to increase.

Each of these areas need further public education, and further research to tease out the factors involved.

Economic well-being, as Illich points out with salutory effect, is basic for improvement of public attitudes. This is as applicable to the area of sexuality and marriage among the handicapped as the delivery of medical care. Where the able-bodied in society are hungry, it is an axiom that the handicapped go more hungry. Where the able-bodied are reasonably housed, the community builds better quarters for the handicapped. Were I talking even forty years ago the best I could have done would be to ask for better cottage homes in colonies for the handicapped. Now, I can talk of the right of the handicapped to have sheltered housing and to marry, and persuade local committees that it is cheaper to educate people in their own homes, than to treat them once they are ill in hospital.

Medical education is advancing. Further knowledge has led to a reversal of medical attitude within the field of genetics. Previously it was thought that the damaged 'germ plasm' of the high-grade defective led to defects among the children produced; now it is known that lethal or handicapping genes are very widespread in the population so that each of us is likely to carry at least one lethal gene, and three handicapping genes among the five million which each cell in our body possesses. Thus, one-sixth of all pregnancies to which we are party will die *in utero* and are spontaneously aborted; if we happen to fall in love with a fellow carrier of our three handicapping genes, one in four of our children will be so handicapped. It is true that those untreated, being severely physically and mentally handicapped are unlikely to reproduce at all, and it is no consolation that attempts to improve the gene pool of the country by genetic counselling on the above lines is likely to make little statistical difference to the frequency in the gene pool, or in the birth-rate of recessive inherited abnormalities. Thus there is a reversal in attitude towards dissemination of damaged 'germ plasm', compared with that seventy years ago. In addition, psychological and social research has now clearly shown the causation of mild mental handicap and how it may be reduced, as opposed to the severe mental handicap discussed in the previous paragraph now known to be a more medical responsibility. This is important, because mild mental handicap is ten times more common than severe mental handicap, and four times as common as the frequency of severe physical handicap in childhood. It has been clearly shown that mild mental handicap occurs almost exclusively, not necessarily among the dullest, but among the economically worst off in the community, usually the Registrar General's IV and V. Recent research has also shown that a substantial improvement in food, environmental and teaching levels among disadvantaged children substantially reduces this level of mild mental handicap, defined in terms of those finally scoring under IQ 70 in adult life.

My conclusion is that the fears of the community at the turn of the century concerning the sexuality, marital and child problems of the handicapped were based on data gathered in the economic, social and medical climate then prevailing. The difference today is in attitudes that arise from the improved economic, medical and social climate. The economic climate allows the handicapped to be well fed and have sheltered housing, together with Day Centres to occupy them, and social workers to counsel them. Medical advances have allowed exactly the same case studies told with woe at the turn of the century, to be analysed more optimistically, taking into account environmental as well as strictly genetic variables, and to allow for the reversal of attitudes within the field of genetics on the transmission of 'damaging genes'. Contraception allows the prevention of unwanted children, and whilst the prevalence of mentally handicapped people is rising due to longevity, and the prevalence of physically handicapped people is also rising, due mainly to the increasing number of road and work accidents, the incidence at birth is decreasing due to therapeutic abortion of major handicapping conditions, such as muscular dystrophy and Down's syndrome, and the improvement of perinatal care. It is in the social field that the greatest advance is now possible. Recent medical research shows that physically and mentally handicapped girls now start their menarche earlier than normal girls, at 10·5 years compared with the normal 12·5 in the UK; statistically an extremely significant finding (Dalton and Dalton, 1978). This supports one's plea that sex education for the handicapped should start earlier than with the non-handicapped, quite apart from the fact that the former are more vulnerable than the latter to exploitation. Apart from sex education, personal counselling for the mental health of such people shows dividends both in the number of families that can be kept healthy and intact, and in their decreasing level of mental ill-health, as defined in terms of general practitioner consultations requested for this reason by handicapped people. But we are straying now both into the fields of general health education and public attitudes, and so at this juncture I had better conclude.

References

Board of Education and Board of Control (1929). *Report of the Mental Deficiency Committee*. (Wood Report). London: HMSO.

British Medical Journal (1976). Sexual development in mentally handicapped children. **ii,** 71–72.

Craft, M. J. and Craft, A. (1978). *Sex and the Mentally Handicapped*. London: Routledge and Kegan Paul.

Dalton, M. E. and Dalton, K. (1978). Menarchial age in the disabled. *British Medical Journal*, **ii,** 475.

Departmental Committee on Sterilization (1934). *Report* (Brock Report). Cmnd. 4485. London: HMSO.

MacKenzie, N. and MacKenzie, J. (1977). *The First Fabians*. London: Weidenfeld and Nicolson.

Ministry of Health (1949). *Memorandum on the Licensing of Mentally Defective Patients from Institutions*. 60021/74/79/1. London: HMSO.

Wootton, B. (1959). *Social Science and Social Pathology*. London: Allen and Unwin.

Sex and the Handicapped: II
Changes in Policy and Practice

ANN CRAFT

Bryn y Neuadd Hospital, Llanfairfechan, Wales

Dr Craft has touched upon the upsurge of concern during the 1960s about the sexuality of the handicapped and this has had widespread implications for policies and practice. In fact, the whole subject of the sexuality of handicapped people has swung towards the rights of the individual, the recognition of the inherent sexuality of all humans, impaired or otherwise. There has been a growing movement away from the essentially negative aspects of strict control, towards a more positive view—how can we help those in our care to develop their full potential, including the ability to make and maintain social and sexual relationships? Parents, special school teachers, adult training centre staff, hostel and hospital personnel began to ask for help in finding constructive ways to respond to the sexual curiosity and behaviour of those in their charge. Official bodies, national organizations and health authorities had, for the most part, ignored the sexuality of the handicapped people within their jurisdiction. But a ground-swell of opinion began to make itself felt. One can quote the example of the National Society for Mentally Handicapped Children, the major parental pressure group, whose secretariat were themselves pressured by parents with maturing children into giving advice on all aspects of sexuality. Very basic questions troubled them, "How can I stop my son masturbating in public?" "Our mongol daughter is so loving and trusting, how can we protect her from exploitation?" "What should I tell my daughter when her periods start?" "My son has got friendly with a girl at the training centre, should I encourage this? I don't want either of them to be hurt." Various other organizations also responded, notably the Family Planning Association, the National Association for Mental Health (MIND), the Spastics Society and the Committee on the Sexual Problems of the Disabled (SPOD). Workshops for staff have been held, conferences organized, pamphlets written and teaching programmes and counselling sessions set up. Quite a contrast to the silence of fifteen years ago.

Attitudes, policy and practice are inextricably linked. All are general concepts, but all three have an enormous impact on individuals. In the context of our subject the individuals are handicapped people and those who look after them. I am going to try and illustrate what changes in attitudes, policy and practice can mean to individuals by telling you the story of two mentally handicapped people.

Bill is now 52, an amiable, timid man whose face usually wears a slightly anxious expression. He has lived in hospitals and hostels for most of his adult life, needing constant reminders about personal hygiene and much help with his finances. In the 1950s, he met Ida, a small, thin, mentally handicapped woman with a pronounced squint and a stutter. She was the illegitimate child of a mentally defective mother and has been in hospital from the age of eight. They liked each other, but courting was well nigh impossible. At hospital dances a nurse sat by the door to make sure couples did not slip out, and male patients got a warning tap on the shoulder from matron if they attempted to dance more than three times with the same partner. Despite these and other official precautions their friendship grew. Then, quite arbitrarily, the system separated them and Ida was moved to another unit. Bill said "I broke my heart", but in the 1950s even if anyone was aware of their friendship it would have been almost unthinkable that it should be allowed to blossom. The whole weight of public and professional opinion was specifically against such an outcome.

Bill and Ida's story might have ended there, plenty of others did. But some fifteen years later, the workings of the system brought them together again, in the workshops of the same hospital. By chance they were in the right place at the right time, for a new bi-sexual hospital was due to open in a year's time. The siting, building and commissioning of this new hospital, incidentally, measures changes in attitude, policy and practice in the mental handicap service as a whole. Part of that is a different story, but it impinges significantly on Bill and Ida, for the new hospital, opened in 1971, had in-patient accommodation set aside for married couples, had operational policies covering all aspects of life including the interpersonal relationship of residents and, above all, an enthusiastic and hopeful staff.

By the late 1960s as I have mentioned, attitudes had changed, and people talked of the quality of life the handicapped were leading, and the concept of normalization was much in vogue (Nirje, 1976). Bill and Ida now did their courting, if not quite with official blessing, at least without censure and disapproval. They became engaged, and had premarital counselling. Bill had a vasectomy and they married in 1971. Their wedding was an affair of some moment, with staff and fellow residents enthusiastically witnessing the event. The consultant psychiatrist gave Ida away, the hospital chairman stood beside Bill as his best man. They were in fact the first couple in the new hospital's married quarters, itself the first in an NHS mental handicap hospital. A large reception was held in one of the wards, with the refreshments and wedding cake organized by the hospital catering department. It was such a huge success that for weeks afterwards mentally handicapped males and females looked speculatively at each other with a view to repeating the event. And some did later.

We have followed up our hospital residents who have married, and also circularized all local authorities in Wales for details of handicapped married couples under IQ 70 that they might know about (Craft and Craft, 1976). We are still accepting referrals within Wales, and analysing our data. So far we have collected some forty-five married couples of whom one couple are separated by death, two temporarily by prison and hospitalization, respectively, one by divorce. This is a substantially lower rate of break-up than the current national average of one marriage in three ending in divorce. We were impressed with the quality of most of the forty-one intact marriages out of forty-five, but, as I say, we are still analysing our data, and we want to carry out a further assessment of the children of these marriages(Craft and Craft, 1979).

I have mentioned the concept of normalization which played a not inconsiderable part in challenging parents and professionals to ask themselves whether those in their care were leading as normal a life as they possibly could, a normality that logically had to include social and sexual areas of behaviour. This rethinking had been facilitated by one of the social revolutions of our time, the advent of efficient, free and readily available methods of birth control. No one now, handicapped or otherwise, need produce children they do not want or cannot cope with. Vasectomy is fashionable, I believe there is even a neck tie which proclaims membership of the now not-so-exclusive male club. When the question of children was discussed with Bill and Ida, they decided they did not want the responsibilities of parenthood. What they did want was to marry and be safely together for always, giving each other love and companionship.

Another revolution which weighted the chances for, rather than against, Bill and Ida was the move towards community care for handicapped people. The government White Paper, *Better Services for the Mentally Handicapped* (Department of Health and Social Security and Welsh Office, 1971), was simultaneously a response to a new stream of thought, a statement of official policy, and an exhortation to planners. It estimated that about one-third of the residents in mental handicap hospitals did not require such specialized care and accommodation, and called for alternative community settings. As it happened, Bill and Ida's hospital was ahead of the government and staff were already operating a scheme whereby a number of ex-hospital residents lived in local boarding houses, backed up by a 24-hour emergency service and support by a social worker (Craft, 1976). This group used the hospital as a work centre by day and, if they chose, as a social centre during the evenings. Bill and Ida were able to move into a boarding house flatlet and have been happy ever since.

Now, you might think that talking about community care and social work support is all very interesting, but hardly germane to our subject of sex and the handicapped. In fact they are extremely pertinent issues for the first questions most engaged handicapped couples are concerned with are "Where will you live?" and "How will you manage?". In the past we have all too often made the assumption that marriage is an independent state with partners suddenly becoming personally and economically self sufficient. In reality we know that it is not the case, most young couples get a great deal of practical, emotional and financial support, usually from parents. But our official services for the handicapped are geared to care for individuals, not couples. Indeed, the actual design of establishments for the handicapped makes it difficult for two people to pursue an intimate friendship. In general, accommodation is arranged for observation, not privacy, so that a goldfish bowl effect is almost inevitable. A physically handicapped woman describes the lack of dignity which results:

"There is nowhere for the patient to go with his or her friend. It is humiliating to have to hide in cupboards or crawl in culverts like dying elephants—embarrassing to have to ask friends to stand and watch by the door as if one were committing a burglary. There are no rooms for lovers to be in, no guest apartments for visiting families to stay in." (Enby, 1975.)

When a couple, despite such difficulties, do reach the stage of marriage and thus of wanting to share a room, this can throw all the sleeping arrangements into confusion. As most rooms are 3- or 4-bedded and a couple will displace one or more people: should male or female beds be lost? What about the toilet facilities? What about night-time observation? The ramifications of two handicapped people in care wanting to marry are endless.

It is not only the handicapped who come up against this obstacle, it can happen to the elderly too. One of the couples on our survey met at an old people's home. He was then 72, normal in intelligence but needing care when his wife died. She was a mentally handicapped widow, some twenty years younger. There were no provisions for married couples in the home, so Jack and Eliza, who had insisted on going ahead with their marriage, had to continue sleeping apart. Jack's letters to councillors and the social services scorched the page, but nothing was done. Eventually the couple took matters into their own hands, located an empty house in a nearby town and moved in as squatters. The local papers loved it. At the height of the public outcry Jack and Eliza were able to graciously accept the offer of a council flat.

Jack, despite his age, had enough strength of character and will to exercise his right as a citizen to marry despite official disapproval and all obstacles. Our disabled citizens, by virtue of their mental handicap or physical dependence, are all too often imprisoned by the care system instead of liberated and encouraged to reach their full potential. Changes do not happen overnight, but over time things do improve.

Ten years ago in a hostel for the mentally handicapped two residents fell in love. They began to court with enthusiasm and little inhibition. Because staff had found it easier to deny the sexuality of the residents, such overt sexual interest and behaviour was seen not only as disruptive but was reported as a matter of urgency to the consultant psychiatrist as "extreme behaviour disorder", with terms such as "shocking" and "gross indecency" thrown in for good measure. The psychiatrist's solution of counselling, permission to court and eventually permission to marry, was not at all what the staff had in mind! Sadly, pills to decrease sexual drive or banishment to separate units would have been acceptable.

In contrast, I am going to describe what one hospital-based care system can offer to the handicapped now in 1978. When a couple have been courting each other for some time and wish to become engaged, a pre-marital preparation service exists to help them appreciate the full implications of marriage. Such preparation includes discussion of sexual and emotional needs; training in budgetting, household man-agement and cooking; counselling on appropriate methods of birth control; and dealing with any special needs which may arise. For example, staff at the hospital may have to teach one partner how to deal with the other's epilepsy or physical handicap. After marriage the couple move into a flatlet on the hospital campus supervised by staff and continue their training. Post-marital counselling can be given as and when required. The couple then move on to appropriate accommodation, be it local bed-sitting room, hostel flatlet, sheltered housing or council flat. The social services then take on the major responsibility for support, but with the back-up of the hospital-based system and out-patient clinics always available.

In the past, the attitude of society, through its caring agents, towards sex where the handicapped were concerned was predominantly this: handicapped people have enough on their plate without complicating their lives further. After all, the able-bodied frequently get into difficulties with their sex lives, how on earth could the handicapped manage? The idea is not only preposterous, but slightly disgusting (Greengross, 1976). Although this view is not uncommon even now, it is far less tenable. Research, both social and medical, has again shown the adaptability of humans. The ways of achieving a mutually satisfactory relationship and mutually satisfactory sexual pleasure are many and various. Most humans can learn and adapt as circumstances dictate.

So what guidelines should current and future policies follow to facilitate enlightened practice? Firstly, health and sex education should be on the curriculum of every special school because handicapped children and adolescents do not have the physical mobility, mental capacity, or independence of their able-bodied contemporaries. They just do not have the same opportunities for informal learning and although they probably know isolated facts about their bodies, sexual arousal and sexual behaviour, they commonly link these half-truths in ways which defy physiology. Physically handicapped children need special help relating to their particular disability and sex; the mentally handicapped especially need knowledge and training to protect them from exploitation (Craft and Craft, 1978).

Secondly, our systems need to be more flexible in their policies. Residents in hostels and hospitals should be accorded the dignity of privacy and of ordering their own lives as far as they possibly can. Simple courtesies, such as a member of staff knocking on a bedroom door before entering, are often absent. Fear that the unit will get a bad reputation and thus bring down censure upon staff gives rise to a negative and destructive atmosphere. What in fact would constitute normal behaviour if in another setting and with able-bodied actors, is seen as abnormal. It is unreasonable, indeed, hypocritical to impose a higher moral standard on the handicapped than pertains in society at large. So the third point is staff training and counselling to help them respond constructively to those in their care.

Lastly we come back to policies affecting accommodation and sheltered housing of all kinds which would offer a choice of niches to suit handicapped people at different stages in their lives. Double rooms and flatlets for handicapped married couples should be included in the forward planning of every new unit.

We may not yet have reached the stage of the Japanese centre for the mentally and physically handicapped which successfully offers a marriage broker service to its clients (Cigno, 1978), but we have reached the stage at which our handicapped citizens can expect, as of right, to develop their full human potential, including the right to love and be loved.

References

Cigno, K. (1978). Welfare centre for handicapped people in Tokyo. *Social Work Today*, **10,** 17–18.

Craft, M. J. (1976). The North Wales Guardianship Scheme. *Apex* (Journal of the Institute of Mental Subnormality), **4,** 19–21.

Craft, A. and Craft, M. J. (1976). Subnormality in marriage: happiness and the quality of life among married subnormals. *Social Work Today*, **7,** 98–101.

Craft, A. and Craft, M. J. (1979) *Handicapped Married Couples*. London: Routledge and Kegan Paul

Craft, M. J. and Craft, A. (1978). *Sex and the Mentally Handicapped*. London: Routledge and Kegan Paul.

Department of Health and Social Security and Welsh Office (1971). *Better Services for the Mentally Handicapped*. Cmnd. 4683. London: HMSO.

Enby, G. (1975). *Let There Be Love*. London: Elek Scientific Books.

Greengross, W. (1976). *Entitled to Love*. London: Malaby.

Nirje, B. (1976). The Normalization principle. In *Changing Patterns of Residential Services for the Mentally Handicapped*. Washington, D.C.: The President's Committee on Mental Retardation, revised edition.

Lesbianism:
A Changing Phenomenon

E. M. ETTORRE

Addiction Research Unit, Institute of Psychiatry,
London, England

The purpose of this paper is to re-examine and possibly to question our ideas not only about lesbianism but also about women and sexuality. A pivotal point of looking at these ideas will be through an analysis of the patterns of social relationships in society or, more simply, through an analysis of social power. We will examine conflicts or contradictory forces which emerge in society with this patterning of social power.

Society, Social Relationships and Power

What do we mean by society? Society is a system of social relationships. Society is not just 'something out there'. We create 'it'. In other words, we, as social actors, have the ability to affect social activities and social relationships. Within this view of society, everything which is 'social' appears to be based upon power. Students of society or those who analyse power and its affect upon the organization of social life say: "Power is not a thing possessed by social actors, but rather a dynamic process that occurs in all areas of social life." (Olsen, 1970) or "Every social act is an exercise of power, every social relationship is a power equation and every social group or system is an organization of power." (Hawley, 1963.)

From the above, we see that power filters through all areas of social life. However, how do we view power as it emerges historically? What is our hindsight vision of power? Perhaps we see it developing in two ways according to the structure of society. It emerges, therefore, consistent with sex relations and class relations in a patriarchal capitalist order.

On the one hand, there are 'sex relations' in which men are dominant and women are subservient, or within which men are viewed as primary and women are viewed as secondary. This leads to paternalism or to a patriarchal view of society. It appears as oppressive to women, anti-women or 'anti-feminist'. This occurs because women reproduce but, more importantly, because when women reproduce, they appear as 'naturally inferior' in relation to men.

On the other hand, we have a system of class relations which divide workers from non-workers. This leads to a capitalist view of society which appears as 'anti' the labouring class. Within this view, workers are oppressed because they have to be productive in order to survive. In other words, they must sell their labour for a wage in order to exist.

These two opposing systems of social relationships (patriarchy/capitalism) create a *sexual division of labour*. Simply, labour is divided by sex. Men become visible as primarily productive (making things necessary for themselves, their families and 'present society' to survive). Women emerge as primarily reproductive (making babies necessary for society to survive in the future). In light of these roles, we see the ultimate example of the sexual division of labour within the family unit. There, the social functions between men and women are clearly delineated (Oakley, 1974).

The sexual division of labour is based upon the basic biological differences between men and women as well as the divisions which exist in the labour process. Together, these social arrangements create further splits in society between sex and society; the private and the public; the family and society; the home and the work-place; women's work and men's work and domestic labour and 'productive' labour.

Both systems of social relationships appear to oppose each other and to perpetuate social division. Patriarchal capitalism seems to divide worker from non-worker as well as productive labour from reproductive labour. In the final analysis, men and women become divided through the sexual division of labour.

Now that we have established this view of society and the nature of social relationships within it, let us ask ourselves the following: "Where does sexuality fit into this framework?"; "What is women's position?" and, furthermore, "How is all of the above relevant to lesbianism?"

Sexuality, Women and Lesbians

Sexuality has become a part of the 'natural order of things'. It is organized as if some providential design set up divisions between men and women. Sexuality is privatized, isolated and hidden from social view. (Again, the family becomes a primary example, but in this context, of a privatized unit for 'legitimate' sexual practice.) Heterosexuality becomes 'normal', 'natural' or the 'order of the day'. Sexuality or views about how sex *per se* should be arranged totally supports or maintains the patriarchal capitalist system.

Women are expected to be subservient to men. They are primarily reproductive. Even if women 'work' or are in any way productive outside the home, they are not looked upon as being 'real' workers. Women are 'secondarily' productive. Beyond the family context, their 'jobs' tend to be orientated towards servicing men or a male-directed society (i.e. domestic workers, secretaries, catering services, etc.). Women are usually concentrated in low status occupations and become visible "as a secondary labour force" (Barron and Norris, 1976).

Whether women work outside of the home or reproduce and work within the home, they are viewed as 'sexual creatures'. In other words, it is feminine or like a woman "to be able to gratify a love object and to arouse males sexually. . . ." (Bernard, 1968). All of these views underpin women's social position.

Lesbians are viewed as 'over-sexed women' or totally asexual beings. Lesbians are expected to be 'sick', 'biologically inferior', 'naturally inferior' or 'deviant' women. These ideas put emphasis upon the individual. They are consistent with dominant ideas about sexuality as isolated from the mainstream of social life.

As a result, lesbians are isolated from women. They are viewed as 'social males' and as individuals who want to be men and who are "penis envious" (Freud, 1920).

Yet, in reality, lesbians are women. They belong to this social group of 'structural females' because they have the potential to reproduce. And, as I have discovered in my research (Ettorre, 1978), many lesbians are acutely aware of this potential.

In order to focus upon a clearer picture of lesbianism, let us ask ourselves the question, "How does lesbianism emerge throughout history?". Remember that the underlying assumption of this paper is that lesbianism is a changing social phenomenon. Also, within this perspective, it emerges as a dynamic and conflicting process. Today, all forms of lesbianism are present within society in varying degrees and levels of awareness. (The three forms of lesbianism are the traditional, the social and the ideological.) However, it appears that the most predominant form is social lesbianism (the development of a group identity for lesbians). Lesbianism at a social stage of awareness probably characterizes the 'lesbian experience' for the majority of contemporary lesbians. As a result, we see that whether lesbians may be orientated towards a traditional view of themselves or an ideological one, many, if not most, are social-orientated. Therefore, if lesbianism is changing, social lesbianism becomes the key to understanding how this change is occurring. Let us look briefly at the three historical stages of lesbianism. Then let us examine the social implications of one of these stages—social lesbianism.

The Three Stages of Lesbianism

The initial stage of lesbian awareness is embedded in tradition. In this context, a lesbian, isolated and secluded from society, remains in the closet and is, therefore, hidden from public view. Aware of her 'sickness', she is denied social recognition. Those (social workers, doctors, psychiatrists, etc.) who may express 'curative concerns' for the lesbian not only deal with her on an individual level, but also prescribe treatment for her 'disease'. She is "in need of help". Society must take responsibility for its unfortunates who are born 'deformed', 'genetically inferior' or who are 'socially abnormal' or 'deviant'.

'It' (lesbianism) becomes a personal problem or a disease which is characteristic of a genetic quirk, a psychological malfunctioning, a mental illness, immaturity, an individual abnormality or, simply, a perversion. Analysts conceptualize notions such as 'arrested heterosexuality', 'dominant mother', 'dominant father', 'abnormal hormones' or 'faulty genes'—all of which either caused the 'disease' and 'problem' or, at least, helped 'it' along.

Within this stage, lesbianism becomes an individual thing and it merits scientific observation similar to studying the effects from a rare, isolated bacteria strain in a pathology laboratory. When the 'cause' of lesbianism is discovered, 'it' is treated accordingly. Lesbians who are bound up within this treatment process experience guilt, fear, frustration or misery. 'Sick lesbians' appear to suffer most from their 'affliction' as well as from society's image of them. In effect, they are prevented from having a 'lesbian awareness' or group identity. Not only do they tend to accept a negative self-identity and a 'deviant' or unacceptable social label, but also they perpetuate these images throughout society. Unknowingly, they collude with tradition as well as with a rigid, unbending opinion of themselves within that self-same tradition.

During the first part of this century (after the initial wave of feminism through the suffragette movement), it became apparent that lesbians organized socially as lesbians and in group settings (bars, clubs, etc.). Becoming more visible, lesbianism was and is thrust into the public sphere of society (Abbott and Love, 1973). Whether or not lesbians consciously questioned traditional images, they manifested themselves (if only in a partial manner) in and through group contexts. As a result, lesbian group identity emerges. A lesbian becomes aware that not only do other women similar to herself exist, but also that there are places in which she can be 'herself'. Extreme isolation breaks down and if only for a brief moment, a lesbian is able to step out from behind the closet-door confinement.

With the rise of social interaction amongst lesbians, society becomes increasingly more unable to individualize or personalize the phenomenon. Containment is thwarted; individual treatment is transformed into a supposed 'social understanding'. In turn, lesbianism is 'upgraded' to the 'status' of a social problem. Implicitly, it achieves social recognition. Yet, in reality, this recognition is merited only within socially designated areas—the subculture of deviance. Any attempt to break down the barriers between the subculture of deviance and the dominant culture of normality is opposed. Thus, once again, lesbianism is secluded from society, but this time on a larger scale than before. Gradually, lesbians persist and emphasize a group orientation rather than an individual one. This emphasis provides them with a framework which is potentially political. By appearing to be less closeted than traditional lesbians, social lesbians begin to challenge social norms. They gather the power to confront society. Their current stage of challenge breeds resistance and a shift towards ideology or 'lesbian politics'. This shift represents the final stage of lesbianism.

Today, ideological lesbianism appears in seed form. As a social force, lesbianism becomes visible at a politically conscious level. Gradually, lesbianism becomes linked up to the total struggle against women's subservient position in society. While their emphasis is upon group struggle and an 'out life', lesbian feminism outwardly exposes major divisions in the struggle against power. Lesbian feminists are split in two. These divisions reflect disagreement on the level of political struggle and as a result, two groups emerge. While lesbian allies (those allied to the Left) maintain the importance of class relations (critique of capitalism), lesbian separatists (those who relate only to women and, therefore, 'separate' themselves from men) place priority upon sex relations (critique of patriarchy). Yet, both groups together illustrate a lesbian feminist stance. This stance is a progression towards political consciousness for all lesbians. It also represents a consciousness with all women as well as with all oppressed groups within society.

Social Lesbianism: A New Consciousness

Previously, I stated that social lesbianism is the most predominant form of lesbianism today. It manifests itself as a new form of consciousness for lesbians. In this way it becomes a source of encouragement for lesbians who were previously overpowered by tradition. In effect, it creates and establishes an important link between one's experience as a lesbian and as a woman.

> "I see myself first as a lesbian or as a woman. Now to me the two are almost synonymous, so I feel very whole I suppose. I feel myself. I mean I don't feel at one with society, but I'm beginning to feel more real, more strong than I have ever done before . . . which is very exciting."[1]

> "Lesbianism is still an emotive word. Yet, it does describe what it means to be a woman, a woman-identified-woman and a woman-loving-woman. It filters right out into the things that really upset women about being women. This is that they are unable to be the same."

> "The lesbian identity is woman and I'm thinking more and more that I'm less and less a lesbian and more and more a woman. I find the two labels so interrelated. Whereas, before I thought being a lesbian was a total separate thing than being a woman."

Lesbianism has the potential to challenge society (become political) when it actively exposes the tensions between sexual practice and society, or between a private notion of sex and a public conception of sexuality. It also makes visible those problems which exist between women's productive role (which seems minimal) and women's reproductive role (which, although important for the continuance of society, is underestimated).

As a social construction, lesbianism implies a variety of interactions for a woman in society. She changes not only as the networks of lesbian activity expand and grow into more socially visible forms, but also with the development of social lesbianism. In effect, it may transform dominant ideas about the sexual and women's role or social function. Resistant to these dominant ideas, groups create alternative forms of sexual practice. They present a direct challenge to the monolithic structure of the sexual. Because lesbians are oppressed by the ways in which society organizes sexuality (into rigid roles), they are able to develop a unique consciousness as lesbians/women.

As a result, contemporary lesbians need not remain isolated in the closet as did their predecessors. Many are emerging from the privacy of their cocoons in order to challenge society. The metamorphosis occurs when public declarations of their newly-found awareness are made. Yet, contradictory feelings still remain for some.

> "I feel right out of society because I don't like it anyway, not just because I am a lesbian. I mean in real terms it (society) is a counter culture. I feel strongly that ours could be a predominant culture but then I think how much I am living in cloud-cuckoo land. How many other people in counter groups think that they are just or it's just a short time before they come to fruition? All sorts of small groups feel that. The point is that society is growing so fast you just can't pretend anymore."

Social lesbianism becomes the key to opening the closet door. Through it, lesbians don't have to pretend anymore. Rather, they are better able to be themselves. Remember that ideas about homosexuality (and, therefore, lesbianism) are consistent with society's attitudes towards sexuality in general. These attitudes uphold 'essentialism' which is the view that sexuality or sexual practice is an 'essence', a 'part of human nature' or 'inherent'. Homosexuals and heterosexuals alike suffer from the oppressive features of essentialism. In other words, the sexual is viewed as having to do with a permanent characteristic which is grounded in one's biological makeup. It is fixed and unchanging. If one is born a woman, one should *be* a woman or 'female'. The same applies to a man. Culture influences 'it' (sexuality) in a marginal or minor way. The social construction of sexuality is ruled out! Social lesbianism as a group response tends to negate essentialism; yet, individual social lesbians may uphold this view. Thus, contradictions are ever present in the realm of the sexual, the social, the personal and the political.

Sick, but not Sorry and Sorry, but not Sick

'Essentialism' may compel some women to treat their lesbianism as a 'fixed entity', 'something they are stuck with for life' or a 'purely sexual thing'. Usually, however, these lesbians admit that their lesbian practice grew from emotional relationships with women. They contradict themselves. On the one hand, lesbianism is a purely sexual *thing*. On the other hand, lesbian feelings are not necessarily sexual but they always include strong ties with women. (It is interesting to note here that in a study of social lesbians, 75 per cent established a close relationship between their identity as lesbians and their identity as women, while 83 per cent viewed themselves as either totally or primarily committed to women (Ettorre, 1980).) Some lesbians have said:

> "I had no choice in the matter, but it is a commitment to women. It is basically inherent."

> "My lesbianism hasn't really changed. I have always accepted myself. I've always had crushes on women. Immediately, I accepted this. People used to say, 'Well, there is a name for people like you!'. I used to think, 'Bloody idiot, there isn't at all'. This was because I knew that my feelings weren't at all sexual. The fact that they became so when I was fifteen was just something different. But, I was never really upset about how people would react. I have always had a strong mind about this and pleased when I sorted out what I was."

Social lesbians who express the above ideas and attitudes are, what I would term, the 'sick, but not sorry type'. In varying degrees, they accept traditional lesbian images. In this way, they lend support to the dominant 'normal' culture even though they are excluded from it. Yet, ironically, they do not regret their 'infirmity' or 'condition'. As born lesbians, they accept 'it' as a fact of life. They were born with 'it'. However, they appear to enjoy 'it' as they meet others in the social contexts of bars, clubs and discos.

As a group, the above social lesbians reveal some interesting implications. On one level, not only are their social lives 'ghettoized' (removed from the mainstream of social life), but also they lend deaf ears to any discussion of lesbian 'politics'. On another level, by coming somewhat out of the closet, they break down a rigid historical tradition and unconsciously further the 'lesbian cause'. Thus, a contradiction between a personal life and a political one is present. This presence illustrates a pre-political stage of lesbian consciousness. In other words, it is the point before which lesbianism achieves recognition as a social force (accepted as a political movement). At this stage, it seems socially impotent. Yet, regardless of this apparent weakness, it implies a movement or shift towards politics. By the very fact that this practice actively questions social norms (and ultimately challenges society itself), it contributes to a new understanding of sexuality, if not lesbianism (in an immediate sense).

Another group of social lesbians, the 'sorry, but not sick type', further this critique of society. They not only come out of the closet, but they go out into the streets. They appear as neither sick nor really sorry for being lesbian.

On the one hand, this group polarizes the sexual and social definitions of both lesbians and women. In other words, they point out the necessity of questioning 'social femininity' for women; sexual being for 'women'. On the other hand, while upholding the importance of being a woman, they do not act in a way which is acceptable for a woman. For them, lesbianism is not primarily a sexual practice and women are not primarily sexual creatures who exist for men's pleasure. Rather, lesbianism is a committment to women in a male-orientated society. Furthermore, all women have the potential to be lesbian-orientated. Perhaps this is their ultimate threat to society. Caprio in his study of lesbians (Caprio, 1955) discusses this 'threat'. He says:

"Lesbianism is capable of influencing the stability of our social structure. Much of the incompatibility of the sexes is closely allied to this problem. Unconscious or latent homosexuality in women affects their personalities and constitutes an important factor in marital unhappiness being responsible for our present increasing divorce rate."

Although Caprio does not relate lesbianism to a male-orientated society, he does see it emerging as a phenomenon with 'structural implications' (i.e. it has the potential to influence "our social structure"). Social lesbians become aware of this potential, if not their ultimate threat.

"I suppose I see the lesbian as one who stands up to all who don't want to be defined by their roles. I suppose that's why we are so persecuted because men are afraid of women who can live independently of them."

"I used to think of lesbians as women who had sex with other women but now I don't think that this is so crucial. I think it's a question of being physical with women but it's not the sex. . . ."

"Lesbianism is that I have a feeling with other women—a feeling of empathy and putting them first and relating to them on a primary level, rather than in a secondary way—in the usual way that women relate to other women or in the way that men relate to us generally. . . . Yet, men are usually their primary relationships and I suppose I have changed my views. I don't see it (lesbianism) in purely sexual terms."

"As a lesbian, you totally reject the heterosexual way of living and you look upon your relationships as being with women. In other words, you count men out of it all together. Not that you can't be friends with a man, but you take a friendship only so far with a man, then, it stops. This happens normally when the sexual part of a relationship comes into it. You can become close friends with a man but the moment when there is some sexual involvement, you back off. Then you just associate yourself with women. At that point in time, you can only associate closely with other women. There is no way in which you can see yourself with a man. Whether you have in the past doesn't matter. You've decided you're a lesbian and you know that you must totally commit yourself to women."

'Sorry, but not sick' lesbians (who were quoted above), emerge from tradition because they are social lesbians. Yet, they challenge tradition and society's stereotype of the lesbian as being 'sick'. Lesbianism is a choice which is grounded in a variety of factors (social, political, psychological, emotional, etc.). As a result, they are 'self-chosen' lesbians who tend to see lesbianism as a total commitment to women or as a way of life rather than as a sexual 'entity'. Their proposed element of choice confuses the lesbian issue, specifically, the 'traditional lesbian issue'.

Social Lesbianism: A Dialectic[2]

As we have seen from the above discussion, both types of social lesbians polarize ideas on lesbianism and sexuality in society. They point out how lesbianism has developed from an individual experience to a social one and from a totally closeted life to a relatively open life-style.

Earlier in this paper, I mentioned the sexual division of labour or how labour is distributed between men and women. Now let us see how lesbianism (as it becomes more visible through social lesbianism) affects this division.

In light of the sexual division of labour and its relationship to women as a social group, lesbianism drives a wedge between the role to reproduce and the role to produce, women's primary function in society and women's secondary function or women as reproducers and women as producers. Its very existence causes this opposition. Furthermore, in society's eyes, lesbianism minimizes women's role to reproduce in favour of a productive role (which is usually reserved for men). Many lesbians desire economic independence from a man. As a result, their jobs may become very important to them.

A labour force which provides a better bargaining position as well as a greater potential for organization may be emerging for women and for lesbians. (It is interesting to point out that 49 per cent of the total sample of social lesbians were included in the three highest occupational levels—higher managerial or professional, lower managerial or professional and skilled or supervisory.) Perhaps these lesbians are included in the group of women who:

"Have been drawn into the greatly expanded, further and higher educational system, encouraged through that process to expect equal job opportunity with men and able, subsequently, to get sufficiently highly paid employment to remain economically independent of marriage." (Gardiner, 1977.)

Lesbians are 'biologically women' or 'structurally females' and 'culturally men' or 'social males'. In society's view, they have the biological potential to reproduce (whether they use it or not). Society's vision is blurred because as 'social males', lesbians should not reproduce. Yet, some do.

For most women, this biological potential becomes a reality in the traditional family unit. The family exists primarily for procreation. Through marriage, the family unit is established. The marriage contract itself reflects a legal contract which transforms a relationship between a man and a woman into a permanent sexual bond. For lesbians, they tend to reject the necessity of the family unit for them as well as the priority of the husband/wife relationship. Ultimately, lesbians may deny motherhood. Yet, because motherhood is usually attainable through the traditional heterosexual family, society denies it for her.[3]

As women, lesbians experience society's command to be dependent upon men for protection and money. The husband's wage is a symbol of this dependency and it characterizes women's relationship to money in advanced capitalistic societies.

It therefore becomes evident that lesbianism rejects the sexual division of labour as well as traditional forms of power (within patriarchal capitalism). As a social force, it contradicts social values and norms.

Previously, I stated that lesbians are viewed by society as being 'social males'. Yet, within the general category 'male' or in relationship to men, they are not primarily productive (viewed as workers). Also, in relationship to women as a social group or to 'structural females' (whom lesbians are as well), they do not become visible as primarily reproductive (viewed as mothers). This ambivalent state contributes to making lesbianism a distinct social category which is isolated and divorced from meaningful social life and which appears as politically impotent.

In a state of confusion and fear, society wants to get rid of lesbianism. It utilizes 'scare tactics'. It tells men that lesbians are competing for 'their women'. Thus far, society has not seen how they compete for 'their jobs'. In reality, however, lesbianism is changing and, hopefully, society's ideas along with it. Perhaps, more and more people will see that the lesbian struggle is for people's liberation as well as a struggle which is linked up with all conflicts with power in modern human life.

Notes

1. All material quoted directly from lesbians was collected on tapes. This information was used as data to support the findings for my Ph.D. research which was completed from 1973–77.
2. In this context, the term, dialectic, implies the presence of opposing forces within social lesbianism as well as within the *total* historical emergence of lesbianism.
3. However, there are ways for lesbians to get pregnant and become mothers. One way is through AID, a method of artificial insemination. Recently, a journalist in England exposed the fact that lesbians use this method of conception. As far as I know from my own research, this method has existed for years.

References

Abbott, S. and Love, B. (1973). *Sappho was a Right-on-Woman*, pp. 13–16. New York: Stein and Day.

Barron, R. D. and Norris, G. M. (1976). Sexual divisions and the dual labour market. In *Dependence and Exploitation in Work and Marriage*. Edited by D. L. Barker and S. Allen, p. 52. London: Longman.

Bernard, Jessie (1968). *The Sex Game*, p. 46. London: Leslie Frewin.

Caprio, F. S. (1955). *Female Homosexuality: A Psychodynamic Study of Lesbianism*, p. 8. London: Icon Books.

Ettorre, E. M. (1978). *The Sociology of Lesbianism: Female 'Deviance' and Female Sexuality*. Unpublished Ph.D. thesis. University of London.

Ettorre, E. M. (1980). *Lesbians, Women and Society*. London: Routledge and Kegan Paul.

Freud, S. (1920). The psychogenesis of a case of female homosexuality. *International Journal of Psychoanalysis*, **1**, 125–149.

Gardiner, J. (1977). Political economy of domestic labour in capitalist society. In *Class and Class Structure*. Edited by Alan Hunt. London: Lawrence and Wishart.

Hawley, Amos (1963). Community power and urban renewal success. *American Journal of Sociology*, **68**, 422–431.

Oakley, A. (1974). *Housewife*, p. 45. London: Allen Lane.

Olsen, M. (1970). Power as a social process. In *Power in Societies*, p. 2. Edited by M. Olsen. New York: The Macmillan Company.

Transsexualism

KURT SCHAPIRA

Department of Psychiatry, The University,
Newcastle upon Tyne, England

Introduction

There can be few conditions among the so-called sexual minorities —the theme of this session of the symposium—about which there is more ignorance, confusion and popular prejudice than there is about transsexualism. In the minds of most people it conjures up sensational newspaper stories illustrated by provocative photographs intended to shock, surprise and titillate. Over the last twenty years some sober publications have offered more detailed and less emotive accounts of the difficulties and anguish endured by transsexuals before they eventually achieve the dominant goal in their lives, that is, the attainment of a sexual identity in accord with their own feelings.

This paper will consider the problems of diagnosis or, more accurately, examine the phenomenon of transsexualism in relation to other kinds of sexual behaviour, such as transvestism, fetishism and homosexuality, with which it is often confused. After defining transsexualism, the prevalence of the condition, its possible origins and finally, the evaluation of its treatment and management will be examined. It will soon become apparent that our understanding of transsexualism remains imperfect and that the management of the transsexual patient leaves much to be desired. Our subject therefore constitutes a challenge and stimulus to further research, both in the scientific and social fields.

Definitions and Classifications

In his classical study of the transsexual phenomenon, Dr Harry Benjamin (1966), whose contributions have formed the basis of much work in this field and to whom, more than anyone else, transsexuals owe a great debt for drawing attention to their predicament, proposed a classification in which transsexualism is distinct from transvestism and yet part of a continuum containing both. He recognized three groups of patients. The first group includes individuals who merely wish to dress in the clothes of the opposite sex. Sometimes such cross-dressing is done in secret, but usually they wish to appear in these clothes in public and to be accepted as women. Although the transsexual phenomenon is found in both men and women, it is far commoner in men and because of this, as well as for convenience, the rest of this paper will refer to the case of the male transsexual. Difficulties and problems when they arise are entirely social in kind, in that when their cross-dressing is recognized it occasionally causes social disruption and a breach of the peace. This group corresponds to that described by Roth and Ball (1964) as 'simple transvestism'. The majority of these individuals feel, work and live as males, leading normal heterosexual lives as husbands or fathers. In contrast, the second group are individuals with a severe emotional disturbance resulting from a confusion of gender identity. This group can be seen as an intermediate stage between the first group and true transsexualism. Indeed, such patients' feelings and hopes may alternate between those characteristic of transvestites and transsexuals, respectively. Thus, they are no longer content with cross-dressing and desire to approximate to the feminine role much more closely than cross-dressing will permit. Moreover, they may demand hormone therapy to enlarge their breasts and so fulfil their need for some degree of gynaecomastia. As a rule, they do not ask for surgery, although some may have fantasies of being without their male genitalia. Like the true transsexual patient they come to doctors for help in changing their body configuration to that of their desired gender. They frequently refuse psychotherapy or fail to benefit from it. This group differs largely in degree from the truly transsexual patient, although there are some qualitative differences. The latter group shows a much greater degree of sex and gender role disorientation and much deeper emotional disturbance. To the true transsexual his sex organs are a source of disgust, he hates his male body-form and all the other physical attributes that are commonly regarded as male.

He considers that his 'female soul' is trapped in an alien body and strives for the day when he can function as a female socially, legally and sexually. Although there would appear to be a continuum between the last two groups it is generally agreed that in transvestism cross-dressing is entirely pleasurable, that it often contains a fetishistic element and that it occurs in biologically normal males, who neither question nor deny their maleness. However, the two conditions share an abnormally strong identification with the opposite sex which results in cross-dressing. Stoller (1968), in his book *Sex and Gender*, deplores the loose use of the term transsexual to include all those seeking sex reassignment, since such requests may come from a variety of individuals wishing to have surgical operations for a number of reasons. True transsexuals are those with an extreme reversal of gender identity and such individuals form only a small proportion of those who at one time or another may express a wish for sex reassignment.

Gender identity as well as sexual object-choice must form the basis on which conditions involving cross-dressing may be distinguished from one another. In transsexuals, gender identity is incongruous, that is, it is contrary to genital morphology, whereas in transvestism and homosexuality this is not the case. Thus, the male transsexual feels uncomfortable dressed as a man but relaxed when dressed as a woman. He feels entirely as a woman with the exception of his male genitalia which are a burdensome anomaly to him. Cross-dressing itself provides no sexual excitement for him but is considered to be merely the appropriate form of dress. He considers his attraction to males an entirely normal result of his female personality. Indeed, the majority of true transsexuals will strenuously reject the idea of a homosexual relationship with another man. On the other hand the homosexual although he may have some feminine identifications considers himself primarily a male and uses his genital organs in sexual relationships, deriving pleasure from their use. He accepts and enjoys his homosexuality. The transvestite, when dressed as a male, considers himself to be male, although when dressed as a woman he may at the same time consider himself to varying degrees a female; he remains typically heterosexual. The fetishistic element may in some cases be present when cross-dressing becomes sexually exciting. Although it is possible to classify most cases into one of these groups it may be difficult to do so in individual cases. The distinction between these groups is likely to remain blurred until there is a better understanding of the causes and origins of these sexual deviations.

Prevalence

Because of its nature, any assessment of the prevalence of transsexualism is an underestimate, since such figures can only be based on the number of patients presenting for treatment. The first systematic study of the prevalence of transsexualism was reported by Wålinder (1968), and was based in part on a national postal inquiry involving all doctors in psychiatric practice working with adults.

Of the 91 cases of transvestism and transsexualism reported, 67 were judged to be cases of transsexualism by criteria based on Benjamin's (1966):

1. a sense of belonging to the opposite sex, of having been born into the wrong sex, of being one of nature's extant errors;
2. a sense of estrangement with one's own body; all indications of sex differentiation are considered as afflictions and repugnant;
3. a strong desire to resemble physically the opposite sex via therapy, including surgery; and
4. a desire to be accepted by the community as belonging to the opposite sex.

Although the fundamental disturbance is a reversal of gender identity, around which all other symptoms seem to cluster, Wålinder points out that the most reliable of these, when it is not possible to interview the patient personally, is the desire for surgical change of sex. Adding 43 personal cases of his own, the number of transsexuals on the census date could be set at 110, giving an overall prevalence of 1 in 54,000 (1 in 37,000 for men, and 1 in 103,000 for women).

Employing similar criteria, Hoenig and Kenna (1974), report their findings of a regional epidemiological study confined to patients aged 15 years and above, resident in the area of the Manchester Regional Hospital Board. These patients had been referred to the University Department of Psychiatry which serves as a Regional Centre for referral of patients by general practitioners and for cross-consultation with other specialists. Although the methods of data collection differed in the two investigations—all cases in the English study were seen personally and one study covered a whole country and the other only a region—figures obtained by these authors are remarkably similar, as is shown in Table I. Extrapolating their results to England and Wales as a whole, Hoenig and Kenna produced a rough estimate of 717 transsexuals aged 15 and over of which 537 are males and 180 are females. The estimate of overall prevalence is similar to that derived by Pauly (1969), who estimated about 2,000 cases in the United States. All investigators in this field have stressed that the true prevalence of transsexualism must be a great deal larger than is suggested by these figures based on individuals who had sought help of a medical or social kind. They are likely to represent the tip of an iceberg.

Table I
Prevalence rates

Authors	Male	Female	Both sexes
Wålinder (1968)	1:37,000	1:103,000	1:54,000
Hoenig and Kenna (1974)	1:34,000	1:108,000	1:53,000

Aetiology

Before considering the problems of aetiology the criteria which have been used to establish sexual identity need to be considered. Armstrong and Hall (1972), in discussing a clinical approach to disorders of sex, used four previously defined criteria (Armstrong, 1964). These are:

1. chromosomal sex: sex determination is by chromosomes, female 46/XX and male 46/XY;
2. gonadal sex: the histological structure of the gonad, either ovary or testis;
3. external genitalia and body form; and
4. psychological sex and sexual behaviour.

These criteria are similar to the seven variables of sexual identification listed by Money (1963):

1. chromosomal sex;
2. gonadal sex;
3. hormonal function;
4. genital morphology (internal);
5. genital morphology (external), and body image;
6. assigned sex; and
7. psychosexual differentiation.

In transsexualism there is no persuasive evidence of abnormality in the first five of the latter variables, but there is a disturbance of body image in some cases and a severe disturbance in psychosexual differentiation in all of them. Orientation is entirely heterosexual, although the sexual drive may be of low intensity.

The Concept of Gender Identity

"What are little girls made of?
Sugar and spice and everything nice,
That's what little girls are made of.

What are little boys made of?
Slugs and snails and puppy dogs' tails,
That's what little boys are made of."

Childhood Ditty.

The term 'gender identity' refers to an individual's sense of masculinity or femininity. Thus it differs from 'sex' which is the sum of the biological attributes that contribute to the making of a male or female (Stoller, 1976). Stoller considers gender identity as arising from the interaction of three forces: the biological, the biopsychic and the intrapsychic response to the environment. The biological components derive from prenatal endocrine influences. Jost (1972) demonstrated that in mammals the basic state of tissue is female and that male organs are produced only under the influence of androgens. Moreover, androgens must be added at a critical time, specific for each species, if the brain is to be organized towards maleness (Money and Ehrhardt, 1972).

However, as we ascend the evolutionary scale the influence of environmental factors becomes increasingly important and the behaviour repertoire of an organism exhibits increasing flexibility. Thus, the general rule that masculinity and male behaviour or femaleness and feminine behaviour inevitably go together is most often broken in the human species (Stoller, 1968).

The second group, the biopsychic factors, are poorly understood. They are believed to originate as stimuli arising from the external and the internal environment, creating changes in the nervous system that determine behaviour. The extent to which these changes contribute to the formation of adult behaviour patterns remains to be determined, but phenomena like imprinting and classical conditioning may be important. The third group contains factors of two kinds. The first of these are influences that do not lead to intrapsychic conflict while the second do so. The latter form an important part of Freudian pathology, being those conflicts that must be resolved satisfactorily if the individual is to reach a mature adult sexual state. Thus, according to Freud, in order to attain proper gender identity a boy must resolve the oedipal conflict, i.e. the desire for his mother against the threat of castration from his father. In contrast a girl finds her femininity by entering into the conflict, that is by turning to her father and risking her mother's anger.

The aetiology of transsexualism remains to be defined. As with other sexual deviations, there are two schools of thought. The first incriminates social and psychological factors in the rearing of the child (Money et al., 1957), while the second regards the condition as organic and due to pre-natal endocrine influences on the developing thalamus (Baker and Stoller, 1968).

That in certain animal species a female pattern of behaviour can be reproduced in anatomically male animals by pre-natal or early post-natal hormonal manipulation has been well established (Harris and Michael, 1964). In humans the only study relevant to this issue is that reported by Yalom et al. (1973), who examined a number of boys aged 6 years and 16 years, whose mothers were diabetics and who were given large doses of female sex hormones during pregnancy in order to prevent abortion. In a double blind study, the children resulting from these pregnancies were compared with a control group. They showed a significant reduction in their aggressivity, sex-linked interests and activities, athletic ability and sexual behaviour. However, it is noteworthy that none of these boys showed any transsexual features. Reviewing the evidence from neuroendocrinological experiments, Levine (1971) defined the five essential and sequential stages in gender and sex differentiation in the human male as follows:

1. X and Y chromosomes are present in the genes, the addition of a Y chromosome to make the XY pair initiates the very process of maleness;
2. if the medulla of the embryological genital ridge develops and the cortex atrophies, then the resulting organ will be a testis;
3. the secretion by the foetal testes of the duct-organizing substance, distinct from androgen, causes the Wolffian ducts to differentiate into male structures;
4. the presence of androgens during development acts upon the brain to programme male patterns of behaviour; and,
5. at least where human beings are concerned, an additional process takes place during development which involves the establishment of gender-role as a function of learning; gender role in the human is also dependent upon rearing.

Such a sequential scheme incorporates the psychological theories and the organic theories into a working hypothesis by recognizing their effect and action at different stages of development. Thus, sex and gender differentiation in human beings is not a question of nature versus nurture, but of nature and nurture acting together at different stages of development by processes that take place with 'exquisite timing' (Levine, 1971).

Clinical Features

When the definition of transsexualism is confined to individuals who fulfil the above criteria a fairly consistent history is obtained. The sexual characteristics at birth are male and the child is given a boy's name, the sex assignment is clear-cut and in accordance with the anatomical evidence. A very close, loving, and in some histories a pathologically intimate relationship, develops between the mother and the child to the exclusion of other relationships. The father is often absent or insignificant as regards the emotional development of the boy. Patients often give an account of behaviour more appropriate to a girl than to a boy, dating back to as early an age as two or three years. General behaviour and demeanour is characterized by gentleness, lovingness and gracefulness, rather than the more usual rough and boisterous activities of boys. However, such personality traits are not interpreted as being feminine, but are welcomed by mother, an approval by which they are reinforced. At a slightly older age the little boy begins to dress in girls' clothing, and is readily accepted by girls who allow him to join in their games, a remarkable phenomenon, since at this age mutual exclusion from each others' games is the rule of the day.

Once at school with other boys problems inevitably arise. His different interests and shy and rather gentle nature, as well as his other personality traits which distinguish him from other boys, make life difficult for him and cause him to become isolated. It is not surprising, therefore, that poor school achievement is common in the history of many patients, some of whom also develop frank neurotic symptoms, such as enuresis. These symptoms may continue into the late teens when problems of gender identity cause difficulties in employment and in social relationships.

Therapeutic Considerations

It is well to remember that transsexualism has been the subject of medical interest for less than twenty-five years and of scientific research for even less than that. Although arousing the interests of sociologists, anthropologists and the bewilderment of many sections of society, not to mention the condemnation of these unfortunate human beings as perverse, it is to the medical profession that the patients have turned for help. To say the least, they have received a mixed reception by a profession that has hitherto regarded sex and gender as identical sides of the same coin. Apart from the very rare cases of inter-sex, where there has clearly been a developmental error of physical sexual development, the phenomenon whereby a person who, from the biological point of view, was clearly of one sex but claims to have the mind of the opposite sex is startling and inexplicable. It is hardly surprising, therefore, that such individuals were referred to psychiatrists in the first instance. Whatever the results of research into the transsexual phenomenon so courageously pioneered by Dr Harry Benjamin, there is little doubt that it has given real meaning to the term gender in stimulating interest and research into the nature of gender identity in normal human beings. Although much remains to be learned about the development of gender identity, the awareness of oneself as male or female, it is accepted as a fundamental characteristic and a basic component of personality. In the public mind as well as in uninformed professional circles, transsexualism is still closely linked with sexual surgery, often preceded by indiscriminate hormone therapy, both being employed merely because the person requests a 'sex change'. In practice, reputable centres dealing with such problems carry out a most rigorous and careful assessment at all stages of therapy. In spite of minor local differences, a basic regime of management appears to be emerging and this is likely to offer the greatest relief to the sufferer, as well as to represent a reasonable and sane policy. All are agreed that a transsexual is not merely a person who requests surgical sex change but someone who genuinely suffers from a reversal of gender identity.

A Plan of Management

A history in which an assessment of the patient's gender identity forms a prominent part must be the core of the preliminary investigations. A careful history of childhood, particularly with regard to behaviour and fantasy life, and of real and imaginary social and sexual relationships, is most important. Similarly, of crucial importance is the question as to when conflict over gender behaviour was first experienced and then to determine to what extent. The time of onset of cross-dressing, its relation to sexual excitement and fantasies are important, as are the individual's own image of his body and his attitude to his genital organs. One of the difficulties is the reliance that can be placed on the history given by a patient known to be determined to obtain a sex reassignment operation. Statements from relatives should, if possible, be obtained to complete the history and also to allay the anxieties about possible retrospective distortions. Two further important considerations have to be taken into account. The first concerns any periods during which the individual has been able to relate adequately as a male and, if so, for how long and how successfully. The second, which in the view of many has an important bearing on prognosis, relates to the extent to which the patient can convey an impression of his desired gender by his physical behaviour. Finally, it is essential for any plan of systematic treatment that the patient must fully understand the implications of such treatment and must be determined in his desire to live in his new gender role. The difficulties likely to occur in social settings and the anguish and distress experienced by the families must be fully understood and accepted by the individual. These are problems which only the transsexual is able to deal with and he will have to resolve them as best he can; few can expect to find the kind of tolerance and understanding which Jan Morris describes in her book (Morris, 1974).

History-taking followed by psychiatric formulation and evaluation, which will continue throughout the first phase of treatment, is essential if serious psychiatric conditions, such as psychotic depression, schizophrenia or psychopathy, are to be detected, since these conditions are likely to be aggravated by sex reassignment procedures.

Treatment may be considered in four stages. To begin with, the patient is assisted in developing modes of behaviour and actions appropriate to his preferred sex role. This would involve the learning of skills and habits, of feminine deportment, of speech, of mannerisms and many of the subtle aspects of behaviour which distinguish women from men. It is remarkable how often an individual may be totally unware of these and although considering himself as entirely feminine will look grotesque in female clothes. Yardley (1976) gives an excellent account of the training in feminine skills of a male transsexual, the procedure which in this instance preceded operation. The patient, a 20-year-old male, was referred for specific help with sex-role skills as part of an overall programme, with a possibility of a sex change operation as the final step of the programme. Extensive use was made of video film of the patient cross-dressed before treatment and interacting with both women and men. The film was viewed by 20 student teachers, a therapist and four clinicians. The comments made immediately after the showing and relating particularly to the patient were recorded. From these comments certain target areas for behaviour modification were chosen. These included body movement, head movement, facial expression, lip movements, gaze, posture, body tonus, gestures, voice, control of interaction, content of conversation, manner of relating to others, appearance and general impression. All these were rated before and after the treatment which helped the patient adopt the sex-role behaviour of his preferred sex. Of particular interest was the finding that the exaggerated feminine behaviour so typical of transsexuals decreased with improved role behaviour. The importance of the relationship with the female therapist and the male psychiatrist, who were both able to accept and relate to the patient as a woman, notwithstanding behavioural anomalies, was considered to be an important aspect of the treatment as well as a good prognostic sign for the patient's successful adaptation. The procedure consisted of twenty consecutive sessions, each lasting for two hours and taking place weekly (see Table II).

Table II
Treatment programme in feminine skills in a male transsexual (Yardley, 1976)

Time (weeks)	Focus of work	Techniques
1–2	Assessment and evaluation of problem	Psychometric behavioural observation
3–5	Body and head positions	Modelling/instruction, rehearsal, video feedback
6–7	Facial expressions	Modelling/instruction, rehearsal, video feedback
8–9	Hand movements	Modelling/instruction, rehearsal, video feedback
10–20	Voice	Voice training (Bruford)
11–12	Overview	Video feedback
13–14	Content of social interactions	Social skills training: audio/video feedback modelling/rehearsal role play/reversal
15–17	Courtship behaviour	As above
17–20	General social situations	As above

Advice from a beautician about make-up and mode of dress is an essential part of social skill training. The concept of femininity in the mind of the transsexual often differs widely from the appearance and behaviour of natural women. Thus, often without appropriate help, clothes are chosen to underline and highlight the femininity of the wearer. The result is often more appropriate to the theatre than everyday life. Also, it is very difficult for transsexuals to choose female garments that reflect their appropriate chronological age; they almost invariably tend to dress as much younger than they are. Such mistakes often make the transsexual highly conspicuous, a particular feature which he wishes to avoid because of his desire to pass as a normal female in society. In essence then, he will have to learn to wear clothes just as natural women do, for comfort and to improve their appearance, rather than to exhibit their femininity. It may be this tendency to focus upon their femininity that leads many transsexuals and transvestites to take up careers as models and actresses where such an emphasis and the wearing of exotic dresses is not only more readily accepted but, may indeed, be positively advantageous.

Hormone Therapy

The second phase of management involves medical treatment in the form of hormone therapy. This may often be started at the same time as the social skills training and adaptation of the patient to his new gender-role is being developed. The patient must understand what hormone therapy is likely to achieve and what it can never achieve, and just as 'sex change' operation is a misnomer, in that no operation can convert a male into a female, so oestrogens cannot produce a female from an anatomical male. What results may therefore be expected from the administration of oestrogens? There will be development of the breasts brought about by a thickening of the glandular tissue behind the pigmented area around the nipple. These changes are followed by an increase in the amount of fatty tissue and by an accumulation of water, giving an overall effect of something like a female breast, in that the breasts will now be more prominent. However, in only a few cases will oestrogens produce the shape and contours of a normal female breast, and the breasts will never function as they do in a normal female, because their increased size is almost entirely due to extra deposits of fat. Oestrogens will not raise the pitch of the low masculine voice, often a considerable practical problem, but vocal practice may help in this respect. The effect of oestrogens on hair growth is variable, but some subjects report that the scalp hair grows longer, becomes softer and more luxurious, while in others these changes are less striking to the objective observer. Beard growth will not be affected by oestrogens and will require electrolytic hair removal. This is currently readily available outside medical clinics and modern techniques produce very satisfactory results. It represents a very important part of treatment since often the patient with thick dark hair growth requires extremely heavy make-up to obscure this growth and so draws attention to himself.

Patients given oestrogens will also develop a deposition of fat around the hips and thighs and in addition there may be a slight increase of fat deposits at other subcutaneous sites around the body, notably the face, which may result in some rounding of the face giving the general effect of a more youthful and feminine appearance. However, it must be made very clear to patients that these hormones will not transform them into someone of perfect female proportions. They need only be reminded that there are many naturally born females who, though exposed to the influence of oestrogens since puberty, have not achieved this ideal!

Psychosexual changes produced by hormone therapy are confined to a reduction of sexual interests and drive. Some also claim a general decrease in assertiveness as well as describing themselves as being more 'emotional' in that they weep more easily and generally experience greater lability of mood. Both these features are welcomed by the patient and considered desirable as representing feminine personality traits.

Side effects occasionally occur and include nausea, vomiting and dizziness. Other more serious complications such as the development of tumours and cancer of the breast have been described and although patients must be made aware of these complications, the risks will rarely deter the transsexual.

The female wishing a change to the male gender will require testosterone (male hormone), and again the effects of such therapy should be made clear to the patient. A degree of hirsutism, occasionally complicated by acne, can be expected, as can a lowering of the voice. The size of the clitoris will increase but will never develop into a phallus of male dimensions. Under the influence of testosterone, menstruation will cease but breast size will not appreciably diminish and may require cosmetic sugery at a later stage. As for libido, unlike oestrogens which diminish libido, testosterone often increases it.

Surgical Intervention

The surgical aspects of sex change caused an uproar in society and created great anxieties and difficulties within the medical profession. Apart from the natural repugnance a surgeon feels at mutilating a normal body, there is also the question of justification on medical, or other grounds, for doing so (Ostow, 1953). Furthermore, it goes against the medical ethic to prescribe treatment of any kind merely because the patient demands it. When the demand for treatment is based on an idea which is clearly contradicted by every available objective evidence of sexuality, then such a demand seemed nothing short of preposterous. As one London practitioner in the early 1950s put it: "It was as though a man, who believed himself to be Nelson, demanded that his arm should be cut off, since then his appearance would be more in conformity with his delusion". It was argued that in complying with such a request the surgeon would be doing no more than he does in cases of transsexualism. The dilemma with which the medical profession was faced then, as indeed it is now, was with an individual who, suffering great anguish and misery and who, apart from his unshakable belief that nature had played him a trick by enclosing him in an alien sexual body, shows no evidence of any other significant psychiatric abnormality. Furthermore, the transsexual is convinced that it is his anatomical sex that requires to be changed so as to conform with his gender identity, rather than the reverse. To support his claims and demands, he cites not only the misery and unhappiness of his life but the difficulties and the failures he has endured whilst a man, and his happiness and contentment in his new gender role, in which he has also achieved some degree of success as judged by employment as well as by social and economic status. He is unwilling to accept any form of psychiatric treatment and will support his attitude by the currently available evidence that formal psychiatric treatment has not been able to achieve worthwhile results for this condition, except possibly in one case (Barlow et al., 1973).

In her book Conundrum, Jan Morris describes the criteria for operation as these were explained to her and which she basically accepted. These were that the patient must not be psychotic, but must be able to understand the procedure and be physically compatible with the new role which is sought. Furthermore, he must already have acquired the secondary female characteristics by protracted hormone therapy and show few, if any, traces of male characteristics. Above all, he must have lived for some years in the role of his preferred sex and

Table III
Criteria qualifying for surgical intervention (from Laub and Fisk, 1974)

1. Ages 21–58
2. Successful endocrine feminization
3. One to three years of total cross-living and working in the gender of their choice
4. Success in social, psychological, employment and sexual spheres
5. Not married in the gender of their anatomy
6. Freedom from psychosis or significant sociopathy (jail or drugs)
7. No life-limiting medical disease (e.g. diabetes or hypertension)

proved that it was socially and economically possible. Most physicians dealing with cases of transsexualism would agree with these selection criteria.

In an interesting paper, Laub and Fisk (1974) give an account of the experience at Stanford of providing a rehabilitation programme for patients with 'gender dysphoria syndrome', by surgical sex change. They define the syndrome as, "an emotional state characterised by anxiety, depression and restlessness", arising in patients from displeasure and disgust of their genital anatomy, the heritage of their chromosomes and the effect of their endocrinal secretions. Such individuals, including groups other than the classical transsexual described by Benjamin, may also seek sex reassignment procedures. The authors define five diagnostic categories which may be subsumed under the syndrome of gender dysphoria:

1. classical transsexualism (of Benjamin);
2. transvestism;
3. effeminate homosexuality;
4. psychosis, and
5. extreme sociopathy and psychopathy.

Operations were carried out only in the first three categories. Although 769 patients were involved in the programme as a whole, only 74 (9·6 per cent) were considered suitable for gender surgery. Of these, 50 had surgery in the male-to-female direction and 24 in the female-to-male direction.

Perhaps the most surprising result of this study was that transsexuals were not the only group to benefit from this type of surgery. In a careful assessment, both pre-operatively and post-operatively, with a follow-up period ranging up to six years (mean follow-up time of 23 months), the authors found that the diagnostic grouping was less important as regards prognosis than the patient's pre-operative adjustment in a one- to three-year trial of living in the gender of choice. Such adjustment was measured in economic, social, psychological and sexual terms.

This paper presents, in a scientific and humane way, the dilemma of these patients, the criteria of selection for surgery and the pre-operative treatment and care they had received. The interdisciplinary approach is stressed. The authors also describe in some detail the surgical and non-surgical complications that may follow the operation. The incidence of surgical complication in patients undergoing surgery in the male-to-female direction was 47 per cent as compared to only 25 per cent in the female-to-male direction. The majority of complications were of a physical kind such as rectovaginal fistula or vaginal infections, but a few psychiatric 'complications' were also noted, ranging from 'an excessive emotional attachment to the surgeon', to 'a desire to shoot the genitals off the surgeon with a shotgun'.

Although supporting the general view that, on the whole, the operation was beneficial, it is clear from a careful reading of this study, as indeed of one or two other carefully conducted investigations, that neither the enthusiasm and expectations of those demanding sex surgery nor their unequivocal satisfaction with its results, are shared by the medical attendants. Little is known for instance, of the operated individuals who are not traced at follow-up or indeed about those who are rejected for surgery and who travel from one clinic to another in search of such radical treatment. These are important aspects which will be considered when the current status of our knowledge about transsexualism and of the implications this has for possible future management and treatment is examined.

Legal Issues

Without social and legal recognition of his new gender identity the transsexual patient remains as disadvantaged as ever in spite of the medical measures, including surgery, which may have been undertaken. The transsexual needs a good lawyer as much as he needs a good physician (Hoenig, 1977), because his lawyer would have to advise his client in a situation where there is no legal definition of sex, and where the legal meaning of 'man' or 'woman' has never been established. Society, reflecting the view of the law considers people as either male or female, the decisive characteristic being the entry on the birth certificate. This in turn is based on the apparent and obvious anatomical sex of the child. In the very rare cases of intersex, the sex assigned at birth becomes the criterion and also determines the subsequent rearing of the child. Since the legal and social attitudes vary from country to country I shall confine myself to the practice in the United Kingdom.

The first occasion on which a court in this country was called upon to rule on the sex of an individual was in the case of Corbett *v.* Corbett (otherwise Ashley), which concerned the validity of a marriage. The case was heard in the High Court of Justice, London, before Mr Justice Ormrod, in 1969. In his judgement (Corbett *v.* Corbett, 1970) Sir Roger Ormrod held that the marriage of a male-to-female transsexual and a man was a nullity. Referring to sex assignment, however, he stated that this was no more than a doctor's decision as to the gender of the individual, by which such a person can best be managed. When there was a contractual relationship where 'sex' was a relevant factor, such as life insurance, pension schemes, and other contracts involving personal documentation, there was nothing to prevent the parties from agreeing that an individual could be treated as a man or woman. However, when it came to the definition of 'woman' in the context of marriage, and this was the crucial issue in this case, then only biological criteria were relevant. Namely, chromosomal constitution, the character of the external genitalia, and the nature of the internal gonads. If these three criteria were congruent then for the purpose of marriage they determined the sex of the individual and no operative intervention or change consequently had any bearing on the matter. The importance of this judgement lies in the fact that it acknowledged the difference between sex and gender, and indicated those areas of human activity where the legal sex is entirely governed by biological sex and other areas where gender assignment, even when contrary to biological sex, might be legally recognized.

Returning to practical issues, a change of name will be one of the early matters requiring legal consideration. In this country it is not necessary to apply for a legal change of name since one is entitled to assume a new name as long as it is not done for criminal purposes. However, it is advisable to apply to the Courts with the support of a medical certificate for a legal change of name, since the granting of such a petition facilitates subsequent changes in other documents such as national insurance card, driving licence, passport, and sometimes also school reports and records of examination and qualifications.

Apart from these, a medical certificate should be given to the transsexual stating that he is under medical care and receiving treatment for sex reassignment. Although such a certificate has little in the way of legal value it does show that a medical practitioner considers the individual to be a responsible member of society who is seeking a change-over to a preferred sex but does not intend, by his cross-dressing behaviour, to cause either social disharmony or to commit a criminal offence. Indeed, it is the patients' desire to pass unnoticed in their preferred gender role and such certificates are often a means of providing them with considerable reassurance should anything go wrong and should they be challenged. However, it should be remembered that cross-dressing by itself, is, in this country, as indeed in most, not a criminal offence. When charges are brought they are for behaviour likely to cause a breach of the peace or in some cases for loitering with intent. In the latter, cross-dressing is seen as a method of disguise. Although some progress has been made in obtaining legal recognition for the transsexual, the state of affairs remains basically unsatisfactory except in Sweden where, from 1972, a law has been in force which puts the responsibility of sex reassignment into the hands of a national board, which in turn calls upon specially appointed expert committees, including endocrinologists, psychiatrists and lawyers for assistance. If an application is successful, the registration of birth in the parish register is appropriately altered and authorization is also given to effect appropriate changes in other personal documents. Furthermore, the law sets out fairly strict criteria for sex reassignment. It also insures that once the new gender role has been assigned it cannot be challenged in court and applies to every aspect of the person's life.

Second Thoughts?

It may seem to the casual reader that transsexualism, although perhaps initially bedevilled by doubts and difficulties, is a fairly straightforward phenomenon for which a reasonable aetiology has been proposed and for which a satisfactory regime of management has been suggested. Nothing can be further from the truth. The condition is one in which individuals, in spite of all the evidence to the contrary, believe themselves to be of the opposite gender. They base this belief entirely upon their feelings and demand that the medical profession should help them achieve a reversal of gender and that society should accept them in their new gender without reservation. At the same time we are asked to believe that these individuals do not suffer from any psychiatric abnormality and that their belief is non-delusional in nature. Moreoever, the majority, if not all of the patients, present to the medical profession not so much for advice and help, but with a *demand* for a 'sex change'. This is the only way, they insist, in which they can achieve tranquillity and nothing short of surgery will satisfy them. Both the nature of their complaint as well as the persistent demand for treatment of a particular kind, are both new and unfamiliar phenomena in general medical practice. It is not surprising, therefore, that the vast majority of doctors feel themselves utterly unable to cope; they hope that these individuals will go elsewhere.

Psychiatrists and neuroendocrinologists fare little better. The former are asked to pronounce upon an individual who denies any psychiatric illness and who maintains that his belief of being of a particular gender (contrary to all anatomical evidence) is not a delusion but a fact. He neither asks for psychiatric treatment, nor indeed appears to benefit when such treatment is attempted. Apart from the one reported instance to which I have already referred (Barlow *et al.*, 1973), the consensus of opinion is that psychiatric treatment has little to offer such individuals. Is it surprising, therefore, that when faced with these individuals whose anxiety, depression and often suicidal behaviour demands some action, the doctors with requisite expertise are willing to provide it. Thus, with the advent of hormone therapy the opportunity presented itself to go some way towards helping the patient to achieve his aim. Surgery, the patient's next demand, proved both morally and instinctively a great deal more difficult, since by no stretch of the imagination can the necessary procedure be considered anything other than a mutilation. The repugnance felt by surgeons when amputating a limb is amplified many-fold when it comes to genital amputation and castration. Moreover, even the most modern plastic surgical reconstructive techniques can never reverse the anatomical sex in anything but the most primitive and crude manner. Thus, the term 'sex change' is a misnomer for a surgical procedure which allows an individual to physically identify more closely to his preferred gender. The nature of the operation and its complications should be clearly explained to the patient. They should also receive more attention in popular articles dealing with so-called 'sex change' operations.

Even if surgery were more successful, the criticism could still be levelled that it is nothing more than symptomatic treatment, in contrast to treatment which focuses on underlying psychiatric problems of anomalous gender identification. The strength of this argument is undeniable but the protagonists of surgery would point out

that there are many medical conditions of obscure aetiology where
only symptomatic treatment is possible. That the allaying of human
suffering cannot, and should not, await a perfect understanding of the
causes of their disease, is one of the fundamental tenets of medical
practice. Nevertheless, few would claim that our present state of
knowledge about gender and the treatment of transsexuals is satisfactory. There is still much to be learned about the nature of transsexualism and new methods of treatment should constantly be explored and
evaluated. At the same time, improvement of current management as
outlined in this review calls for carefully conducted longitudinal studies
to determine both the prognosis and to define the pre-operative
features that best correlate with outcome. In this connection it should
be borne in mind that in some individuals the drive for gender reversal
may well not be as fixed as we have been led to believe. One hears of as
yet unpublished reports of patients who seem to have reverted to the
gender congruent with their sexual anatomy.

Since adult transsexualism is a serious condition which presents
such formidable therapeutic problems and since cross-gender behaviour is often clearly evident in children under the age of five, follow-up
of such children and even therapeutic intervention at an early stage
may well prove to be beneficial, not only in terms of understanding
the condition, but also in achieving a more satisfactory result of
treatment with less drastic measures. Prospective study of the young
'incipient transsexual' may also provide more useful information than
retrospective study of fully developed transsexualism in the adult.
Such an early therapeutic approach, were it successful, would also
pre-empt the thorny problem of the effect the transsexual has on his
family and in particular on his children. There is little information
about this aspect except from the accounts given by the transsexuals
themselves, and these are likely to be less than objective. It is
remarkable, however, how rarely a history of transsexualism in a
member of the family is elicited from psychiatric patients. This
contrasts strongly with other forms of sexual difficulty, such as a
history of sexual assault by parents or relatives.

If the phenomenon of transsexualism has posed a real challenge to
the therapeutic skills of the medical profession, it has also stimulated
research that has thrown much light on the understanding of 'normal'
gender, a concept almost entirely derived from the evidence produced
by examples of abnormal development. Although the history of
mankind records examples in antiquity of individuals who desired to
assume the role of the opposite gender, it was not until the work of
Benjamin, a mere twelve years ago, that the transsexual phenomenon

really began to attract medical attention. It is a twentieth century disorder in that the sufferer calls upon the physician for physical treatment, upon the psychiatrist for help with his psychological difficulties and exclusion of psychiatric illness, and turns to the psychologist for assistance with behaviour modification, psychotherapy and counselling. A lawyer is required for legal advice and administrators are involved in providing the necessary documentation. Where sexual difficulties clash with religious belief the help of clergy may be appropriate. Perhaps most important of all, as far as the transsexual is concerned, is the acceptance and tolerance by society of his predicament. The notion of a multi-disciplinary approach has 'come home to roost'!

The question that needs to be asked concerns the doctor's part in the management of these patients. The mere development of potent and radical methods of medical treatment is a poor justification for their use and, as with other advances in the field of medicine, such as organ transplantation and, more recently, the first successful 'test-tube baby', such advances have brought with them problems for the medical profession and indeed for society as a whole, which would have been unthinkable only three decades ago. It is both the advances in medical and surgical technology as well as a wider acceptance by society of sexual diversity, that is responsible for demands made by sexual minorities to be allowed to live in the life-style that they believe and feel to be natural to them.

References

Armstrong, C. N. (1964). Intersexuality in man. In *Intersexuality in Vertebrates Including Man*. Edited by C. N. Armstrong and A. J. Marshall. London and New York: Academic Press.

Armstrong, C. N. and Hall, R. (1972). Endocrinology. In *Medical Progress 1971–1972*. Edited by Sir John Richardson. London: Butterworth.

Baker, H. J. and Stoller, R. J. (1968). Can a biological force contribute to gender identity? *American Journal of Psychiatry*, **124**, 1653–1658.

Barlow, D. H., Reynolds, E. J. and Agras, W. S. (1973). Gender identity change in a transsexual. *Archives of General Psychiatry*, **28**, 569–576.

Benjamin, H. (1966). *The Transsexual Phenomenon*. New York: Julian Press.

Corbett *v.* Corbett (otherwise Ashley) (1970). 2 *All England Law Reports*. 33–51 Probate, Divorce and Admiralty Division. London. Before Mr. Justic Ormrod.

Harris, G. W. and Michael, R. P. (1964). The activation of sexual behaviour by hypothalamic implants of oestrogen. *Journal of Physiology*, **171**, 275–301.

Hoenig, J. (1977). The legal position of the transsexual: mostly unsatisfactory outside Sweden. *Canadian Medical Association Journal*, **116**, 319–323.

Hoenig, J. and Kenna, J. C. (1974). The prevalence of transsexualism in England and Wales. *British Journal of Psychiatry*, **124,** 181–190.

Jost, A. (1972). A new look at the mechanisms controlling sex differentiation in mammals. *Johns Hopkins Medical Journal*, **130,** 38–53.

Laub, D. R. and Fisk, N. (1974). A rehabilitation program for gender dysphoria syndrome by surgical sex change. *Plastic and Reconstructive Surgery*, **53,** 388–403.

Levine, S. (1971). On becoming male. In *Personality and Science: An Interdisciplinary Discussion*. Edited by I. T. Ramsey and R. Porter (a CIBA Foundation Report). Edinburgh and London: Churchill Livingstone.

Money, J. (1963). Factors in the genesis of homosexuality. In *Determinants of Human Sexual Behavior*. Edited by G. Winokur. Springfield, Illinois: Charles C. Thomas.

Money, J. and Ehrhardt, A. A. (1972). *Man and Woman Boy and Girl*. Baltimore: Johns Hopkins University Press.

Money, J., Hampson, J. G. and Hampson, J. L. (1957). Imprinting and establishment of gender role. *Archives of Neurology and Psychiatry*, **77,** 333–336.

Morris, J. (1974). *Conundrum*. London: Faber and Faber.

Ostow, M. (1953). Letter to the Editor. *Journal of the American Medical Association*, **152,** 1553.

Pauly, I. (1969). Adult manifestations of male transsexualism. In *Transsexualism and Sex Reassignment*. Edited by R. Green and J. Money. Baltimore: Johns Hopkins University Press.

Roth, M. and Ball, J. R. B. (1964). Psychiatric aspects of intersexuality. In *Intersexuality in Vertebrates Including Man*. Edited by C. N. Armstrong and A. J. Marshall. London and New York: Academic Press.

Stoller, R. J. (1968). *Sex and Gender: On the Development of Masculinity and Femininity*. London: Hogarth Press and the Institute of Psychoanalysis.

Stoller, R. J. (1976). Gender identity. In *The Sexual Experience*. Edited by B. J. Sadock, H. I. Kaplan and A. M. Freedman. Baltimore: Williams and Wilkins.

Wålinder, J. (1968). Transsexualism: definition, prevalence and sex distribution. *Acta Psychiatrica Scandinavica*, Supplement **203,** 255–258.

Yalom, I. D., Green, R. and Fisk, N. (1973). Prenatal exposure to female hormones. *Archives of General Psychiatry*, **28,** 554–561.

Yardley, K. M. (1976). Training in feminine skills in a male transsexual: a preoperative procedure. *British Journal of Medical Psychology*, **49,** 329–339.

Changing Incidence and Patterns of Sexually Transmitted Diseases

W. H. G. ARMYTAGE

*Division of Education, University of Sheffield,
Sheffield, England*

From Euphemism to Eugenics

The Eugenics Society originated in a breakaway from the Moral
Education League, led by Dr J. W. Slaughter, an American lecturer
from the University of London. It took shape as the Eugenics
Education Society and 1978 marked the centenary of his birth. So I
exercised presidential privilege in offering to give this lecture. For
Slaughter put the matter very neatly when he described it as:

> "Clear that man's struggle for existence is by no means finished and his
> survival is far from assured. The struggle is no longer with the large and
> obvious forms of nature but with the hidden hosts of microscopical
> organisms that perpetually menace the stronghold of life". (Slaughter,
> 1911.)

Just as the discoverer of Salvarsan hoped for a single dose for the cure
of syphilis, the *therapia sterilisans magna*, so the first secretary of this
society, Mrs Gotto, hoped that it would explain the problem of the
feeble-minded. As she put it:

> "Until syphilis was recognised as a cause of apparently inherent defect,
> how could it be seen what proportion of mental defect, insanity, blindness,
> deafness and sterility were due to this removable cause, and what was
> inherent and truly hereditary?" (Neville-Rolfe, 1949.)

For these were the days of euphemism rather than of eugenics. Only
ten years previously, even Rudyard Kipling had to resort to anonym-
ity to complain in the *Saturday Review*:

159

"We asked no social questions—we pumped no hidden shame—
We never talked obstetrics when the Little Stranger came:
We left the Lord in Heaven, we left the fiends in Hell.
We weren't exactly Yussufs, but—Zuleika didn't tell."

"No! No! not a word about that without blushing" said one of the characters in Eugene Brieux's *Damaged Goods*, "but as many dirty jokes as you like. Pornography, as much as you please; science, never!" (Brieux, 1911). Brieux was referring to syphilis, a disease whose origin and nature was so imperfectly understood that it was referred to as 'the social evil' or the 'great scourge'. Even the novelist who explored the possibility of class distinctions being eroded by the prime instincts was a victim: George Meredith himself had VD, according to Bernard Shaw (Winsten, 1951).

Early Estimates of Incidence

Did two-thirds of the male population in this country have gonorrhoea and a quarter have syphilis? That accusation was made by Christabel Pankhurst in a book called *The Great Scourge* (1913). Though she subsequently omitted all reference to this in her autobiography, it should be mentioned if only to point out that fifteen years earlier, when she was fifteen, 36,881 of the 681,331 soldiers in India were hospital cases of venereal disease (Bailey, 1902). And if the soldiers of the Queen were so afflicted, what about her illustrious predecessors? Indeed, an industrious Scottish medical graduate who, after correlating the historical record with what was known in 1913 about venereal diseases, concluded that all the King Henrys—one to eight—suffered from one or other of them (Rae, 1913). Rae's study was published in the same year as the Royal Commission on Venereal Diseases heard the first witness, the Superintendent of Statistics of the Registrar General, Dr T. H. C. Stevenson. He admitted that the statistics for syphilis had no absolute value. Indeed he had to return before it again on 19th December 1913 and admit that doctors would not certify death by 'venereal or other diseases' which would offend friends and relations.

Having instituted (in the census two years before) registration of fertility by what are now well known as the five social classes, he went on to say that the highest and lowest of these classes seemed to suffer most from syphilis, but that textile, mining and agricultural districts seemed remarkably free (Royal Commission on Venereal Diseases, 1914).

The Royal Commission estimated that ten per cent of the population suffered from some form of venereal disease and recommended the establishment of clinics. It did not, if it even could, explore the horror it engendered in two of the most articulate men of the day: the journalist W. E. Henley and the playwright, Oscar Wilde. W. E. Henley told W. B. Yeats that when he was young "syphilis was the terror that walked by night". Henley's brother answered "and quite right too". Henley was a victim: and through him, so was his only daughter, who died early (Yeats, 1973). An even more distinguished man of letters, Oscar Wilde contracted syphilis at Oxford with the result that the mercury treatment of those pre-Salvarsan days discoloured his teeth. Though he consulted a doctor, before getting married, for assurances that he was completely cured, two years later he discovered that the disease had been only dormant. So he discontinued sexual relations with his wife and turned towards homosexuality, researching into Shakespeare's "W.H." and publishing *The Picture of Dorian Grey* (1891) (Hyde, 1960). James Elroy Flecker wrote a gloomy poem about the ravages of venereal disease in 1908:

"I had not thought to see the young
With trembling knees and twitching eyes
Or a boy's brow with torment wrung
If he were old and wise". (Sherwood, 1973, p. 82)

Even James Joyce put a character called Biddy the Clap in *Ulysses* which no doubt contributed to the interest of the censors in his masterpiece (Burgess, 1973, p. 173).

Publicity

Both in the appointment and in the implementation of the recommendations of this commission, the Eugenics Society played no inconsiderable part (Searle, 1976); and with good reasons. Firstly, some of its council were critical of the hereditarian implications implied in the custodial provision of the Mental Deficiency Act of 1913 and realized that syphilis might be a partial explanation. Secondly, its secretary Mrs Gotto—a naval officer's widow—had concluded from her experience as a social worker in a hostel for fallen women, that a more practical course would be to instruct girls in the "facts of life". To this end she tried, before joining the society, to form a Society for Sex Education (Neville-Rolfe, 1949).

Nor was this all, for on her own account she went to see the country's only mass communicator (in that he owned the *Daily Mail* and the *Times*) Lord Northcliffe, who boasted that he was so rigidly orthodox in his attitudes that dirty thoughts, dirty words and dirty jokes were not allowed in his paper. He would not even allow advertisements in his paper to mention 'rupture' or 'constipation'. Yet she persuaded him to print accounts of the evidence given before the Commission. This may well have been because by 1909 he seems to have acquired syphilis and possibly had been one of the earliest patients to receive the anti-syphilitic drug '606' or Salvarsan (Ferris, 1971).

Certainly Mrs Gotto took a great part in the pressure group formed to inform the public that became the British Social Hygiene Council and later the Social Biology Council. And the clinics' staffs, too, built up techniques of treatment and of contact-tracing which proved so effective that in 1974 the United Kingdom was credited with a lower rate of syphilis and gonorrhoea than any other industrial country (Office of Health Economics, 1974). As a result the Office of Health Economics wished to change their name from VD clinics to Genito-Urinary Clinics: a proposal endorsed by a *British Medical Journal* editorial on 11 January 1975.

Despite the inevitable susurrus of protest from the British Association of Urinological Surgeons, one who did change the name of his clinic claimed that statistics justified the change, as only fourteen per cent of patients with the major sexually transmitted diseases seen in his department in 1974 were suffering from either syphilis or gonorrhoea, whereas 51 per cent suffered from other genital infections, some of them not sexually transmitted. These included non-specific genital infection, trichomoniasis, candidosis, genital warts and genital herpes. The remaining 35 per cent of his patients proved to have no infective diseases even though suffering urino-genital complaints (Oriel, 1975).

Changing Carriers

Josephine Butler and Mr Gladstone would be pleased to hear that the

Table I

Sexually transmitted diseases: new patients (in thousands) seen at British hospital clinics (Compiled from Social Trends, Nos. 7 (p. 145), 8 (p. 144), 9 (p. 140) and 10 (p. 177) HMSO. 1976, 1977, 1978, 1979)

	1949	1959	1961	1966	1969	1971	1973	1974	1975	1976	1977	1978
Cases (in all stages) dealt with for the first time at any centre												
Syphilis:												
Male	9	2	3	3	2	2	3	3	3	3	4	4
Female	7	2	2	1	1	1	1	1	1	1	1	1
Non-specific infections:												
Male	25	38	26	32	44	64	75	76	76	80	84	84
Female	10	14	—	—	—	14	15	16	17	20	21	23
Gonorrhoea:												
Male	24	28	32	30	39	42	42	42	41	41	42	39
Female	5	7	8	10	16	20	23	23	24	24	24	21
Other conditions, not requiring treatment:												
Male	36	26	31	32	40	49	58	57	57	61	69	68
Female	17	10	13	17	21	27	32	33	35	36	40	39
Total:												
Males	94	94	92	97	125	157	178	178	177	185	199	192
Females	39	33	23	28	38	62	71	73	77	81	86	83
Young people under 20 years dealt with for syphilis or gonorrhoea:												
Male				3		5		6	6	5	6	5
Female				3		7		8	9	8	8	7

role of the prostitute as a carrier of what they knew as 'contagious diseases' seems to have declined, for in London the percentage of heterosexually infected men acquiring gonorrhoea from a paid source fell by more than half between 1961 and 1969, from 31 to 14 per cent (Dunlop *et al.*, 1971). So, too, in Newcastle the percentage of those acquiring gonorrhoea similarly declined from 27 to 17 per cent (see Table I).

But in the inland towns the non-professionals appeared in the areas where immigrants settled. Capitalizing on the boredom and loneliness of immigrants in the industrial cities, before their wives and children came to join them, local girls (some of whom were emotionally unstable and infected with symptomless gonorrhoea or untreated syphilis) were active and in the late fifties doctors began to report rarer diseases such as lymphogranuloma venereum (Galbraith *et al.*, 1957) and granuloma inguinale (Knight and Fowler, 1956).

In the early 1960s more than half the men with gonorrhoea in the UK were immigrants. In Bradford, between 1959 and 1968, of the 5,000 men known to have gonorrhoea, 80 per cent in the first seven years were immigrants. However, when their wives and families arrived this percentage declined (Oller and Wood, 1970).

By the 1970s the possibility that new carriers would emerge from the seemingly ever-increasing number of travellers to foreign parts led the DHSS in 1973 to add to their *Notes to Travellers* the significant warning that:

"Sexually transmitted diseases remain a serious threat to health both in this country and abroad. They are easily avoided as their name implies. Persons suspecting they may have contracted such a disease should seek advice and treatment immediately." (Department of Health and Social Security, 1973.)

Changing Nomenclature

The use of the term 'sexually transmitted diseases' goes back to 1961 when the physician in charge of the VD Department at St. Thomas's and St. Bartholomew's Hospital suggested dropping the term venereal disease (and with it the stigma) and referring to a group of sexually transmitted diseases which could be treated by a genito-urinary physician, rather than a venereologist. For, as he argued "if by venereal disease one means any disease *usually transmitted by sex contact* (his italics) then certain non-gonococcal infections in the female, including trichomoniasis and a number of other minor infections or infestations might be considered" (Nicol, 1961).

Trichomoniasis is infection by trichomonas vaginalis, a tiny parasite present in the vaginas of between 10 and 20 per cent of women in their reproductive years (15 to 49). It can be harboured with gonorrhoea, and can be treated with a single dose of the drug Flagyl, which is aptly named, as the globular parasite it kills has four moving flagellae or threads at its front end (Llewellyn-Jones, 1974).

Yet another vaginal infection is caused by the fungus which causes thrush in babies. Known as vaginal caroidiases or moniliasis, this is often found in diabetic women and is particularly common in pregnancy. Though harboured by one in four of every woman of reproductive age it only produces symptoms in 5 to 30 per cent of them (Rosebury, 1971).

More controversial infections, such as warts, scabies and crab lice, can also be transmitted by sexual contact. Crab lice like the pubic hairs, as they are wide enough to cling to an adjacent pair. Hence they are also found in the hair about the anus, the armpits, and even the eye-lashes. Perhaps the most controversial of these infections is the variant type 2 herpes, which seems to have some connection with cervical cancer in women who began intercourse relatively early and have had several sex partners, especially uncircumcized men.

School Children and Young Adults

By the early 60s the 'reservoir of infection' was being topped up not so much by prostitutes as amateurs with gonorrhoea (Nicol, 1961; Fluker, 1970) till in the last four years of that decade the morbidity rates for 18- to 19-year-old women nearly doubled (from 271·22 to 558·8 per 100,000) and those for 20- to 24-year-old women increased by one-third (from 549·41 to 683·29 per 100,000).

Though the level rose higher than that prevailing during the war it was realized at the time that this was due to the pill, and the consequent abandonment of 'armour' by the male; to an unknown number of untreated women who were a constant source of infection; to the increase in the incidence of non-specific urethritis, which is similar to, and often confused with gonorrhoea; and to the increasing mobility of the young. It was also pointed out that with over 121 per 100,000 we had a better record than either the Americans with 308 per 100,000, or the Swedes with 514 per 100,000 (Schofield, 1973). Also, we did not have the American problem of syphilis in high schools. One fourteen-year-old American boy who was investigated led to the examination of 66 other students who had had intercourse with him or his contacts and 14 of these had syphilis (American Social Health Association, 1971). It was also comforting to read that the science correspondent of the *Daily Express* found no evidence to suggest that contemporary teenagers were any more promiscuous than those of his days. Indeed, he suggested they might be less promiscuous as they tended to restrict themselves to the same partners for long periods (Pincher, 1973).

But at the same time, the tripling of the number of annual visits to British VD clinics between 1960 and 1970 was, to one practitioner in north-west England, 'alarming' (Felstein, 1974) and he quoted a suggestion that pill-takers seemed to have coitus more often than non-pill-takers. A Glasgow consultant in the field discerned a teenage behaviour syndrome: leaving home, promiscuity, pregnancy, sexually transmitted disease and suicide attempts. If any one of these five entities was missing, he suggested that it should be anticipated (Schofield, 1965). Noting that the promiscuous "spring from every class of society and every type of home", a Sheffield consultant identified the predisposing factor as "lack of an intelligent and affectionate approach by the parents" (Morton, 1966). He also pointed out that the male/female ratio for gonorrhoea had shifted significantly towards parity for the sexes from 3 or 4:1 to 1·72:1—a phenomenon also observable in both the USA and the USSR (Morton, 1970).

The Homosexuals

The third group figuring in the trends in sexually transmitted diseases were the homosexuals with their infections of the rectum, the pharynx and the crypts of the tonsils. These were found to be more common in homosexual than in heterosexual males and next most frequently found in heterosexual females. They were least often found in heterosexual males. By 1977 Morton thought that the importance of these findings in terms of the spread and control of gonorrhoea in sexually free societies "should not be underestimated" (Morton, 1977).

This, of course, was reflected in the latest Kinsey Survey of the year

1970 in the United States. Published in 1978, this indicates that two-thirds of the male homosexuals had developed VD and two-fifths had more than 500 sex partners. A quarter of them had performed with boys under 16. Yet only one lesbian had VD (Kinsey, 1978).

That, as I said, was America. What of Britain? Here, in five London west-end clinics, 27·6 per cent of the patients were homosexual whereas in other London clinics only 7·7 per cent were homosexual. Outside London the percentage of homosexual clients ranges from 3·1 to 5·6 per cent (Morton, 1977).

What Next?

Twenty years ago an immuno-prophylactic approach to sexually transmitted diseases—as with typhoid fever—was suggested by Dr R. S. Morton, a clinician of great and proven experience in this field (Morton, 1958). But the general feeling that the gonococci are, as Dr Comfort put it, "God's little allies", was strong (Comfort, 1967). Recently, however, Dr Morton has come to think that if patients in the clinics are treated with compassionate care, the information given to them is akin to that of imprinting. To strengthen this yet further, and to prevent 'repeaters', he suggests that there are six dark areas on which some light would be welcome.

1. What degree of co-operation in contact-tracing can be expected from various ethnic groups?
2. Can homosexuals be educated in greater discrimination in the choice of sex partners?
3. What psycho-social characteristics are associated with the patient who brings his or her contact at the first attendance?
4. Why do men with a urethral discharge send their regular girlfriend or wife before presenting themselves?
5. Why do some partners ignore their symptoms and signs of gonorrhoea and continue to have intercourse?
6. What can the educational estate contribute to the cultural, and psychological aspects of the transmission and control of sexually transmitted disease?

At present, as Felstein says, the key,

"if key there is, lies in the development and increasing efficiency of local, national and international contact-tracing, with vigorous follow-up of discovered contacts to help ensure full therapy and the necessary follow-up check" (Felstein, 1974).

"Put not your faith in penicillin" might well be the moralists' motto as evidence of its uncertain resistance to gonococci accumulates. Even by 1958, a microgramme of penicillin (fifty times the largest quantity required to eliminate gonococci ten years before) had to be administered to some patients, and by 1976 cases were being reported from London to Liverpool, of gonococci producing penicillase. If these spread widely, the control of gonococcal infections would have to depend on other anti-bacterial drugs (Phillips, 1976).

References

American Social Health Association (1971). *Today's V.D. Control Program*, pp. 21, 57, 19–20.

Bailey, M. H. (1902). Some problems concerning venereal diseases. *New England Journal of Medicine*, **CXLVI**, 592.

Brieux, E. (1911). *Three Plays*. New York: Coward McCann.

Burford, E. J. (1976). *Bawds and Lodgings: A History of the London Bankside Brothels*, pp. 20–23. London: Peter Owen.

Burgess, A. (1973). *Joysprick: An Introduction to the Language of James Joyce*, p. 173. London: Andre Deutsch.

Cartwright, F. F. and Biddis, M. (1972). *Disease and History*, p. 81. London: Hart-Davis.

Central Advisory Council for Education—England (1959). *15 to 18*. London: HMSO.

Comfort, A. (1967). *The Anxiety Makers*. Sunbury on Thames: Thomas Nelson and Sons.

Cross, A. B. and Harris, J. R. W. (1976). Reappraisal of the problem of British mariners and sexually transmitted diseases. *British Journal of Venereal Diseases*, **52**, 71–77.

Dalzell-Ward, A. J. (1969). Britain's venereal disease education for high-risk age and cultural groups. *Medical Officer*, **121**, 3.

Darrow, W. W. (1975). Changes in sexual behaviour and venereal diseases. *Clinical Obstetrics and Gynaecology*, **18**, 255–256.

Department of Health and Social Security (1973). *Chief Medical Officers Report for 1971*. London: HMSO.

Deutsch, Helen (1968). *Selected Problems of Adolescence*. London: Hogarth.

Dunlop, E. M. C., Lamb, A. M. and King, D. M. (1971). Improved tracing of contacts of heterosexual men with gonorrhoea. *British Journal of Venereal Diseases*, **47**, 192–195.

Felstein, I. (1974). *Sexual Pollution: The Fall and Rises of Venereal Diseases*, pp. 11, 51. Newton Abbot: David and Charles.

Ferris, P. (1971). *The House of Northcliffe*, p. 200. London: Weidenfeld and Nicolson.

Ferris, P. (1978). *Homosexuality*. New York: Simon and Schuster.

Fluker, J. L. (1966). Venereal disease and the public. *British Journal of Venereal Diseases*, **42**, 244.

Fluker, J. L. (1970). Sexually transmitted infection in school children. *Midwife and Health Visitor*, **6**, 91–96.

Galbraith, H. J. B., Graham-Stewart, C. W. and Miller, C. S. (1957). *British Medical Journal*, **ii**, 1402.

Hyde, H. M. (1960). *The Trials of Oscar Wilde*, pp. 368–369. London: William Hodge.

Hyde, J. N. and Montgomery, F. H. (1895). *A Manual of Syphilis and the Venereal Diseases*, pp. 60–65, 68–80. Philadelphia: W. B. Saunders.

Jefferiss, T. J. G. (1966). Recent trends in homosexuality, *West London. British Journal of Venereal Disease*, **42**, 243.

King, A. J. (1958). *Lancet*, **i, 651.**

Kinsey, A. C. (1978). *The Modernization of Sex*. New York: Harper and Row.

Knight, G. H. and Fowler, W. (1956). *British Medical Journal*, **ii**, 980.

Ledbetter, R. (1976). *A History of the Malthusian League 1877–1927*, p. 32. Columbus: Ohio State University Press.

Llewellyn-Jones, D. (1974). *Sex and V.D.*, pp. 16, 53. London: Faber and Faber.

Longford Report (1972). London: Hodder and Stoughton (Coronet Books).

Moore, J. E. (1951). *Lancet*, **i**, 699.

Morton, R. S. (1958). Sensitivity of the gonococci to penicillin. *British Journal of Venereal Diseases*, **34**, 81.

Morton, R. S. (1966). *Venereal Diseases*. Harmondsworth, Middlesex: Penguin Books.

Morton, R. S. (1970). Male:female ratios in the V.D. clinics of England and Wales. *British Journal of Venereal Diseases*, **46**, 103–105.

Morton, R. S. (1977). *Gonorrhoea*, pp. 90–91. Eastbourne, Sussex: W. B. Saunders.

Morton, R. S. and Harris, J. R. W. (1975). *Recent Advances in Sexually-Transmitted Diseases*, p. 374. Edinburgh: Churchill Livingstone.

Neville-Rolfe, S. (1949). *Social Biology and Welfare*, pp. 16–30. London: Allen and Unwin.

Nicol, C. S. (1961). The recrudescence of venereal diseases. *British Medical Journal*, **i**, 445–447.

Office of Health Economics (1974). *Venereal Diseases*. Economics Briefing No. 1. London: OHE.

Oller, L. Z. and Wood, T. (1970). Factors influencing the incidence of gonorrhoea and non-gonococcal urethritis in men in an industrial city. *British Journal of Venereal Diseases*, **46**, 54–57.

Oriel, J. D. (1975). Genito-urinary medicine. *British Medical Journal*, **i**, 514.

Palmer, J. (1972). Permissive statistics. *New Society*, 4th May, p. 237.

Pankhurst, C. (1913). *The Great Scourge*. London: E. Pankhurst.

Phillips, I. (1976). B-Lactamase-producing penicillin-resistant gonococcus. *Lancet*, **ii**, 656.

Pincher, C. (1973). *Sex in Our Time: The Frontiers of Modern Research*, p. 291. London: Weidenfeld and Nicolson.

Power, D'Archy (1938). Clap and the pox in English literature. *British Journal of Venereal Diseases*, **14**, 105–118.

Rae, J. (1913). *Deaths of the Kings of England*. Manchester: Sherratt and Hughes.

Rogers, R. (1971). The effects of sex education. *New Society*, **17**, 949.

Robinson, J. A. T. (1972). In *Sex and the Love Relationship*. Edited by F. Spicer. Hove, Sussex: Priory Press.

Rosebury, T. (1971). *Microbes and Morals: The Strange Story of Venereal Disease*, pp.192, 237. New York: Viking Press.

Rowntree, F. St. D. (1975). The health education. In *Recent Advances in Sexually Transmitted Diseases*. Edited by R. S. Morton and J. R. W. Harris. Edinburgh: Churchill Livingstone.

Royal Commission on Venereal Diseases (1914). *Appendix to the First Report*, Cd. 7475, pp. 1–10, 108–121. London: HMSO.

Schofield, C. B. S. (1975). *Sexually Transmitted Diseases*, Second Edition, pp. vi, 44. Edinburgh: Churchill Livingstone.

Schofield, M. (1965). *Sexual Behaviour of Young People*, p. 63. London: Longman.

Schofield, M. (1973). *The Sexual Behaviour of Young Adults: A Follow-Up Study of Young People*. Harmondsworth, Middlesex: Allen Lane.

Searle, G. R. (1976). *Eugenics and Politics in Britain, 1900–1914*, p. 11. Leiden, The Netherlands: Nordhoff International Publishing.

Sherwood, J. (1973). *No Golden Journey: A Biography of James Elroy Flecker*, p. 82. London: Heinemann.

Slaughter, J. W. (1911). *Adolescence*, p. 59. London: Swan Sonnenschein.

Social Trends (1976). No. 7, p. 145; (1977). No. 8, p. 144. London: HMSO.

Turner, G. C., Ratcliff, J. G. and Anderson, D. (1976). Penicillinase-producing neisseria gonorrhoea, *Lancet*, **ii,** 793.

Willcox, R. R. (1972). A venereological panorama. *Transactions of the Medical Society of London*, **88,** 156–164.

Winsten, S. (1951). *Salt and his Circle*. London: Hutchinson and Co.

Yeats, W. B. (1973). *Memoirs*. Edited by D. Donoghue, p. 81. London: Macmillan.

Incest: Changing Patterns of Social Response

K. L. SOOTHILL

Department of Sociology, University of Lancaster, Lancaster, England

Introduction

Over the past decade or so there has been a remarkable rise of various sociological perspectives on deviance. Central among these has been 'labelling theory',[1] which introduced the innovation of looking at the phenomenon of the social reaction to a deviant act as a separate phenomenon and so attacking the positive criminology approach which looks for causal explanations in terms of the biological or behavioural characteristics of persons seen to be guilty of deviant activities.[2] Hence, labelling theorists insist that deviance is the product of social interaction between those who engage in acts *and* those who label the behaviours as deviant. They also insist that discrediting labels are not automatically conferred upon persons who violate norms.

Probably the most influential early work outlining this new approach within the study of deviance was Howard Becker's *Outsiders* (1963) and it is interesting that he took incest as his first major example to illustrate that deviance is "the product of a transaction that takes place between some social group and one who is viewed by that group as a rule-breaker". In fact, Becker cites the example of a suicide case taken from Malinowski's (1926) study of the Trobriand Islands. The case concerned a youth who commits suicide after being publicly accused of committing incest and thus violating the clan rules of exogamy. The crucial aspect which Becker draws attention to is that incest is tolerated, though perhaps accompanied by a certain amount of disapproving local gossip, provided that the culprits are not publicly accused. When knowledge of incest is made public in the Trobriand Islands, it seems that the guilty parties are ostracized by

171

insult and degradation to such an extent that suicide by one or both offenders is seen as the only proper solution. Hence, this example illustrates the social process of definitions of deviance (e.g. whether an act is deviant depends on how other people react to it) as well as the effects of public labelling on the deviant.

Labelling theorists are essentially saying that there is no automatic, fixed and invariant relationship between behavioural acts and societal reactions to the conduct as deviant. Instead, the likelihood that behavioural occurrences will be identified publicly as deviant varies in accordance with the time at which they occur, the place where they transpire, and the individuals who observe the conduct (see Gibbons and Jones, 1975; Gibbs, 1966).

Historically, the priorities which people assign to social values change over time, e.g. it could be argued that petty theft was on a par with homicide in the nineteenth century or at least in terms of the potential sanctions which could be imposed. What I aim to do in this paper is to consider whether any changing pattern of social response towards various types of incest can be recognized over the comparatively short period of the last two or three decades. In an attempt to do this I consider the population of persons appearing as incest offenders in the higher courts of England and Wales in various years (1951, 1961 and 1976) during this period. These are persons who are, in effect, being publicly denounced for their behaviour although the numbers of the public who actually attend the ceremony (i.e. in the public gallery at the courts) or who read about the case in the newspapers (in fact, incest cases are comparatively rarely reported) are small in practice. However, a court appearance has a symbolic importance far beyond the numbers of the general public who observe the event either in court or through secondary sources, such as the media.

Labelling analysts have certainly tended to stress the importance of public labelling, especially of "status degradation ceremonies" (Garfinkel, 1956), in the development of a "deviant identity", but as Erikson (1964) has stressed, public labelling also has the function of maintaining group boundaries:

"The deviant is a person whose activities have moved outside the margins of the group, and when the community calls him to account for that vagrancy it is making a statement about the nature and placement of its boundaries. It is declaring how much variability and diversity can be tolerated within the group before it begins to lose its distinctive shape, its unique identity."

Hence, deviance can be considered as conduct which is thought to require the attention of social control agencies—i.e. conduct about which "something should be done" (Erikson, 1964)—and it can further be suggested that societies will invariably display high rates for those patterns of deviation about which its members are most "concerned" (Gibbs, 1972).

While in the late nineteenth century incest was frequently dealt with in England and Wales as rape (although in many cases it was admitted that there was no evidence of force), incest only entered the English statute law with the Punishment of Incest Act 1908. Some sources have suggested that the 'moral entrepreneurs' who brought some pressure to bring the matter of incestuous behaviour within the ambit of the ordinary criminal law were the newly developed moral welfare organizations who complained that they had no means of dissuading fathers from persisting in this behaviour. Clearly, here were social control agencies who felt around the turn of the century that incest was conduct about which "something should be done". Within these terms, how has the offence of incest fared? Has there been any indication of a modification in the boundaries or, in other words, a lessening or an increase of tolerance in this area. With the submission of evidence to the Criminal Law Revision Committee which is currently considering sexual offences, there is clearly a revival of interest in the crime of incest; the range of opinion already expressed to this Committee rather suggests that incest may be an area where the boundaries of social response have been changing or at least will be in a state of negotiation for some while yet.

Method

To consider whether and, if so, in what ways the views of social control agents have modified in the period since the Second War, the three basic samples we used were obtained from the *Criminal Statistics for England and Wales* in the years 1951, 1961 and 1976,[3] and consisted of those who were charged with incest in the higher courts. In 1951, 102 cases were recorded and in 1961, 178,[4] while in 1976 the comparable figure was 143. While most authorities would recognize that there are very different kinds of incest (e.g. father–daughter, mother–son, brother–sister, etc.) these distinctions are not made in the published *Criminal Statistics*. By studying the court calendars and information from the criminal record office, the aim has been to separate out the main groups of incest relationships for those charged in the two sample years of 1951 and 1961, and the Home Office Statistical Division kindly carried out a similar exercise for 1976.

Public Disclosure

There are probably large numbers of incest cases which never come to the attention of anybody outside the family setting. There will be other cases which may be a topic of gossip (among these will be some who are being falsely accused even at this informal level) but which never come to the formal attention of the police either because of the consent of both parties (perhaps particularly so in brother–sister incest) or because of the fear of the consequences of disclosure (perhaps more typically the case with parent–child incest). Even among parent–child incestuous relationships, while perhaps generally disapproved of, others may not necessarily regard the behaviour as important enough to 'blow the whistle'; Lukianowicz (1972) argues to the effect with regard to father–daughter incest that

> "incestuous behaviour on the part of some fathers should not necessarily be regarded as an expression of a real sexual deviation (paedophilia), but rather as an expression of a morally and socially accepted type of behaviour in some 'oversexed' and under-inhibited males in the sub-culture of certain social groups."

Even where cases of incest are disclosed many are dealt with outside the criminal law, perhaps by the family doctor, a priest, a social worker or even a close friend (James, 1970). Furthermore, no prosecution for incest can be commenced except by or with the consent of the Director of Public Prosecutions, and perhaps partly for this reason the police may sometimes prefer to use other charges— such as indecent assault or unlawful sexual intercourse—where there is not this constraining procedure (Hughes, 1964). Of those reported to the police but not brought to trial, sometimes the evidence will simply be insufficient to sustain a prosecution while in others a deliberate decision may be taken not to prosecute. Although Sir Arthur James could quite rightly stress in his talk to the Royal Medico-Psychological Association (1970) that "the offence could vary in gravity between the most vicious and revolting abuse of a position of trust, and the manifestation of true and deep affection", some recent cases involving brother–sister relationships have indicated that this is not necessarily the basis by which a decision to prosecute or not is reached. This exercise of considerable discretion is clearly an untapped future area for study. Unlike most other offences, the problem is not one of detection; once the offence becomes known to the police, in nineteen cases out of twenty the offence is 'cleared up'. However, as Table I demonstrates, only about nine or ten cases out of every twenty actually reach the stage of a trial at a higher court.

Table I

Relation between cases known to the police as incest and eventually tried as such in the higher courts

Year	Known to the police (No.)	Tried in higher courts	
		(No.)	(% of original total[a])
1951	209	102	49
1961	335	178	53
1971	307	147	48
1972	323	119	37
1973	288	129	45
1974	337	147	44
1975	349	191	55
1976	338	143	42

Source: *Criminal Statistics England and Wales*

[a] It should be remembered that in some instances the eventual classification of an offence at the trial stage may not be the one used initially by the police. A negligible proportion of incest cases are completed in the magistrates' courts but these tend to be very youthful offenders.

Table I indicates that between 1951 and 1961 there was a sizeable increase in incest offences as known to the police, but this figure has remained remarkably stable since then. Bearing in mind the increase in population over the last decade or so, this represents a proportionate decline in terms of the offence as recorded by the police. Interestingly, this largely follows the pattern in recent years of sexual offences recorded by the police, contrary to the trend for other types of offence.

Types of Incest Relationships Coming Before the Courts

Over the past three decades since the Second World War there have been changes in the type of incest cases which have been seen in the courts. The main change, however, seems to have occurred between the early 1950s and early 1960s.

Table II
Type of incest offences with which charged or found guilty in 1951, 1961 and 1976

Type of offence	1951 series (No.)	(%)	1961 series (No.)	(%)	1976 series (No.)	(%)
Parent (or grandparent) and child						
Father–daughter	55	54	124	70	116	77
Son–mother	1	1	6	3	2	1
Grandfather–granddaughter	—	—	1	1	—	—
Brother and sister						
Brother–sister	31	30	38	21	28	19
Half-brother–half-sister	4	4	4	2	2	1
Unspecified	11	11	4	2	2	1
Total	102	100	177	100	150	100

Note: Both the 1951 and 1961 series include the seven persons acquitted in each of these sample years.
Percentages do not always add up to 100 because of rounding up.

Table II indicates that in 1951 just over half the cases (55 per cent) coming before the courts were parent–child incest while around one-third (34 per cent) were brother–sister relationships. (The type of incest for the remaining 11 per cent could not be specified from the information available—in fact, if these were known, the subsequent argument about the declining proportions of brother–sister cases could only be strengthened.) However, by 1961, three-quarters of the cases coming before the courts were parent–child (or grandparent–child) incest while the proportion of brother–sister cases had fallen to less than one-quarter. The figures for 1976 suggest that the pattern for 1961 has been roughly maintained, with over three-quarters of the court cases being parent–child incest with the proportion of brother–sister cases falling still further to one-fifth. In fact, the actual numbers of court cases involving brother–sister relationships were the lowest in 1976 compared with either of the two earlier years. Within a general social context of rising crime rates this is indeed a remarkable decline in both proportional and real terms.

The change in proportions between 1951 and 1961 in father–daughter and brother–sister cases—with father–daughter cases more than doubling while brother–sister cases remain about the same—suggests two possibilities; either it reflects a change of proportions of such cases recorded by the police or a definite change in the prosecuting policy of the DPP. However, if brother–sister cases were systematically not being 'passed through' to the courts by the DPP after notification by the police, one would rather have expected a lower proportion of trials at higher courts in 1961, but this does not seem to be the case—in fact, if anything, the opposite happened in 1961, as Table I has shown. Hence, one rather suspects that proportionately fewer brother–sister cases were being reported to the police by the year 1961.

In a similar manner, the number of parent–child cases has remained remarkably steady since 1961 and so represents an apparent decline in this type of offence over recent years. Hence, the question becomes one of why has the offence of incest (rather like some other sexual offences) failed to follow the pattern of increasing crime rates over recent years—since the 1950s in the case of brother–sister incest and since the 1960s in the case of parent–child incest. There are perhaps three major possibilities which need to be considered.

1. *The incidence of the behaviour changed during the period.* Whether or not the incidence has actually changed is, of course, impossible to assess, but if one assumes (as the author does) that the number of cases of incest which reach the notice of the police is only a minute proportion of the total, questions of incidence are hardly relevant.

2. *The activity of the police changed during the period.* Unlike some other areas of illegal sexual activity (e.g. homosexuals using public lavatories for fleeting impersonal sex acts; see Humphreys, 1970), where the police can be involved 'pro-actively' (i.e. they go out and seek 'trouble'), the police can only be involved 'reactively' with incest (i.e. they react when they hear a complaint). In other words, incest is hardly an area where the police can act as, to use Becker's phrase, 'moral entrepreneurs', and so the activity of the police will not in itself be the main source of fluctuation in the figures of incest.

   There are, of course, other ways that the police may have altered their response to incest. It could be argued that nowadays the police may fail to take any relevant complaint as seriously or simply refer the matter elsewhere (e.g. to social work departments). However, when an offence of this nature is alleged to have been committed, such a response by the police is extremely unlikely in general terms. In clear-cut cases of incest the police certainly continue to see it as their duty to pass the matter on to the DPP for his decision of whether or not to prosecute. In less clear-cut cases (e.g. where there is, among other investigations, only a suspicion of incestuous activity) it is plausible to suggest that there may be an increasing reluctance by the police to follow up their suspicions if other, perhaps more appropriate, charges can be brought. This is understandable within the context of the police recognizing the high cost of higher court trials, the dangers of the shaky case being challenged by defence lawyers (after all, the complexity of some family relationships may make it difficult to know the exact blood-ties among the members), as well as the knowledge or belief of a more liberal attitude on the part of the DPP, which makes the submission of cases where there is a substantial element of doubt begin to be regarded as a waste of everyone's time and money.

3. *The number of incest cases reported to the police has proportionately declined.* While the above considerations, such as the soaring cost of higher court trials in the 1970s, are certainly relevant, not reporting to the police seems the most likely explanation as to why incest has not contributed to the general rise in crime rates since the Second World War. It is likely that people have been for some time beginning to reassess the apparent seriousness of many incest cases and have been becoming less willing than ever to involve the police. More specifically, the reactions of professionals, such as family doctors and social workers, who have had greater access to all sectors of the population since the Second World War, is probably the key variable. Alternative courses of action, whatever they may be, which do not mean reporting the matter to the police, probably first became prevalent in the 1950s for brother–sister cases (that is, parallel with the development of the National Health Service and the general rise and interest in social work) and then in the 1960s these professions possibly felt that it was inappropriate to report their suspicions to the police in a much wider range of incest cases. Hence, with incest, there has probably been developing a screening network so that the police only hear of the more serious cases or those where there is an involvement in other types of criminal activity.

The next section considers whether there has been any parallel change in the attitude of the courts towards incest offenders over the past three decades.

Disposal of Incest Offenders
Coming Before the Courts

The vast majority of incest cases which are tried in the higher courts result in a conviction—most are guilty pleas and only one in twenty are acquitted (seven persons in 1951; seven persons in 1961; eight persons in 1976).

Table III
Disposal of those dealt with for incest in 1951, 1961 and 1976

	1951 series		1961 series		1976 series	
	(No.)	(%)	(No.)	(%)	(No.)	(%)
Unfit to plead, detained during HM pleasure	1	1	1	1	—	—
Bound over, absolute or conditional discharge	6	6	9	5	5	3
Fine	—	—	—	—	1	1
Attendance centre	—	—	—	—	1	1
Supervision order	—	—	—	—	2	1
Care order	—	—	—	—	4	3
Probation order	14	15	27	16	13	9
Hospital order	1	1	5	3	1	1
Detention centre	—	—	1	1	—	—
Borstal	1	1	1	1	3	2
Suspended sentence	—	—	—	—	15	10
Immediate imprisonment						
Up to 1 year	5	5	5	3	2	1
Over 1 year but less than 2	18	19	25	15	21	14
Over 2 years but less than 3	11	12	28	16	16	11
Over 3 years but less than 4	19	20	34	20	24	16
Over 4 years but less than 5	10	11	17	10	15	10
Over 5 years but less than 10	9	9	16	9	25	17
10 years or over	—	—	—	—	2	1
Preventive detention	—	—	1	1	—	—
Total	95	100	170	100	150	100

Note: The disposals do not tally exactly with the *Criminal Statistics, England and Wales* for the categories have been changed slightly. The marginally different base for the 1976 series[3] may explain some of the higher prison sentences for this series.

Table III considers all those dealt with for incest in the three sample years. What is interesting is, despite the increase in the numbers convicted from 95 to 170, the similarity in the proportions receiving various sentences in 1951 and 1961 (in both years, 21 per cent received non-custodial sentences). However, by 1976 there are several new characteristics which have emerged. There is a marginal increase in the use of non-custodial sentences, but the use of the probation order has actually declined way below the 1951 and 1961 levels and the most frequent non-custodial sentence has become the *suspended* prison sentence. In an age when the rhetoric of rehabilitative and supportive measures is rampant, the most striking feature shown in Table III is the continued reliance on imprisonment (including suspended sentences where the reliance is on imprisonment as a deterrent) and, indeed, the increasing severity of some prison sentences in 1976.

So, rather surprisingly, the use of imprisonment for incest is as high today as it has ever been. There was actually a fall in the population receiving prison sentences in the early 1970s (more specifically, 1971–73) as Table IV shows, but this was short-lived. The increase in *non-custodial* sentences in the early 1970s was occasioned by an increased use of the suspended sentence and the continued use of the probation order in appropriate cases. Since 1973, the increase in custodial sentences for incest has not been, as one might perhaps have expected, through any disenchantment with the efficacy of the suspended sentence, but through something of a decline in the willingness to impose probation orders (in 1971, the *Criminal Statistics, England and Wales* show that there were 34 probation orders imposed by the higher courts, but by 1976 the number had fallen to 13).

Table IV
Use of sentence of immediate imprisonment by the higher courts

Year	Total found guilty in higher courts (No.)	Immediate imprisonment imposed	
		(No).	(%)
1951	94	73	78
1961	170	128	75
1970	109	76	70
1971	140	76	54
1972	107	68	64
1973	122	73	60
1974	143	100	70
1975	181	125	69
1976	133	98	74

Source: *Criminal Statistics England and Wales*

Note: 'Immediate imprisonment' includes borstal training and detention centres as well as sentences of imprisonment.

Tables III and IV, however, mask the considerable difference which has always existed between the disposals of father–daughter and brother–sister cases and also, in particular, the trend in dealing with the latter. Thomas (1970) has pointed out how, in all cases of incest involving parents, the Court of Appeal "takes a stern view of the offence and sentences in the region of six years' imprisonment are common". Thomas is, of course, talking of those cases which reach the Court of Appeal and this length of sentence is by no means the norm. However, as Table V demonstrates, virtually all father–daughter cases have received custodial sentences. The only modification by 1976 was that about one in ten (11 per cent) who in previous sample years would almost certainly have received immediate imprisonment were given *suspended* prison sentences. Although in one sense this is an interesting shift to a non-custodial sentence, the abiding concept of the higher courts for this type of incest behaviour is that essentially a term of imprisonment (albeit now a suspended one

Table V
Sentences imposed for father–daughter and brother–sister cases in 1951, 1961 and 1976

	Father–daughter cases			Brother–sister cases		
	1951 (%)	1961 (%)	1976 (%)	1951 (%)	1961 (%)	1976 (%)
Bound over or conditional discharge	4	2	1	12	12	4
Fine	—	—	—	—	—	4
Attendance centre	—	—	—	—	—	4
Supervision order	—	—	—	—	—	7
Care order	—	—	—	—	—	11
Probation order	—	3	2	36	54	36
Hospital order	—	2	—	3	7	4
Detention centre	—	—	—	—	2	—
Borstal	—	—	—	3	—	11
Suspended sentence	—	—	11	—	—	4
Immediate imprisonment						
Up to 3 years	31	39	31	45	22	11
Over 3 years but less than 5	50	40	33	—	2	4
5 years or more	15	13	22	—	—	4
Preventive detention	—	1	—	—	—	—
Total	100	100	100	100	100	100
Total no. of persons	52	117	116	33	41	28

Note: In this table, son–mother, grandfather–granddaughter and unspecified cases have been disregarded (see Table II).

for a small minority of those offenders) is the appropriate sentence.

In contrast to father–daughter cases, where there has been little change in sentencing policy so that, since the Second World War, the choice of imprisonment remains steadfastly virtually the only option in the thinking of the judiciary, there have been noticeable differences with regard to sentencing brother–sister incest cases. Between 1951 and 1961 the proportion sent to prison had almost halved (from 45 to 24 per cent) while there was a considerable increase in the use of probation (from 36 to 54 per cent). In fact, by 1961 probation was used more than any other type of disposal for brother–sister incest cases. However, by 1976, while non-custodial sentences continued to predominate over custodial sentences, the actual use of probation had declined even below the 1951 level—12 cases were placed on probation in 1951, 22 cases in 1961 and only 10 cases in 1976 (the increase in other types of disposal, e.g. care and supervision orders, is largely the result of including some cases dealt with by magistrates' courts in the 1976 sample but which were excluded in the earlier series).

To summarize the view of the courts, it would appear that a consistently serious and punitive attitude has been taken towards father–daughter cases throughout the period, while a more lenient and social work oriented attitude towards most brother–sister relationships developed in the courts during the 1950s, and by 1961 a straightforward custodial sentence was becoming rather unusual for the latter type of incest offence. By 1976, however, while the general reluctance to impose custodial sentences for brother–sister cases remained, the use of the probation order had declined somewhat. Perhaps the brother–sister cases which eventually reach the courts tend to be those for whom social work intervention has already been tried in some form and failed. What, of course, is not known from the information available for this study is the type of case which is in fact coming before the courts. A brother–sister case where there is the consent of both parties is likely to be regarded in a somewhat different light by the courts from a case where there is a clear-cut perpetrator and victim.

Criminal History of Offenders
Appearing Before the Courts

With such a high element of discretion relating to whether or not it is regarded as appropriate to prosecute, it is of interest to know whether there is any difference in the criminal history of the offenders who actually appear before the courts in the three sample years. One of the possibilities is that prosecution may be seen increasingly as the way to handle cases where there is evidence of previous convictions or findings of guilt, while persons with no previous convictions may, other things being equal, tend not to be sent for trial and simply be given a formal warning. Certainly, in recent years where the dangers of labelling persons as criminals have been stressed, one might expect such a trend for offences where there is discretion to prosecute. Table VI begins to suggest that something of this pattern was beginning to emerge between 1951 and 1961, for whereas in 1951 over two-thirds of those before the courts for incest had no previous convictions, this proportion had fallen to 57 per cent by 1961. However, this apparent change should be regarded with considerable caution; the fact that only 71 per cent of the criminal records could be traced for the 1951 series compared with 94 per cent for the 1961 series and all those in the 1976 series could be a serious source of bias. More significant is the really quite remarkable similarity in the criminal history of the 1961 and 1976 series, where 57 per cent of the former and 56 per cent of the latter had no previous criminal convictions. These figures certainly seem to undermine any belief that a rather different (and perhaps more serious) group of incest offenders are coming before the courts these days. At least in terms of their *previous* criminal record there has been remarkably little change and no evidence at all that there has been any change in prosecution policy in this direction.

Table VI
Total number of previous convictions for standard-list offences[a] for 1951, 1961 and 1976 incest cases

	1951 series		1961 series		1976 series	
	(No.)	(%)	(No.)	(%)	(No.)	(%)
None	50	69	94	57	84	56
One	13	18	32	19	36	24
Two	0	—	17	10	13	9
Three or more	9	13	23	14	17	11
Total	72	100	166	100	150	100

[a] In this and Table VII only standard-list offences are counted as these are recorded systematically by the police and include all the more serious offences.

The similarity between 1961 and 1976 still holds if, as in Table VII, father–daughter and brother–sister cases are considered separately. It has already been noted elsewhere with regard to the 1961 series (Gibbens et al., 1978) that "a surprising feature is that the convicted siblings, though the great majority were not over 20, had many more previous convictions or findings of guilt than the fathers". In fact, previous offences of violence or sex were quite uncommon among the siblings and

> "the high rate of juvenile and young adult property offences may indicate that the supervision of probation officers had made (incest) behaviour more visible or more readily brought to light by parents who were under 'social observation'."

The group of fathers had a distinctly higher rate of previous convictions for sex offences (13 per cent) than the siblings (5 per cent) but the age factor could, of course, be important.

Table VII
Total number of previous convictions for father–daughter and brother–sister cases in 1951, 1961 and 1976

	Father–daughter cases			Brother–sister cases		
	1951 (%)	1961 (%)	1976 (%)	1951 (%)	1961 (%)	1976 (%)
None	76	61	59	63	46	43
One	17	16	20	20	27	39
Two	—	10	8	—	15	14
Three or more	7	14	13	17	12	4
Total	100	100	100	100	100	100
Total no. of persons	41	114	116	30	41	28

Note: For ease of presentation, cases other than father–daughter or brother–sister incest have been excluded from this table.

Of the 166 persons in 1961 where the complete criminal record was traced, 20 individuals (or 12 per cent) had previous sex offences but only three of these cases were unequivocally shown from the criminal record to have previous incest-type offences (in two cases, incest was the charge while in the remaining case the conviction was for 'indecent assault on daughter aged 5'). By contrast, among the 150 persons in the 1976 series there was a slightly higher proportion with previous incest-type offences—four of the fathers had a previous conviction for incest, one had a previous conviction for attempted incest and one had a previous conviction for raping his daughter; in addition, two of the brothers had a previous conviction for incest.

The Impact of Societal Reaction on the Incest Offender

In the present study we have no information on the detailed impact of the court appearance on the lives of these publicly accused incest offenders. Unlike Malinowski's Trobriand Islander, guilty parties will probably not see suicide as the only proper solution for any ostracism they may suffer. However, a central claim among most labelling theorists is that the stigma of the criminal label drives persons further into deviance. In addition, the vast majority of father–daughter incest offenders (almost certainly regarded as the more dangerous threats to the community) receive prison sentences and labelling theorists often stress how institutions such as prisons actually push persons further into criminality. Undoubtedly such extremely simple and gross claims tend to be polemical rather than backed up by systematic evidence. As Gibbons and Jones (1975) suggest,

> "labelling notions concerning the alleged harmful effects of correctional experiences are at present quite inchoate and, most likely, they are defective. Stated another way, whatever the relationships between correctional intervention activities and deviant careers, they are complex and multi-faceted".

Table VIII demonstrates that for the majority the incest conviction is their last conviction. In fact, three-quarters of both series are not reconvicted for any standard-list offence during the follow-up period up to 1974. Despite the different lengths of follow-up for each series the similarities are quite striking. This seems quite surprising in view of the more extensive previous records of many offenders in the 1961 sample. While this could be (and probably is) a function of the shorter follow-up period of the 1961 sample and one might therefore expect a further build-up of reconvicted cases in the next few years, this is by no means the only explanation; instead the different contributions of the two main sub-groups should be considered.

Table VIII
Total number of subsequent convictions for 1951 and 1961 series

	1951		1961	
	(No.)	(%)	(No.)	(%)
None	53	74	129	78
One	8	11	20	12
Two	6	8	8	5
Three or more	5	7	8	5
Total	72	100	165[a]	100

[a] In addition there was one person who was deported, so the subsequent reconviction check is not fully available.

As Table IX shows, the proportions of the father–daughter group reconvicted for some offence is really quite low for both series—one should stress that for the 1961 series the prison sentence received by the majority somewhat curtails the follow-up period for many, but there is not this problem for the 1951 series. By contrast, four out of ten of the brother–sister group (1951 series) are subsequently reconvicted and this rises for the 1961 series, despite the shorter follow-up period, to one-half of the group; however, as we have shown in Table VII, the previous record of the 1961 series is somewhat worse, so this is not an unexpected finding.

Table IX
Total number of subsequent convictions for father–daughter and brother–sister cases in 1951 and 1961

	Father–daughter cases		Brother–sister cases	
	1951 (%)	1961 (%)	1951 (%)	1961 (%)
None	85	88	60	51
One	7	8	17	24
Two	5	3	13	12
Three or more	2	2	10	12
Total	100	100	100	100
Total no. of persons	41	114	30	41

The question arises with respect to parent and sibling incest how much of the difference is largely due to age. Certainly an inspection of the subsequent records fails to suggest that the stigma of the criminal label of incest and the severe sanction of imprisonment will tend to push the father–daughter incest offenders further into criminality. In fact, it is perhaps questionable whether the routinely heavy sentences for some of these men are justified (the subsequent criminal records for both groups in the 1961 series have already been considered more fully elsewhere; see Gibbens *et al.*, 1978).

Discussion

During the past quarter of a century there have been several occasions when there has been formal examination and discussion of the intersect between the criminal law and sexual behaviour. In the 1950s there were the deliberations of the Wolfenden Committee which set the scene for some legislative realignment in the 1960s of what should be included under the criminal law. In 1975 we had the report of the Heilbron Committee on ways to protect the interests of the rape victim prior to and during the court process. Now the Criminal Law Revision Committee and the Policy Advisory Committee on Sexual Offences are currently considering sexual offences, including incest.

However, changes do not await the counsels of such committees which probably tend to codify rather than make innovative suggestions. By a detailed analysis of material derived from the *Criminal Statistics* one can already begin to plot some changing patterns of social response towards types of incest since the Second World War.

Certainly labelling analysis has been particularly useful in border-line forms of deviance (e.g. drug use) where there is a lack of social consensus on how such behaviour ought to be regarded and dealt with, and labelling processes have become crucial in shaping outcomes, but as Schur (1971) mentions, "those deviations on which widespread consensus exists (homicide, incest, and so on) (seem) less promising candidates for the emphasis on labelling". However, elsewhere Schur stresses that "it is true that within a given society there may be widepsread consensus on negative evaluations of certain forms of behaviour, though not necessarily on the intensity and methods of implementing such evaluations". It is precisely a certain measure of change in the intensity and methods of implementing the negative evaluations that the present study has begun to chart.

More specifically, there have almost certainly been changes in the social response to incest although there are considerable variations according to the type of incest involved. The category of incest seemed to follow the general increase of crime rates between 1951 and 1961, but this study reveals that there was a sizeable fall in the proportions of brother–sister cases which actually reached the courts. It is suggested that this reflects a fall in cases reported to the police rather than a change in prosecuting policy. Hence, there is probably the beginning of a reluctance by members of the public to 'blow the whistle' in cases of brother–sister incest, although there is little doubt that a widespread consensus continues to exist regarding such incestuous relationships. The reluctance to involve the police in such cases has continued so that, by 1976, brother–sister incest has become an almost residual sub-group in the offence category of incest. Only by a careful study of these individual cases can one fully understand the type of behaviour which is still felt officially to need the intervention of the criminal law, but this exercise was beyond the scope of the present study.

The proportional decline of brother–sister cases in the decade between 1951 and 1961 was matched by a further shift towards non-custodial sentences awarded by the courts and so there is clear evidence that 'official labellers' (i.e. the courts) were tending to take a less punitive line in such cases. Hence, it would seem that both the general public and the courts were taking a more tolerant attitude towards brother–sister incest by the early 1960s. Perhaps not surprisingly, this seems to have continued up to the present time. Whether or not there has been any change in actual behaviour over this period is almost pure speculation. However, during a period when premarital sex became more acceptable, it could well be that both brothers and sisters were tending to look and find sexual satisfaction outside the family (a decline in brother–sister incest among those aged between 21 and 29 does, in fact, emerge in this study and goes some way to substantiate this point).

By contrast, there seems to have been no comparable change of attitude towards father–daughter incest during the earlier period (1951–61). The number of such cases reaching the higher courts had more than doubled in the ten-year period. Again, assuming no change in prosecution policy, this suggests that many more of these cases were being reported to the police by the general public. The stability of father–daughter cases in terms of numbers between 1961 and 1976—going against the general trend of rising crime rates—is somewhat more problematic to explain. Certainly the police are probably more reluctant to involve themselves in high court cases (which are expensive in terms of both cost and police time) where there is much element of doubt and may prefer, where appropriate, alternative charges which do not involve the DPP. However, this can only be a partial factor and it could well be that fewer such cases do in fact come to the notice of the police these days.

What should be considered more fully in any future study of incest are the possibly changing attitudes of the medical and social work professions towards this offence since the Second World War. Nowadays, it is probably these professions rather than the police who mediate the social response to this behaviour. In the 1950s the development of the National Health Service and the beginnings of the expansion of the social work professions perhaps provided the source of many complaints about father–daughter cases—after all, it had similarly been the newly developed moral welfare organizations at the turn of the century who had complained that they had no means of dissuading fathers from persisting in this behaviour and who had provided some of the thrust for the 1908 legislation. Subsequently, however, it could well be that, except in the more extreme cases, these same professions have been more and more reluctant to involve the heavy instrument of the criminal law. To some extent this could be seen as a reaction to the attitude of the courts who have, throughout the period, taken an extremely serious view of the father–daughter cases, almost invariably imprisoning the offender. To the interested professional observer of these cases, the simple distinction between a formal warning if the DPP decides not to prosecute and a long term of imprisonment if he does proceed may seem a very blunt instrument indeed. It is certainly a dilemma for doctors and social workers, for, apart from being involved in this particular offence, paternal incest offenders do not appear generally to engage in a range of other types of criminal behaviour. A study of the previous and subsequent criminal history of these offenders rather indicates that whatever machinery of control might be imposed on these persons they are not such a general menace to the community as some stereotypes of sex offenders might suggest. Whatever truth, if any, there is in such stereotypes the parent–child incest offender should not be part of them.

Conclusion

The current review of sexual offences by the Criminal Law Revision Committee will almost certainly open up the question of whether, or in what form, to retain the crime of incest. Already, for example, the National Council of Civil Liberties has recommended in its evidence to the committee that the crime of incest should be abolished. This type of question raises a whole plethora of issues which cannot be considered here. However, some points can be stated which seem to emerge from the present study.

1. During the 1950s persons probably began to be less interested in reporting cases of brother–sister incest to the police. In other words, brother–sister incest should not too readily be regarded nowadays as behavioural transgressions necessarily exceeding the tolerance limits of the community (whether it should be so regarded, say, on genetic grounds, is a totally different issue). Since the early 1960s there is some evidence that with parent–child cases, too, there is an increasing reluctance to involve the police.

2. The increasing tendency towards non-custodial sentences suggests that by 1961, the courts already thought of brother–sister cases generally as needing help (i.e. in the form of probation orders) rather than punishment (i.e. prison sentences) (Whether the help offered is appropriate—perhaps keeping the couple separate—is again a totally different issue). By contrast, the punitive attitude of the courts towards parent–child incest offenders has been remarkably consistent throughout the period.

3. Finally, it is recognized that the question of what *should* be our response to incest offenders has been deliberately avoided. However, one point is perhaps helpful to note in forming the appropriate response. Elsewhere (Gibbens *et al.*, 1978) we have considered the 1961 series in more depth and it seems that brother–sister offenders are more of a threat to property values and there is little evidence at all that they are general sexual predators. In a similar manner, the vast majority of father–daughter offenders do not seem the general threat to the community as some may have assumed. It should be clearly recognized that if these type of incest cases continue to be treated harshly this should not be because they are thought of as a *future* threat for they rarely are. It means that their behaviour is regarded as requiring retribution from society, for they have abused their parental rights and responsibilities. Certainly the criminal law is an extremely clumsy instrument in the sphere of sexual behaviour. However, there are certain situations which are, by almost universal agreement, extreme and where the

criminal law must then intervene. The problem remains one of recognizing those situations.

Acknowledgements

This study derives from a larger study (under the general direction of Professor T. C. N. Gibbens and originally supported by a grant from the Social Science Research Council) on the recidivism of serious sexual offenders. The coding and basic analysis was carried out by Mrs C. K. Way, B.Sc. (Econ), formerly Research Assistant, Institute of Psychiatry, London.

The author is grateful to the Home Office Research Unit and the Home Office Statistical Division for providing the material for this study. The paper is published with the consent of the Home Office but this does not imply agreement with the views expressed.

Notes

1. Variously called 'societal reactions approach', 'interactionism', 'social processual approach' etc. (see Becker, 1974; Schur, 1971).
2. See Taylor *et al*. (1973, Chapters 1–4) for a discussion and critique of the positivist approach.
3. The material for the years 1951 and 1961 derive from the work undertaken for a long-term follow-up study on the recidivism rates of serious sexual offenders (see Gibbens *et al*., 1977, 1978; Soothill *et al*., 1976; Soothill and Gibbens, 1978). The Home Office kindly agreed, for the purposes of this paper, to supplement our data with comparable material for a more recent year, namely 1976. The Home Office, in fact, followed up *all* persons convicted in 1976 of incest, including those who were convicted of incest at the Crown Court where some other offence was the principal offence; hence the figures do not tally exactly with those published in the *Criminal Statistics* for 1976 as they are compiled on a slightly different basis. The Home Office did not consider those who were acquitted of incest in 1976.
4. *Criminal Statistics, England and Wales 1961* show 178 cases of incest (classification 23), but we suspect that an individual who had two multi-punch cards (though appearing only once in the court calendars) had been wrongly counted twice. Therefore, we have taken 177 as our base number.

References

Becker, H. S. (1963). *Outsiders.* **New York**: Free Press of Glencoe.

Becker, H. S. (1974). Labelling theory reconsidered. In *Deviance and Social Control*. Edited by P. Rock and M. McIntosh. London: Tavistock Publications.

Criminal Statistics for England and Wales for the years 1951, 1961 and 1976.

Erikson, K. T. (1964). Notes on the sociology of deviance. In *The Other Side*. Edited by H. S. Becker. New York: Free Press of Glencoe.

Garfinkel, H. (1956). Conditions of successful degration ceremonies. *American Journal of Sociology*, **61,** 420–424.

Gibbens, T. C. N., Way, C. K. and Soothill, K. L. (1977). Behavioural types of rape. *British Journal of Psychiatry*, **130,** 32–42.

Gibbens, T. C. N., Way, C. K. and Soothill, K. L. (1978). Sibling and parent–child incest offenders. *British Journal of Criminology*, **18,** No. 1.

Gibbons, D. C. and Jones, J. F. (1975). *The Study of Deviance: Perspectives and Problems*. Englewood Cliffs, New Jersey and Hemel Hempstead: Prentice–Hall.

Gibbs, J. P. (1966). Conceptions of deviant behaviour: the old and the new. *Pacific Sociological Review*, **9** (Spring), 9–14.

Gibbs, J. P. (1972). Issues in defining deviant behaviour. In *Theoretical Perspectives on Deviance*, p. 39–68. Edited by R. A. Scott and J. D. Douglas, New York: Basic Books.

Heilbron Report (1975). *Report of the Advisory Group on the Law of Rape*. Cmnd. 6352. London: HMSO.

Hughes, G. (1964). The crime of incest. *Journal of Criminal Law, Criminology and Police Science*, **55,** 322–331.

Humphreys, L. (1970). *Tearoom Trade*. Chicago: Aldine.

James, Sir A. (1970). Address given to the Royal Medico-Psychological Association. Reported in *The Guardian*, 21.11.70.

Lukianowicz, N. (1972). I. Paternal incest. II. Other types of incest. *British Journal of Psychiatry*. **120,** 301–313.

Malinowski, B. (1926). *Crime and Custom in Savage Society*. London: Routledge and Kegan Paul.

Schur, E. M. (1971). *Labelling Deviant Behaviour*. London: Harper and Row.

Soothill, K. L. and Gibbens, T. C. N. (1978). Recidivism of sexual offenders: a reappraisal. *British Journal of Criminology*, **18,** No. 3.

Soothill, K. L., Jack, A. and Gibbens, T. C. N. (1976). Rape: a 22-year cohort study. *Medicine, Science and the Law*, **16,** 62–69.

Soothill, K. L., Way, C. K. and Gibbens, T. C. N. (In press). Rape acquittals. *Modern Law Review*.

Taylor, I., Walton, P. and Young, J. (1973). *The New Criminology*. London: Routledge and Kegan Paul.

Thomas, D. A. (1970). *Principles of Sentencing*. London: Heinemann.

Wolfenden Report (1957). *Report of the Committee on Homosexual Offences and Prostitution*. Cmnd. 247. London: HMSO.

The Development of Sexual Function Therapies after Masters and Johnson

P. T. BROWN

Frederick Chusid and Company Limited,
London, England

I propose to address the title of this paper under three particular heads.

Whilst the publication of *Human Sexual Inadequacy* by Masters and Johnson in 1970 marks the beginning of an explosive clinical and popular interest in what at that time started to be called the treatment of sexual dysfunctions, its autochthonous aspects reveal, on close examination, antecedents that potentiated the uptake of Masters' and Johnson's work. I shall in the first place, therefore, offer a brief historical view of the main streams of socio-clinical thinking which I believe caused this effect in the acceptance of their work.

In the second place, and as the central theme of the paper, I shall digress upon the actual state of the development of sexual function therapies in the eight years since *Human Sexual Inadequacy*. In this I have been helped by the timely appearance of a review of the effectiveness of sex therapy in the American literature by Hogan (1978), of the State University of New York at Stony Brook. However, I shall hope to make some observations upon the situation from a particularly British point of view.

Thirdly, I propose to speculate a little, again from a somewhat culturally bound perspective, upon the future development of sexual function therapies in the context of our rapidly changing times.

From an historical viewpoint we could hardly avoid starting with Freud—not only because of the centrality of his work in our dawning awareness of the aetiology of the sexual life, but because the publication of Masters' and Johnson's physiological work in 1966/7, and its antecedent papers, occasioned a good deal of critical reappraisal of the psychoanalytic position in the psychoanalytic literature of the middle and late sixties.

The psychoanalytic model of sexual difficulties rests upon the observations of Freud that the maturation of sexuality from infancy to its reproductive capacity involves the inseparable and interrelated processes of physiological maturation and psychological development. In normal development these processes lead to an integration which enables the individual to find expressions of sexual drive within the requirements of the culture in which he or she is raised and/or lives. Thus men and women reach their psychosexual maturity through the reconciliation of sexual drives within the requirements of their super-egos.

Particular odium has attached to the Freudian discussion of female sexual function. Deriving its model of female functioning from the genital primacy of male functioning, in which the reproductive function requires an act which is consummated in sexual coitus and orgasm, the psychosexual maturity of women was unwittingly characterized by a genital primacy that, parallel to male function, was to culminate in vaginal orgasm. Accordingly, vaginal orgasm implied a transfer of clitoral sensation to the vagina, thus eliminating the "residual male organ" called the clitoris (Freud, 1933; in Benedek, 1968). This concept was made the measure of psychosexual maturity, was often the goal of psychoanalytic treatment, and gave rise to the vaginal–clitoral transfer theory of female psychosexual development.

In *Beyond the Pleasure Principle* Freud (1920) recorded the hope that there might one day be an explanation of female sexuality from biology which would ". . . be of a kind that would blow away all of our artificial structure of hypotheses . . ." about female sexuality. In their physiological work Masters and Johnson (1966) made some claim to have provided the explanation for which Freud hoped. Indeed, Sherfey (1966) asserts that Masters and Johnson met that hope more than adequately by describing the function of the clitoris as a receptor of sensation, and delineating the physiological processes and anatomical consequences arising from the vasodilative effects of sexual arousal which culminate in the perceived sensations of orgasm through the mediation of the orgasmic platform. As a psychoanalyst, however, Helen Deutsch had expressed her conviction in 1961, based upon her clinical insights, that:

"the female sexual apparatus consists of two parts with a definite division of function. The clitoris is the sexual organ and the vagina primarily an organ of reproduction. The central role of the clitoris is not merely the result of (infantile) masturbation but serves a biological destiny. Into it flow waves of sexual excitement which may more or less successfully be communicated to the vagina".

Pines (1968) observed that these views seem compatible with Masters' and Johnson's finding, and observes upon the marked concordance of laboratory and psychoanalytic evidence. In 1961, Benedek also asserted her clinical view that the sexual sensations that begin in the clitoris spread to the vaginal walls and finally encompass the whole body in orgasm and that it is the women's personality (her ego organization) that allows the clitoral stimulation to spread and be experienced as orgasm.

In this country (England) the most widespread effect of Freudian thinking has been in the brief psychotherapy work developed by Balint and reported by Friedman (1961) for (especially) female psychosexual difficulties, and it is this school of thought that has been the prime inspiration of the training of medical practitioners in the remedy of psychosexual disorders under the auspices of the Family Planning Association. Before 1970, therefore, and whatever the outcome of the discussion as to whether Freud and his followers were right or not, and whether Masters and Johnson have disproved or supported these observations and whether or not the analysts had described it all correctly from a clinical standpoint before Masters and Johnson provided the laboratory evidence, the psychoanalytic stream of thought inspired the only widespread systematic approach to the treatment of sexual difficulties.

The second antecedent to Masters' and Johnson's work is perhaps best thought of as a sociological stream. It derives its importance from the presentation of factual data which establish the basis for normative thinking within the culture. Of prime significance is the work of Kinsey in the States (Kinsey *et al.*, 1948, 1953), and of Chesser (1956) and, more recently, Schofield (1968) in this country. While Freud might have begun to develop the understanding of sexuality in relation to the integration of adult development, it was Kinsey and his colleagues who told us what these adults did with their integration. Whilst certain explicit cultural sexual conventions might be one thing, Kinsey showed that private sexual practice might be quite another and his work paved the way for a concordat between public and private understandings of sexuality. Whatever the strength of the rejection of Kinsey's observations at the time of their first presentation, and of the criticisms that derived from pedantic approaches to the methodology of sampling and interviewing, there can now be no doubt that Kinsey's work established an acceptance of normative observations about sexual behaviour. Of course, there are those who questioned, and still question, whether the providing of factual information might not simply provoke a whole new range of sexual problems. I suppose that for a time it might. But we can recognize and properly guard against a too-mechanical view of sex, which is not the case if we do not know the mechanics. Ignorance in the sexual function field is not a happy state, nor conducive to any kind of bliss.

There is a third stream which defies classification, but is best exemplified by the work of Marie Stopes (e.g. 1923) and, more recently, Dr Martin Cole (personal communication). The essence of this stream is that, from outside the established helping professions, occasional individuals respond to the needs of society as they see it at the time and focus upon themselves and their actions a good deal of the prevailing conflicting attitudes about the active expression of sexuality in the sexual behaviour current at the period. Stopes, of course, centred her interest upon contraception and the resulting possibilities for the enjoyment of sexual expression. Cole has centred his most recent interests upon the systematic exploration of the use of surrogate partners in sexual function work, and in a series of 59 males using female surrogates and 16 females using male surrogates has established immediate outcome rates of 80 per cent success in males and 72 per cent in women.

The importance of this stream lies in the development of discussion about sexual matters within the society of the time, and in both the examples quoted above providing a lead to inherently cautious clinical professions. Perhaps in an analagous way, though not by such clear intention, the influence upon sexual attitudes of physiological research in the field of reproduction should not go unrecorded. Francoeur (1974) has observed that current research into reproductive biology is increasingly separating the concept of reproduction from the sexual act. He notes that artificial insemination, frozen human sperm banks commercially accessible, embryo transplantation, artificial wombs, asexual reproduction and cloning, predetermination of foetal sex, uterine transplants, embryo fusions and even transsexual operations, are all now matters of active scientific pursuit and popular knowledge which impinge extensively but often unconsciously upon our under-standing of ourselves as sexual beings. Where once the sexual act itself was the only means of establishing reproduction, and was entirely bound up with the mysteries of generation, current scientific advances can make it increasingly irrelevant for that purpose. It leaves us with a vacuum as to what the sexual act is *for*.

The resurgence of behaviour therapy in the late 1950s, under the stimulation of Wolpe's (1958) contribution regarding the principles of systematic desensitization, contributes the fourth main stream in establishing the groundwork for Masters' and Johnson's acceptance. Rachman (1961) provides an early review of behaviour therapy in sexual disorders, though the term 'sexual disorders' included difficulties now distinguished as sexual dysfunctions as well as sexual variations, among which latter in the context of the time homosexuality was included. Feingold (1966) set the behaviour therapy approach to sexual problems in the wider context of the treatment of social problems and it is not surprising that by 1972 the behaviour therapists had begun to incorporate Masters' and Johnson's ideas into a much clearer behavioural approach to the treatment of sexual difficulties, with the development of modifications of Masters' and Johnson's treatment programmes for a National Health Service setting (Bancroft, 1972; Brown and Kolaszynska-Carr, 1972; Kockott *et al.*, 1975).

I am making the case, of course, for the appearance of Masters' and Johnson's work in 1970 as the apotheosis of these streams. In actual fact the case is only a fabrication. It was an extraordinary facet of the appearance of *Human Sexual Inadequacy* in 1970—at least to this excited observer on this side of the Atlantic—that their clinical work was presented in such a well developed form *de novo*. It is a weakness of *Human Sexual Inadequacy* that it proposes an essentially a-theoretical treatment procedure yet, at the same time, a tremendous strength that its pragmatism is so firmly underpinned by laboratory investigations of normal sexual behaviour from which the treatment package was derived. It is this, of course, which established Masters and Johnson in their apotheotic position. For the first time in the clinical literature we have the description of treatment procedures for sexual difficulties which are based upon observations of a most rigorous and replicable kind. Thus Masters and Johnson institute the scientific stream, as well as being the inheritors, whether they like it or not, of those precursors that I have noted.

When we look at the development of sexual function therapy since 1970, four broad generalizations may be made. In the first place there has been a trend towards setting Masters' and Johnson's work in a wider clinical context. In the second place there has been an increased impetus towards the development of specific behavioural techniques. In the third place there has been a boom in the provision of treatment packages. In the fourth, there has been a small amount of work designed to investigate the effectiveness of the component parts of Masters' and Johnson's treatment proposals. I shall exemplify all four categories.

So far as setting Masters' and Johnson's work in a wider clinical context, Helen Singer Kaplan (1974) is pre-eminent in this field. Her book *The New Sex Therapy* will, I suspect, be recognized as the classic work on sexual function therapy in this decade. Without providing detailed statistical results in her work she has provided extensive clinical details which widen the basis of Masters' and Johnson's formulation of the aetiology of sexual difficulties. Masters and Johnson, you will recall, considered ignorance and fear, whether singly or in combination, the main progenitors of sexual difficulties in adult life. Kaplan ranges over the available psychological and psychiatric knowledge to demonstrate the multiple causes of sexual difficulties, whose remedy may nevertheless lie in a relatively simple and structured approach to the learning or relearning of sexual behaviours and attitudes.

Kaplan has also sought to clarify the diagnostic concepts in the field which Masters and Johnson themselves had reformulated. Masters and Johnson, it will be recalled, classified four main sexual dysfunctions in each sex: in the male, primary and secondary impotence, premature ejaculation and ejaculatory incompetence; in the female, primary orgasmic dysfunction and the three categories of situational orgasmic dysfunction (coital, masturbatory and random). They noted that dyspareunia appeared in both sexes and that, in the female, vaginismus and dyspareunia might be precursors to orgasmic difficulty. Kaplan observed that Masters and Johnson had not entirely followed the logic of their physiological findings and indeed had overcomplicated their physiological findings in describing the sexual response cycle. Again I am sure it will be remembered that Masters and Johnson described a four-stage process of sexual arousal in the now commonly referred to stages of arousal, plateau, orgasm and resolution. Kaplan felt that this four-stage process refined their observations without due cause, and that in fact they had observed a two-stage process of sexual function—arousal itself, which at an appropriate and variable degree of intensity results in the trigger response of orgasm. The first part is dependent upon increasing vasodilation in both male and female while the second is dependent upon an appropriate intensity of stimulation provoking involuntary muscular reflexes which are experienced as orgasmic ejaculation in the man and orgasmic pulsing in the woman.

In consequence of these observations Kaplan felt that a revised diagnostic formulation would be helpful in which disorders of arousal would be clearly distinguished from disorders of response. In the male, therefore, she called disorders of arousal erectile insufficiency, in the hope of abolishing the pejorative word 'impotence' and, again in the male, the responsive disorders were agreed as premature and retarded ejaculation. In the female she observed that the sexual response is both more complex and widely diffused throughout the body than in the male, and refers to the disorders of sexual arousal as being those of general sexual dysfunction, while disorders of response are referred to as disorders of general orgasmic dysfunction. Masters and Johnson had concentrated in their formulation upon the orgasmic difficulties of the woman rather than arousal difficulties.

In the work that I completed for the National Marriage Guidance Council in 1976 it was felt that both these systems of categorization, though an improvement upon such previous concepts as frigidity, were in fact too limited. They isolated vaginismus, which is a specific, inhibiting reflex response in the woman upon attempts at intromission, and also failed to deal in a classificatory way with disorders of drive. In consequence I have proposed a classificatory system (Brown, 1976; Brown and Faulder, 1978) in which we observe not only disorders of arousal and disorders of response in both male and female, but also disorders of intromission which, as I have already observed, is called 'vaginismus' in the woman. In the male we observe circumstances in which there is a catastrophic loss of erection upon the attempt at intromission. It appears to be the male analogue of vaginismus, rendering effective penetration impossible, and it is likely that its aetiology is similar. We have in consequence referred to this disorder as a specific diagnostic category in its own right and as it is the opposite of the disorder which involves permanent erection, called priapism, we have labelled it 'anapriapism'.

It is also apparent that some couples, as Masters and Johnson observe, present with disorders of sexual drive. This is of course a problem when one member of a partnership has a level of drive which is much higher or lower than the other. While the concept of drive is a difficult concept to elucidate, we may for the sake of argument assume that it is distributed within the population as if fulfilling the characteristics of a normal curve, so that we might expect to see difficulties associated with low sexual drive (hyposexuality) and disorders associated with high drive (hypersexuality). Thus we have taken the view that the adequate development of sexual function therapy will, in part, depend upon an adequate classification structure which not only allows proper discussion to proceed but permits the comparison of results. The view is offered, therefore, that a categorization which included disorders of arousal, disorders of response, disorders of intromission and disorders of drive will adequately exhaust the phenomena that present as disorders of sexual function, and will be distinguished from those disorders of sexuality that used to be called perversions and are now called variations (Kaplan, 1974). Despite limitations in classification, however, Kaplan is pre-eminent as a clinician who has integrated Masters' and Johnson's work into the broad stream of our knowledge about psychological disturbance.

On the behavioural side, Annon (1974) has provided a structured approach which attempts to offer a broad-span behavioural approach therapy based on differing levels of therapist intervention. He develops a mnemonic called 'plissit'. At the first level the therapist acts as a source of permission (P). It is alright to be sexual. At the second level limited information (LI) may be provided. At the third level—the level encompassed by Masters' and Johnson's work—specific suggestions (SS) for the development of sexual behaviours will be provided. At the fourth level intensive therapy (IT) is indicated, which in behavioural terms might also involve wide-span training in social and sexual assertiveness. Lobitz and LoPiccolo (1972) have been particularly active in developing detailed behaviour programmes for the remedy of specific disorders, and their masturbatory training programmes emphasize the use to which observations of normal sexual development can be put in a social context freed from fear and inappropriate guilt concerning the pleasurable functions of the mature body.

Varieties of packages for the development of more effective sexual responses have also been offered. Masters' and Johnson's two-week therapy programme is the archetype, I suppose. Hartman and Fithian (1972) have adopted a technique not unlike Masters' and Johnson's, but which includes therapist involvement in stimulating sexual responses. The National Sex Forum in California has been pre-eminent in the developing of visual material in its Sexual Attitude Restructuring and Reassessment programmes (*SAR Guide*, 1975). By the introduction of a wide variety of explicit visual information about sexual function both patients and clinicians are encouraged, over periods of 24, 48 or 72 hours, to re-evaluate their own sexual defences and reassess their levels of comfort with their own sexuality. LoPiccolo and LoPiccolo (1978) have published a useful synthesis of the range of treatment procedures now being used in the sexual function field which include programmes for helping elderly couples become liberated, discuss sexual behaviour in pregnancy, sexual adjustment in the post-coronary male, aspects of sexual response in adults with spinal cord injury and sexual function in patients with chronic renal failure. In the same volume, group procedures are discussed when enhancing the relationships of normal as well as sexually dysfunctional couples, and pre-orgasmic workshops for women are not only discussed in the American literature but are the subject of public advertisement in this country. Workshops for the development of sexuality in single men are also beginning to appear in this country (Yaffé, personal communication).

So far as the investigative side of sexual therapy is concerned, the LoPiccolos (1978) have noted that the field of sex therapy is one in which practical applications have been much more emphasized than has research. While sex therapy "... consists of a variety of procedures which are demonstrably effective, ... the reasons for this effectiveness are not known". Two experimental studies have, however, been carried out in this country, one by Bancroft and his colleagues at Oxford and the other under my direction in association with the National Marriage Guidance Council and with the grant support of the DHSS.

Bancroft (Mathews *et al.*, 1976) was concerned to compare Masters' and Johnson's programme, modified for weekly out-patient attendance, with the anxiety reducing procedures of systematic desensitization combined with counselling and directed practice with minimal contact—effectively a postal treatment. Thirty-six couples were seen, and half of the couples were seen by a single therapist while the remaining half were seen by two therapists in the traditional co-therapy format described by Masters and Johnson.

Whilst no significant differences between treatments were found, consistent trends suggested that Masters' and Johnson's procedure modified for the purpose of an NHS setting was generally superior to the postal procedure or a desensitization-based procedure. The benefit of using two therapists as against one therapist was observed to be slight and, on a cost-effective basis, probably of no advantage. It was also observed that the actual change in couples whose treatment was rated relatively successful was often surprisingly unclear, and that this was particularly true where changes in orgasmic function had been expected. Changes often failed to materialize in any directly observable form, even though the general tone of the sexual relationship appeared to improve.

My own work has been directed not only to exploring the usefulness of one or two therapists, but also to try to establish whether sexual function therapies must necessarily be carried out by skilled clinicians, or whether the body of knowledge now available makes it possible and practical for marriage guidance counsellors to involve themselves more directly in the specific treatment of sexual difficulties, thereby increasing the treatment resources available. In a two-year study, 72 couples were treated in treatment/training design, in which six female marriage guidance counsellors were each trained as a co-therapist with me. Subsequently three of these trained co-therapists each trained two male marriage guidance counsellors as co-therapists of their own, whilst the remaining three female therapists each worked as a single therapist, as I then did myself. Thus we were able to observe the effect of a clinician as against trained counsellors as against counsellors in training, and also to observe upon the single versus co-therapy distinction. In our seven-point scale assessments we also tried to distinguish between the nature of the general relationship with which couples were presenting and the nature of the sexual relationship, to assess whether changes in both general and sexual relationships were contingent upon treatment.

Without going into the minutiae of the results it was apparent that co-therapy procedures seemed to have more effect than single therapy procedures upon the functioning of the general relationship, but that co-therapy was no more or less effective than single therapy in facilitating change in sexual function. The general and sexual relationships were quite well-differentiated aspects of the treatment effect and, so far as the differences between the results of the clinician and the counsellors are concerned, the study demonstrated that counsellors could produce treatment results which were as powerful, in terms of the speed of treatment and the effectiveness of treatment, as a clinician.

It has become apparent in more recent work that the treatment population that we are seeing in the UK is very different from that upon which Masters and Johnson conducted their main research. In a further series of 73 couples recently completed under the auspices of the London Marriage Guidance Council, 18 couples simply did not attend in response to the first assessment appointment while, because of waiting lists and pressure for treatment, four couples were referred to sexual function treatment elsewhere. Of this series, then, 51 couples were seen for assessment following referral, and only 25 of these were assessed as suitable for active treatment. Of the 25 couples who did come into active treatment, ten were subsequently referred elsewhere after the inception of treatment. Thus from 73 couples only 15 (20 per cent) continued a course of treatment. Out of these 15, six couples had four or fewer treatment appointments before terminating treatment and of these six, five couples were assessed as showing no change at the time of termination. Thus out of our original 73 couples referred only nine (12 per cent) continued in treatment for more than four sessions without either failing to attend for assessment, putting pressure on us for treatment earlier than was available, being referred elsewhere or terminating. Of these nine, four showed improvement or much improvement; three showed some improvement; one showed no change and one couple has still to complete treatment. Thus in a very small group of couples there is some evidence of the fact that 50 per cent who continue beyond four sessions and who are not further referred show real changes as a result of therapeutic intervention. We have not yet, however, really investigated the reasons which make sexual function therapy less successful or less applicable than Masters and Johnson recorded, though it must also be observed that very little is known in the formal literature about the population that Masters and Johnson assessed but did not take into treatment. Our own observations are in line with those of Mathews and Bancroft and their colleagues in which, even when treatment is apparently relatively successful, the specific consequences of treatment are not terribly clear. We ourselves now think of sexual function therapy as a form of intervention counselling which unfortunately Masters and Johnson have described less than fully in *Human Sexual Inadequacy*. The rapid and intensive treatment programme that is the basis of their report has not, however, been replicated in this country, and so results of sexual function therapy in the UK should not be seen as comparable with those emanating from St. Louis and elsewhere in the USA. This is not to deny, though, that Masters and Johnson have provided an invaluable structural base for the further development of sexual function therapies.

Let me turn in considering the forward development of sexual function therapies to a brief review of what is now the agreed aim of sexual function therapies. The LoPiccolos (1978) have summarized it well. In the first place the concept of mutual responsibility is involved. It is stressed that sexual function is a shared responsibility and that difficulties of function are shared difficulties. Thus treatment is ideally oriented towards what happens between the couple rather than an attack, albeit therapeutic, upon the individualized failure. In the second place there is a good deal of information-giving and education about the sexual function of the body. We continually observe an extraordinary lack of accurate knowledge about how the body works, and have observed elsewhere (Brown and Faulder, 1978) that were we to fail to teach our children to drive in the same way that we fail to teach them about sex we would see as many casualties on the road as we see in relationships. In the third place, sexual function therapy is aimed at attitude change. Negative attitudes induced by society and parents, and the double standard type of morality required of men and women in western cultures often require a good deal of therapeutic effort in the remedying. Then, in the fourth place a great deal of effort is expended on eliminating performance anxiety. To the sex therapist sexual functioning is not gymnastic, nor is it sacramental, though it can be either or both. The focus is on enjoying the process rather than trying for a particular end result. In the fifth place there is emphasis on increasing communication and effectiveness of sexual technique. The best teacher I can have is a partner who knows not only what she wants but how to establish what she wants, and the idea that we can be each other's best teacher sexually underpins a lot of the work that is done. Finally, there are the specific prescriptions for changes in behaviour. Couples are encouraged to explore and discover the potential of their bodies as sources of pleasure to be enjoyed personally and to be shared. Therapists, at least in the UK, do not engage in direct sexual function with their clients nor do they observe their client's actual responses in any direct manner, but they are not afraid to be direct in discussing sexual function.

It will be clear by this stage that sexual function therapies are a largely undifferentiated mix of education and attempts to remedy specific difficulties. To what extent the term 'therapy' should be applied to the broadest of educational processes is a point which has not been elucidated in the literature and which I think is worth tackling. In clinical work it is apparent that couples (not to say clinicians!) presenting in the latter half of the 1970s are much better informed about sexual function than they appeared to be in the early part of the decade and, consequently, are presenting with a very different constellation of complaints than the 'simple' sexual difficulties that Masters and Johnson described. This situation is reminiscent of the late 1950s when the behaviour therapists described monosymptomatic phobias in profusion which were, in fact, much more complex subsequently. It is my strong impression in an out-patient clinic setting, and on the basis of referrals of over 500 couples in the last five years, that probably less than 10 per cent of couples are realistically asking for the straightforward resolution of a well-defined sexual difficulty that is uncomplicated by an absence of communication problems in the relationship. Indeed, 10 per cent seems an unduly high figure. Again, in the setting in which I work, which is now largely under the auspices of the Marriage Guidance Councils though with couples coming from a wide variety of referring sources, it is the case that less than half of the couples referred enter effective treatment for one reason or another. In the 1974/6 series to which I have already made reference, we found that the consequence of referral for 305 couples was that only 41 per cent actually entered treatment.

The case for a continued development of effective sexual function therapies also rests perhaps upon an adequate statement of the incidence of sexual difficulties in the population. Generalized figures proposing that up to about one-half of marriages are sexually less than satisfactory hardly help this argument. Frank *et al.* (1978) collected data on 100 marriages in the USA in which questions about sexual function were part of a much wider study, and noted that although over 80 per cent of the couples reported that their marital and sexual relationships were happy and satisfying, nevertheless, 40 per cent of men reported erectile or ejaculatory dysfunction and 63 per cent of the women reported arousal or orgasmic dysfunction. In addition, 50 per cent of the males and 77 per cent of females reported difficulty that was not dysfunctional in nature (e.g. lack of interest, inability to relax). Although this is a small and totally unrepresentative sample, such evidence argues more for education than specific treatment work, and it is perhaps time that we, in this country, turned our attention more formally to the possible large-scale preventative benefits of a thoroughly planned and well-directed programme of education based on our current knowledge about sexual function.

However, on the remedying side of things we have again tried to assess the incidence of sexual dysfunction in a population by looking at our sources of referral from general practitioners. We found in a series of 305 couples that 169 had been referred by 117 different general practitioners over a wide, but defined, geographical area in the Midlands. Eighty-three different general practitioners had referred one couple each, 27 two, four had referred three couples, one had referred four couples, one had referred five couples and one had referred eleven couples. This referral rate was taken from the planned inception of a new service advertised to all general practitioners in the area at the same time, and the referrals appeared over the course of just two years. By looking at the demography of general practitioners in the area we found that eight per cent of possible general practitioners used the service over the two-year period that it was available and that, by looking at total general practitioner/patient load, we estimated that one general practitioner might be expected to refer three actual patients in any two-year period for the treatment of sexual difficulties. In consequence we estimated that over the UK as a whole we might expect there to be slightly over 50,000 cases presenting as sexual dysfunction from general-practitioner sources in any one year, which means that from this source alone 50,000 *couples* were identified as needing help in the area of either their sexual function or the relationship implicated in the referral.

If a measure of need is also taken on the basis of market forces, it is widely agreed among sex therapists in this country that the offering of any new facility for the treatment of sexual difficulties results in the rapid establishing of an extensive waiting list. As has been noted above, less than half of all referrals are likely to be appropriate for direct help with the sexual difficulty, but nevertheless there is a widely agreed demand for help in the area. One solution to this, of course, is the development of self-help resources and group treatment programmes. As I noted earlier we have begun to see the development of pre-orgasmic workshops for women in this country, sexual consciousness raising workshops for men, and there is a delightfully illustrated small book by Betty Dodson (1974) called *Liberating Masturbation*.

As another move in this direction, Carolyn Faulder and I have recently published a work called *Treat Yourself to Sex* (Brown and Faulder, 1978) which is a response to the pressure of demand for help that frequently means waiting lists extending to six or nine months.

In this country we have not yet seen, beyond the carefully controlled work that Dr Martin Cole has done, the development of so-called surrogates, but it is now quite apparent in the USA that a group of para-professionals has arisen who have institutionalized themselves into an association and who offer treatment resources in the manner of being active sexual partners. In the rather low-key manner which is characteristic of the British style (or English disease, whichever way you look at it) we have not yet seen a booming private sector in sex therapy nor the advent of consumerism in the setting out of widely advertised guides on how to choose one's sex therapist. We are perhaps protected from both by the structure of the NHS and our concept of primary general practitioner care. Nevertheless, I find myself being increasingly sympathetic to the view that sexual function therapies should be considered outside the context of health care as we have it in this country and be seen as part of a movement concerned with developing the quality of life and developing our human resources. Alex Comfort (1974) has neatly summarized the dilemma which is beginning to face us. Observing that we are the first generation in the history of the world to have reliable contraception, and that there is concurrently a demand for zero growth population, he has suggested that while up until perhaps the middle thirties sexual function was almost entirely considered within the concept of procreation, and whilst also between the late thirties and the middle fifties our cultural ideas about sexual function began to place it in the context of the relationship, we are now perhaps moving towards a period of time in which we are in need of adopting a recreational view of sexual function. If we are, then both the sociology and perhaps the theology of marriage are in urgent need of public discussion.

The final observation that I should like to make very briefly is upon the need that I think there now is for the development of well-organized training programmes for sex therapists. Only three bodies have taken an active interest in this field: the three-year-old Association of Sexual and Marital Therapists, which acts as a focus of professional interest and a source of professional stimulation in a newly emerging field; the Institute of Psychosexual Medicine, which is the heir to the brief psychotherapy work of Balint to which I referred at the beginning of the paper; and thirdly the National Marriage Guidance Council, which is the only formal body to investigate the training of sexual function therapists in a UK context and to have subsequently introduced structured training programmes. One London hospital medical school has established a lectureship in human sexuality. We are, I believe, signally failing to meet not only the training needs of current professionals, but the forward training of the next generation. This is an area worthy of great endeavour and both private and public support. As personally involved throughout the 1970s in the development of sexual function therapies I feel we ought to be moving into the 1980s with the intention of developing, in the last twenty years of this century, a population informed, open and relaxed about its sexual function; not licentious, but nevertheless free.

References

Annon, J. S. (1974). *The Behavioral Treatment of Sexual Problems*, Vol. 1. *Brief Therapy.* Hawaii: Enabling Systems Inc.

Bancroft, J. H. J. (1972). Patterns of sexual inadequacy in clinical practice. In *Psychiatric Aspects of Medical Practice.* Edited by B. M. Mandelbrote and M. G. Gelder. London: Staples.

Benedek, T. (1961). Participant in a panel discussion on frigidity in women, reported by B. E. Moore. *Journal of the American Psychoanalytic Association,* **9,** 571.

Benedek, T. (1968). The evolution and nature of female sexuality in relation to psychoanalytic theory. (Discussion of M. J. Sherfey). *Journal of the American Psychoanalytic Association,* **16,** 424–448.

Brown, P. T. (1976). *Report to the Counselling Advisory Board of the National Marriage Guidance Council.* Rugby, England

Brown, P. T. and Faulder, C. (1978). *Treat Yourself to Sex.* London: J. M. Dent and Sons.
Brown, P. T. and Kolaszynska-Carr, A. (1972). *The relevance of Masters' and Johnson's methodology to the treatment of sexual disorders in an out-patient clinic.* Paper read at the second European conference on Behaviour Modification in Wexford, Ireland, 26.9.72.
Chesser, E. (1956). *The Sexual, Marital and Family Relationships of the English Woman.* London: Hutchinson's Medical Publications.
Comfort, A. (1974). Sexuality in a zero growth society. In *The Future of Sexual Relations.* Edited by R. T. Francoeur and A. K. Francoeur. Englewood Cliffs, New Jersey: Prentice-Hall.
Deutsch, H. (1961). Participant in a panel discussion on frigidity in women, reported by B. E. Moore. *Journal of the American Psychoanalytic Association*, **9**, 571.
Dodson, B. (1974). *Liberating Masturbation.* New York: Bodysex Designs.
Feingold, L. (1966). An illustration of the behavioural therapy approach on the treatment of social and sexual problems. *Pennsylvania Psychiatric Quarterly*, **6**, 3–19.
Francoeur, R. T. (1974). The technology of man-made sex. In *The Future of Sexual Relations.* Edited by R. T. Francoeur and A. K. Francoeur. Englewood Cliffs, New Jersey: Prentice-Hall.
Frank, E., Anderson, C. and Rubenstein, D. (1978). Frequency of sexual dysfunction in 'normal' couples. *New England Journal of Sexual Medicine*, **299**, 111–115.
Freud, S. (1920). *Beyond the Pleasure Principle.* London: Hogarth Press.
Freud, S. (1933). *Feminity.* 1964 edition. London: Hogarth Press.
Friedman, L. J. (1961). *Virgin Wives: A Study of Unconsummated Marriages.* London: Tavistock Publications.
Hartman, W. E. and Fithian, M. A. (1972). *Treatment for Sexual Dysfunction.* California: Center for Marital and Sexual Studies.
Hogan, D. R. (1978). The effectiveness of sex therapy: a review of the literature. In *Handbook of Sex Therapy.* Edited by J. LoPiccolo and L. LoPiccolo. New York and London: Plenum Press.
Kaplan, H. S. (1974). *The New Sex Therapy.* London: Baillière Tindall. New York: Bruner Mazel.
Kinsey, A. C., Pomeroy, W. B. and Martin, C. E. (1948). *Sexual Behavior in the Human Male.* Philadelphia and London: W. B. Saunders.
Kinsey, A. C., Pomeroy, W. B., Martin, C. E. and Gebhard, P. H. (1953). *Sexual Behavior in the Human Female.* Philadelphia and London: W. B. Saunders.
Kockott, G., Dittmar, F. and Nosselt, L. (1975). *Systematic de-sensitization of erectile impotence: a controlled study.* Paper presented at the second European conference on Behaviour Modification in Wexford, Ireland, 26.9.72. Reported in *Archives of Sexual Behavior*, **4**, 495–500.
Lobitz, W. C. and LoPiccolo, J. (1972). New methods in the behavioral treatment of sexual dysfunction. *Journal of Behavior Therapy and Experimental Psychiatry*, **3**, 265–271.
LoPiccolo, J. and LoPiccolo, L. (1978). *Handbook of Sex Therapy.* New York and London: Plenum Press.
Masters, W. H. and Johnson, V. E. (1966). *Human Sexual Response.* London: J. and A. Churchill.
Masters, W. H. and Johnson, V. E. (1970). *Human Sexual Inadequacy.* London: J. and A. Churchill.
Mathews, A., Bancroft, J., Whitehead, A., Hackman, A., Gath, D. and Shaw, P. (1976). The Behavioural treatment of sexual inadequacy. *Behaviour Research and Therapy*, **14**, 427–436.
Pines, M. (1968). 'Human sexual response': a discussion of the work of Masters and Johnson. *Journal of Psychosomatic Research*, **12**, 39–49.

Rachman, S. (1961). Sexual disorders and behaviour therapy. *American Journal of Psychiatry*, **118,** 235–240.

SAR Guide (1975). California: National Sex Forum.

Schofield, M. (1968). *The Sexual Behaviour of Young People*. Revised edition. Harmondsworth, Middlesex: Penguin Books.

Sherfey, M. J. (1966). Evolution and nature of female sexuality in relation to psychoanalytic theory. *Journal of the American Psychoanalytic Association*, **14,** 28–128.

Stopes, M. C. (1923). *Contraception*. London: Bale, Sons and Danielsson.

Wolpe, J. (1958). *Psychotherapy by Reciprocal Inhibition*. Stanford, California: Stanford University Press.

Subject Index

F

Family Planning Association,
  and the handicapped, 115
  and psychosexual disorder
    therapies, 195
  and sex education, *see* Sex
    education
Female orgasmic dysfunction, 198
Fetishism, *see* Paraphilias
Frequency of intercourse,
  women in UK, 75–76

G

Gay Liberation, 8, 51
'Gender dysphoria syndrome', 151
Gender identity, 142–144, 145
  aetiology, 142
  cross-gender behaviour in
    children, 156
  transsexualism/transvestitism/
    homosexuality, *see also*
    Transsexualism, 139
Gender relationships,
  and expression of sexuality,
    102–103
  and social power, 123–124
Gonococcus,
  penicillin resistant, 168
Gonorrhoea, 50
  incidence, 163
  incidence: early estimates,
    160–161
Granuloma inguinale, 164

H

Handicapped people,
  attitudes to sexuality in, 107–113
  community care of, 110–113,
    117–119
  contraception and, *see*
    Contraception
  current policies, 120–121
  genetics and, 111–112
  isolation of, 108–110
  normalization of life for, 116, 117
  post-marital supervision, 120

Handicapped people (*contd*)
  practical and policy changes,
    115–121
  pre-marital preparation service,
    119–120
  sex education, *see* Sex education
Herpes genitalis, 49, 162
Herpes type 2, 165
Homosexuality,
  backlash response to law reform,
    55
  and child custody, 54
  female, *see* Lesbianism
  gender identity, 139
  incidence, 50
  'interactionist' perspective, 104
  law and moral outlook, 13–14
  law reform in UK, *see* Sexual
    Offences Act 1967
  law reform in USA, 53
  medical attitudes to, 53
  and NVALA, 8–9, 10, 12
  surgical intervention for gender
    dysphoria, 151
  and venereal disease, *see* Venereal
    disease

I

Illegitimacy, *see* Legitimacy
Impotence, 198
Incest, 171–191
  abolition of criminal status, 190
  criminal history of offenders,
    182–185, 189
  disposal of offenders, 179–182
  figures and police activity,
    177–178
  imprisonment in father–daughter
    and brother–sister cases,
    180–181, 189, 190
  and law, *see also* Punishment of
    Incest Act 1908, 187
  public disclosure, 174–175, 178,
    190
  reconvictions, 186, 189
  societal reaction, 187–188